About the Author

The author is born and raised in central area of south Ethiopia and studied, worked, travelled and lived across four continents. The most important of all, he is a learner who is willing to share his stories. As real-life editors and are also on the queues, we better do good with it.

Club of the Conditioned

Andualem Boltena

Club of the Conditioned

Vanguard Press

VANGUARD PAPERBACK

© Copyright 2023
Andualem Boltena

The right of Andualem Boltena to be identified as author of this work has been asserted by him in accordance with the Copyright, Designs and Patents Act 1988.

All Rights Reserved

No reproduction, copy or transmission of this publication may be made without written permission.
No paragraph of this publication may be reproduced, copied or transmitted save with the written permission of the publisher, or in accordance with the provisions of the Copyright Act 1956 (as amended).

Any person who commits any unauthorised act in relation to this publication may be liable to criminal prosecution and civil claims for damages.

A CIP catalogue record for this title is available from the British Library.
ISBN 978-1-80016-432-1

Vanguard Press is an imprint of
Pegasus Elliot Mackenzie Publishers Ltd.
www.pegasuspublishers.com

First Published in 2023

Vanguard Press
Sheraton House Castle Park
Cambridge England

Printed & Bound in Great Britain

To my lovely first son and the light to my world.

To my mother, King Amado's descendant and the princess from the most honoured among the Tigrayan Dynasty. The wisest, great listener and sharp in character judgment also in discerning a person's intents and actions.

To my father, who is great at foreseeing and forecasting what would work in good time. His simplistic view of complexities helped me see life as open as the sky as deep as the ocean.

To the people of Wolaita, all Ethiopians, and everyone from all walks of life who aspires to see the world a better place.

Acknowledgements

I would like to acknowledge those whose names I cannot list down here as stars of my stories, and to those I could mention, instead I pronounce these as the reasons for fulfilment of my life.
You all are my gifts from God!

Contents

Chapter One
The Who of Me	13
Holozo	10
Gode (Princess) Almaz Geze Dogiso	21
Even Today?	25
Manta (Mr) Tadesse Boltena Zerihun	31
Several Holozo sites	35
Pour Me the Black Milk	37
The Ethiopian Prophet (Hiragawa)	41

Chapter Two
The Walk to Asmara	49
It Is All in the Names	53
Highly Personalised Hostilities	62
Opening a New Clinic	64
Ethiopians Getting Tormented	67
Assassination Threat	77
Between an Affair and a Responsibility	90
Stabbing and Exile	102

Chapter Three
Going Global	113
Smelling like Berbere	110
Saving Birgitta From Suicide	113
Kampala	121
Gods of Africa	133
No Quero	139
What Works in Turkey?	144
Wolaita is the New Jerusalem	148
Our New Holy Planet	152
Bonfire Master	157

Chapter Four
Club of the Conditioned	178
Menelik's Success or Tewodros' Failure?	174
A Government in Auction	177
Was It Always?	184
Her Shadows	191
Sleeping During the Day	202
Void of The Truth	212
The Ethiopian Truth	218
Aggrieved Famers	221
New Players	230
Old Rules	237
Club of the Conditioned	250

Foreword

As a recollection of a personal learning and weaving this into a fabric of a solid record, this memoir is part of life's product thus far and shows the search for the answers to hurtful events and tracing who is responsible for all of it.

This memoir is more loyal to the storyline than chronological flow, while few names and places have been changed for obvious reasons. What started as a journey of an ambitious, highly curious, super sensitive and resistive young boy has turned the author into a person that is in a constant state of searching for the truest meaning of what is happening around himself and many people he has been blessed to have encountered. The author enjoys and questions civilisations, faiths; refuses conserving traditional fundamentals and because of which he sees no reason to look just like the rest.

The author wilfully contributes to holistic social progress of humanity, instead of becoming a player to accommodating only the privileged few. Life has not been boring while tracking and dodging one of Africa's stringent security barriers, which Obama and the former American Ambassador Susan Rice once praised. The author learnt that a lot of suffering would be avoided if people knew painful moments are works of responsible hands, not random incidents as they are told to believe. Outliving torture, extortion, stabbing, jailing and exile, he waited for doctors to call him sane and healthy. It also depends on which doctors we are talking about.

We are in an era where a new culture is arising as guns get infamous, clandestine forces manipulate people's health and wellbeing as a silent form of demographic, political, economic, financial, social, psychological, behavioural, individual and collective decision alteration and population control. In today's world, this simply amounts to global control. This involves governments and businesses and their interactions with machines and intelligentsia.

In this story, the author walked between life and death, peace and war, calm and violence. He calls it a demarcation of love and hate. A relatively humble family boy transformed into a man rejected by systems and rejects them back, and day and night combats deep hate and bad will that runs through the veins of our societies. Embracing people rather than governments, the author would say he loved and was loved, and saw the good in people, though few dare to show it openly.

From eating fruits from bushes near his hometown to five-star hotel treatments in Rio de Janeiro, Brazil and a number of advanced cities, he also saw everything in-between. Life has never failed in testing the limits, setting him up for constant learning by shaking his fundamentals every now and then.

In what can be seen as chasing and escaping from forces of evil, by a one in million chance, the author ended up learning about the might of our women and their daily struggles. What triggered him to engage for the conscious days of his life is what they cope with, how they shrug off their challenges and wait for the next one. To comprehend it all, he had to risk losing himself and fought to reclaim it in the process. This has put the author to reject the normal that is set to pin him and loved ones down and holding him back from reaching out to others. He is a disbeliever of the past penned laws, scrolls and rules of games that his fathers and mothers did not get the chance to voice their opinions for or against.

The quest of which put the author at the centre of healing wounds, mending people to people and people to state relations at the country and international levels.

The author believes in organised and self-sustaining society, only when it does not crush his inner desire to check the essence of creating the just in people. In this story of experiencing love and hate in the society, which one of the two is unforgiving of the other remains unclear. One thing is for sure, good people have always managed to see the best side of him.

Rayond Mujuni
Journalist
Daily Nation Uganda

Chapter One

The Who of Me

Holozo

"Here, they cut heads and roll them down the mountain hills."

As a fifth grader, my parents arranged a trip to our coolest auntie Bontole, who lives close to the mountainous Koyisha area. Bontole is a very deep village name in Wolaita, in the Southern Ethiopia. We were to walk on our feet for about a total of over five hours. First, we left my parent's house and headed to the junction of the Gesuba-Gofa road, that took us almost an hour.

From there you would hitch hike a car and travel up to a Gesuba town. From Gesuba, you would take a very lengthy walk on a mountainous landscape uphill. To make it to Bontole's house, it took us about an hour by a car and some four hours' walk.

While we were climbing the mountain, I knew that I would visit this place at least once again. I even started imagining my second trip for which I may have to remember all the roads, junctions, small rivers, cottages and trees at turning points. After a while of walk, we crossed a river called Maneasa, that often becomes violent and claims lives or takes the donkeys, cows, sheep and goat that people bring to and from the market. The river usually causes the bridge to collapse while carrying wood trunk, large objects even sometimes removing small size cottages is a common place. Even though my auntie is very considerate and walked slowly it was beyond the strength of my muscles to walk up the mountain to make it home without taking a rest or a pause for a cup of tea.

We passed through a narrowly made public passage that crosses through small rivers, open fields, grazing land, lines of cottages and farms. In the farms, you would see sweet potatoes, potatoes, cassava, yam, corn, sugarcane, enset (false banana), wheat and teff among many other crops.

My auntie would pause on our way to greet some people, tell them who I am and of our journey so far. Since there is no any weather forecast or overall information about Gesuba town for the day, people share information verbally with greetings breaking the ice every time we meet someone she knew.

Sometimes, we would greet farmers ploughing lands or harvesting or taking their animals to the riverside. There were kids herding animals and playing football, taser balls, volley balls, hide and seek or some games I had no idea how they play. The men would be dressed up in the usual jean's trousers, jackets or some cheap suits, most of them had somewhat Chinese-made shoes. Older men would have a hat while middle-aged or some styled ones seemed to frequent capes.

Cleanliness is obviously a thing here. Whether they wash at the river or water wells, they must wash before going to a market or paying a visit to towns. They would carry small mobile phones with radio transmission from which they listen to music, local news or programs broadcast in local language, Wolaitic or as they call it Wolaitatuwa. The women would have long dresses in various tropical colours and styles. Some of them would normally have some scarves covering their hairs. Some did wear jewellery made of gold silver or bronze while others adorned handmade simple products available in the markets. Often, the ladies would be singing in a group, especially on their way back headed for home.

There were open fields after every ten- or twenty-minutes' walk where people sit for community meetings, conflict resolution or just chit-chatting and bursting into laugher after some intriguing talks. Mostly, there were either eucalyptus or other trees people would sit under. In some cases, horses could be seen next to the elders, waiting for a ride back home. Nowadays, this has changed completely; it is totally a different story. Cheap Indian-made Boxer motorbikes are calling for people to take them almost to their doors.

Connectivity has changed so fast that there are 4G cell phone connections, and Facebook images are released frequently from these very places. Skipping office hours while clients are told that they are in meetings, several high officials spend enormous amount of time in what appears as profile picture updating contest with the celebrities, opposition figures and people of prominence. Things do change and often very fast.

A question of prioritizing connectivity which seems achievable all across Africa than banks, good roads, clean water, food security, quality education, health care, and overall protection than just improved information-exchange technologies remains highly relevant as of today. At least, you need to eat, have roof over your head, send your children to schools and the pregnant or the sick need to visit health care centres.

How would access to Facebook help if there are no nurses, teachers and service providers in close vicinity, anyway? Among the images I saw, some did not feel ashamed to post images of dirty wards and workplace walls with holes.

You would hear governments in Africa boasting over the coverage of telephone and internet across their countries while over eight hundred million people do not have access to proper electricity.

I stayed for about a month during a very cold and rainy season which often lasts from June through mid-September. The place gets dark green, covered with fresh grass and all trees and bushes coating the area with beautifully decorated plants and flowers. The animals would be grazing, scattered on the hills, separated by huge rocks or lines of trees separating neighbours.

During daytime, the chores must be completed so that the family cool stays pleasant and the evening would be greeted with some jokes, giggles and tales that my auntie or her husband would tell us. The rule has it that you do what needs to be done, whether it is cutting grass, bringing potatoes from the farm or taking out the animals and search for grazing areas.

Somehow, everyone would fit in the daily routines; except me, who had yet to learn a few things here and there. One time, the animals rushed to a neighbour's farm or another time the grass I cut looked like the size of a baby grip. Or I cut my foot trying to cut a tree for firewood or teared my cloth while stretching to lift something heavy.

In Sodo the games my friends and I played and our roles in a family were different. We never fell short of creativity apart from playing with the usual stuff. Close to my parent's home we used to dig to find bullets left during the Ethio-Italian war.

It was not just old-styled bullets the Italians left behind, they instated a sense of hope for restoring dignity and respect for repressed people of Wolaita. A number of young people are now bringing back the trend of speaking in Italian just like during my father's high school age. My father is not much into Italian as much as he is into English. My uncle Eniyew, a soldier just like three of his brothers, takes the prize in my family. He took it to himself to name my little brother, Capelo, a typical Italian name by which my brother is called on Facebook as of the time this is written. Eniyew would utter some Italian words and we know that he is seriously angry with something. It can even be in the middle of a conversation. It appeared that my father knew those words and it would mean a heated debate in our home.

Though they may hesitate to eat pasta, while pizza is the thing in town, people of Wolaita have a fond feeling towards Italians, as they are seen as liberators from slavery and imposed labour, exploitation and inhumane treatments by the then rulers assigned by the Addis Ababa government. For as much as the Americans lived in Wolaita, they have been secluded in their compound while the Italian priests and social workers seem to have integrated much better. You would see them on streets teaching thing or learning in their turn, debating with the poor the rich or anyone for that matter.

I must put this as a reflection of the Wolaita people that Italians have a special place in the hearts of quite several people, young and old alike. Because of this, discussions about Italians are a common place and as children we were told that the bullets were from the war during the Italian occupation.

The city has a reminder of less than a hundred year's history while the rural places kept reminders of over seven thousand years of Wolaita and at times East African history. As historians put Wolaita, unknown land and the Horn of Africa as uncharted territory. For a child's mind the bullet is a simple and yet unforgettable object of a lesson.

While we play, we hide from our parents and gather some wood, bring stones to hold the bullet upright and set fire underneath and run as fast as we can, hide for a coverage and from a distance watch it explode. Sometimes we bring a bullet case, sneak matchstick from home and crush the head to have a combustible powder. We stuff the powder in a bullet case that is also tied with a rubber band, or a rope attached with a metal bar inserted at the top. We usually hit the edge of the metal bar on a hard surface to make it pop very loud. Sometimes this can be very loud and dangerous too.

We would also make cars from metal wire into brands of our imagination and roll them on the streets. We would attach pen cases or a candle and light them to drive during evening times. Much of this is absent in Holozo.

Once I learnt of my unspoken duties of Holozo, I had to come up with some tricks of competing or role play or anything that would allow me to appear like anyone else. These tricks of collecting more firewood or grass for cows were learnt at my extended relatives of my dads' side. It is about thirty kilometres from my hometown. One day, we all woke up, had breakfast, joked about this and that and it was time for daily chores. As the usual suspect to bring the least bundle of grass, I suggested that we play games and earn some grass for it. I did not invent it. They do it all the time and I saw it more widely. It is also a break between work hours to make the day go with a bit of fun. It makes life easier. Its motivational effect is also sensible.

What we all learnt was that missing any of the games was not in my mind, I would learn where all of them were weak and use it to my advantage and score more. The simplest of all games that did not need much of a trick was hitting the target from a distance. This one is more like the Swedish summer game of throwing pieces of wood to hit a target. It is rather a laid-back game, but you got to do it to win.

When we are going back home from the field, I would carry the fattest bundle of grass or wood to the embarrassment of my relatives that are used to bringing this much. It is later said that the game had to be called off or something else needs to be done.

This thing of the games we played for grass bundles or firewood continued; just because it is fun to do and just because one may or may not win the next time, the day should not get boring. So is life.

On a usual day in Holozo, we stayed for a longer time in the field. I would never forget a very terrible thing that happened during that evening. My auntie's stepson got his seizure once again. His epilepsy is so rough that it was very confusing to understand what was actually happening to him. The whole house got so nervous and devastated. My auntie's husband rose up and offered a very long prayer to chase out the devil hurting this young man.

It was when I studied neurology that I understood that this man suffered from seizures and not possession by demons. What is very sad to this day is that most people with such types of illnesses or several others with disabilities are condemned to suffer even more because of superstitions, wrong perceptions and awful practices that are commonly used across Ethiopia.

The nights the seizure happened, I found it difficult to fall asleep. I would wait to see if the demons were going to hurt me and do the same to me too. A few times, I wished if I could catch, choke and finish them all. For some odd reasons, my mind thought the demons would be fended off if I stayed awake. I would try to be watchful for as much as I could before falling asleep.

My difficulty of sleep did not stop in Holozo. I heard of something terrible that took place for almost all the time the Wolaita kingdom, a once-great empire in East Africa named Damot, existed. And I was about to be introduced to what would rock the deepest depths of my soul and shake up all the fundamentals without any sign of stability even when I am an adult.

One day, after a family time with good meal, crooked jokes, church songs and prayers, my causin's seizure happened and I slept very little. The next morning, my head was uneasy and grumpy and yet soon after a quick breakfast, we took the animals to the top of the Mountain Holozo, where animals were grazing at the tip of the hill. When we got there, my cousin Alana asked me if I knew about Holozo and what took place there. Alana was born to another wife of my auntie's husband, and she passed away before Bontole got married with him. But whom your cousin calls a brother is your cousin too. That is how it works. At this very moment I got extremely interesting story to listen to. I asked him to tell me.

"I don't know anything about Holozo," I told him. I asked, "were children playing here, Alana?"

From the look of his face, it was not fun to talk about it at all.

The graphic depictions he was trying to make me picture in my head terrified my young soul and kept me awake every night I thought of it. The feeling of it was much worse than his seizures. The Holozo hill is a very steep place on a top of a mountain that has very large stones here and there, and people would lead their animals to graze or tie them to bushes or trees and keep them there for a while. If one stands on the stones and looks down the hill, it is so steep to the point one would have intense feelings of acrophobia. There are houses, farms and grazing animals or farmers tending their crops at the lower bed of the mountain. One can see them moving and looking as small as the thumb.

"If a stone is rolled from here," said Alana, "it would destroy houses and crops and kill animals or people on the way. Some of the trees here are for protection and derail such stones from getting down there."

"What did people do here?" I asked.

Alana was a bit older than me and knew so many things. He was more relaxed and took a lengthy time before speaking for most part of it. He took it from his father, a very wise farmer who also did trading. His father was known for his distinct manners of speaking.

Alana said, "No. *Ha sohuwan asyi asa seranawu hayitta gidin, kushiya gidin tohuwa qanxiyosa.*" Meaning this is a place where they mutilate or amputate limbs as a punishment.

I was shocked that this happened to the people in this place. Alana was not done talking.

He then pointed towards the edge of rocks on the top of the mountain and said:

"*Hage sohoy asay asa shukidi woriyosane duge zaridi bululisiyosa!*" (Here, they cut heads off and roll them down the mountain hills.)

He was not at ease while telling me about it.

He had difficulty in breathing; he was gasping heavily both because of walking on the hill but also the story felt difficult to process.

I was walking behind him and said to him, *"Aybissi hega ottiyona?"* (I meant, why would they do that?)

"Hega cima asay eres," he said. (Meaning, it is the elders who know about this.)

"Asa woriyage one?" was my next question. (Who are the ones killing people?)

"Hega cima asay eres," he said again. (Meaning, it is the elders who know about this.)

The place has a raw and unwritten history of mutilations, limb dismemberment, horrifying death and blood bath.

I knew that there was nothing he could explain. This was to be saved to ask my father and mother. Especially my mother, as she came from the line of the Wolaita Kingdom, very closely related to King Tona. She must have answers to this.

To get hacked is a serious punishment by the kingdom; this probably means the entire family goes through not only the sorrows and deep hurt of loss, but it would also include condemnation of family members to physical amputations, limb dismemberments, imposed slavery or forced labour for extended period, or even a life-time service. What amounts to such heinous punishment is mostly when a group of people conspire to overthrow the government or are caught in treason or anything that is perceived to be a mistake with grave consequences.

Usually, the legal proceedings begin with several community meetings attended by local rulers and elders as to identify, verify and agree on the identity of the individuals responsible for the accusations. The individuals are given the chance to clear their names, but once the collective has believed you as a criminal, the situation demands that some individuals must be punished anyway. It is a must. This process is called *paxisuwa*, more of an ancient interrogation, as a practice of getting confessions.

In this process, the royal guards representing the king would vent out their furry on the accused and their defendants and witnesses. Hearing the threats from the kingdom of execution or wiping out your entire clans or burning your entire family with their cottage closed while they are inside, you would end up giving yourself up to save others.

It is an unforgiving system of extracting truth, often time yielding a false narrative that is made to be pronounced as truth. The sad reality is that some small neighbourhood skirmishes may put you right there if your neighbour knows the loopholes in the legal system and triggers to spin the kingdom around your head.

The temptation of enjoying the power profits and spoils of the kingdom lures many naïve people to try it out and later realise that they are being played by their own relatives that aim for higher ranks or prominence at the Royal Circle. It is human greed that we see today. Humans never change in this. It is the technology and way of life that advances while human tendencies for selfish wonders seem to feel like the same.

Once the accused are arrested by the local police, called *tondiya*, they are brought before the royal court for proceedings. Once evidence is presented and that verdict is done, the king would announce his verdict. Almost all such alleged criminals are executed in an open field of Holozo while the public witnesses it. Before the execution, the criminals would be kept in prison cottages prepared for this. Word has it that the criminals would stay under the watch of designated rulers of the close area they come from.

The execution process begins with informing the people. There would be a public announcement by horsemen who spread words that criminals would be punished on a date set by the royal guards. The place Holozo is close to Koyisha which is said to be where the Wolaita kingdom was located originally before it was moved to the present-day area of Damota mountain.

The Holozo mountain would be filled by people who are sent from every locality to witness the execution and public announcement of the decisions of the king. You would hear horses gasping and sounds of '*qata*' urging the mules to walk faster. The horses and mules would be decorated with colourful covers and the rulers wearing some smart dresses and a look of royalty. It is said that the king and his royal family members have their horses coated with metal handles and parts of saddle edged with lines of gold and other precious stones. Regular people use items made of metal, ropes, bronze chains and pieces of light wood.

On the scene, people would be seated with their respective ranks and social prominence. While the king and his crew would arrive, the local music club would beat drums, play *dinkiya, cacha-zayiya, ulduduwa* and other equipment. *Dinkiya, zayiya* and *ulduduwa* all are made up of bamboo tree. *Dinkiya* and *zayiya* are very long instruments played with mouth. *Ulduduwa* is a local flute played with almost the same way as the flutes you hear the Roman people (whom some would call gypsies) play on the streets of European cities or any Asian flutes you hear in their music.

The drums of Wolaita are made up of barrels, clay, or wood covered with leather wrapped up with leather ropes that would be dried up and held tight while it was wet during manufacturing. Usually, it is the drums men or women that begin the music followed by others in synchronised fashion. You would have singers in a group while the lead artist would be leading the way.

The loud sound, the cheering crowd and happy faces would make you question if it were crowning ceremony or sort of high-end wedding. People are so happy in such days to my awe. Word has it that it is a relief to know that the kingdom lives on and that their collective way of life would not be disrupted or endangered by anyone for some time to come. And the present threats are to be taken care of. And that they are happy for the assurance of the peaceful and calm future. The only question remaining here is 'at the expense of what?' which would have been important to pose. The haste of the execution proceeding takes over the mind from doing a proper thinking, but then no one would dare say it and end up like the criminals to be killed.

The alleged criminals would be presented to the people, and their crimes would be publicly condemned and that their execution would signify an end to the attempt of the enemies of the kingdom from destroying Wolaita. Two strong and highly fit royal guards would open the metal framed cells and drag out the criminals, tied up with chains on their feet and necks. Three other royal guards would follow them to make sure all is going as planned. They would be asked if they have final words before their last moment. Whatever they say, the crowd is there to boo them, but it is just to the satisfaction of repentance and fulfilling the tradition.

Then the criminals are held down on the edge of wooden stage with both of their legs tied to metal poles, preventing them from making any movement. A metal bar would be placed right below their shoulders, restricting movement of their upper bodies. Both of their hands would either be held by the assigned guards or are also tied to wooden bars to ensure zero resistance. This all is done while the criminals are already fed with some toxic drinks from mix of herbs, snake poison or anything of similar effect of weakening the body into harmless state and absolute docility.

The executioner would use a very heavy and sword or an axe with widened edge sharpened for one-stroke cutting. Standing there, watching, would make anyone puke after too much physical battles to arrange all of this. The mumbling, uttering words, chants and cheers and shouts of the crowd motivate the executioner to rise the axe high up where everyone can see. The second the neck is hit; the blood would be spilled on the stage and the head would roll down like a rounded ball stuffed with flesh. The repeated execution in the day would mean a wet line of blood is drawn by jostling heads spinning downwards. A pile of heads at the bottom field of the mountain joins the old bones before it while their bodies are carried away for mass burial, thrown like a disposed trash. Just like that. This is almost like the Maya styled execution history you hear from the Maya of Mexico.

Some brave men, though, would express their contempt to this process through songs and *zilassa* — a song of sorrow with words of deep meaning condemning the kingdom for cutting human head in a way sheep or goats are not even slaughtered. Or they would perform *geresa* — a mix of pride, resistance and concern vented out through songs.

What happened in this place shaped the fate of the entire people of Wolaita. What I heard here also changed the way I see the world and probably the person I have become shaped by it more than the Bible stories or any other divine contents I have heard of. It was so gruesome that I could not let go of it, day or night during my childhood. My life just changed upside down. It is a curse that inflicted pain on individuals that later became source of our collective tormenting hell. I was very sure that this story was not just some cruel beastly act of some bad people a while back. It is a practice that must mean something today. Looking back, I was very sure something unfair and unbearable happened. And I took it to myself that I must understand who is responsible for this. I needed answers. Real answers.

I still wonder why I ended up at the Holozo mountain top; whether it was by a random chance or if people were teaching me the things that matter to our collective selves, perhaps without meaning it or in some silent communication with each other. One way or another, and thinking of the depth of the situation, I wondered, why me? What is that I can do? How? With whom? Is it something I should just keep quiet about and live my life like the others or is it right to pick a burden so heavy for anyone like me? Is there anything that can be done to change? Does it even mean anything today? How does it affect my daily life, and would it be different if I did not know about all of this? Holozo left me with several questions.

Gode (Princess) Almaz Geze Dogiso

History tells us that the pre-Christianity Wolaita state was established and led by eight consecutive queens that rose prior to 221 kings and rulers that form a total of two hundred and seventy leaders. Scholars would argue that sizing down Wolaita to only fifty kings is a narrative sold by some narrow-minded and biased historians that had a motive of stealing the three thousand years state civilization history of Wolaita and incorporate it into their own under the name Ethiopia.

The people of Wolaita nation are categorised into two lineages of ethnicities; Mala and Dogala. The Mala and Dogala are related lineages in Gamo, Gofa, Dawuro, Wolaita, Konta and Kucha, among others. While I leave the historians' job to them, I would add that the Wolaita nation was ruled for over thousands of years by the Dogala before the Mala took over. There was also time when the rulership alternated from both. Among the Mala, the Wolaita Mala dynasty ruled before the Tigrayan dynasty replaced the kingship. King Tona, the last warrior king of Wolaita, is related to my mother Princess Almaz Geze Dogiso. Her name Almaz means diamond in Wolaitic and Amharic, among others.

Prince Dogiso is my mother's grandfather. Her great-great grandfather King Amado is a father to her father's side who is also forefather of the King Tona. It is important to mention that the Wolaita pronounce themselves as Amado Karetta, meaning the king's black people. The Wolaita pride in their blackness in songs, music dance, clothing and other expressions. Even the Wolaita national flag has black in it below yellow and red. Tona's family members, Mr Abebe Bekele and several people who come to visit my parents and they talk elaborately about Tona's son Prince Fisseha Desta. The Wolaita Prince was buried close to the late American President Wilson Widrow's cemetery in Fair-Fax in the USA.

Geze was married to my grandmother who is also a royal from the Oyates of the Kambata and mix of the Hadiya and Halaba heritage. This is also where it gets very interesting and cool to know that it is not just the royals intermarrying into other ethnicities, but also most people like farmers, merchants and metal smiths that fall in love across the borders. This practice brought my grandmother to marry the Wolaita royal family member whose story she would never get tired of telling. She tells with pride of Dogiso's war in support of the Abyssinian empire against the Somalis, also any foreign invaders.

At the end of her war stories, where she mentions the braveries and spoils, their songs and dances, she would always say war is the work of mad men. I would ask her why she would not mention women's role as most women are also trained soldiers who know the ways of war. She would say, "but it is mostly the men who break the war." I would argue that may be because they love their women, but she would say, "Almaz, I cannot silence your boy in any way" and then she would say, "of course, some wars are instigated by smart and strong women too."

The reason why the Wolaita intermarry with the like of the Hadiya is far more than simple tales of falling in love with some cool beautiful woman. I asked my grandmother the reason why our men would fall for their women, most of whom are tall, have beautiful faces and curves. She is a very wise woman who would adapt to a whole new culture and way of life, risking the comfort of the royal treatment of her parents. It is not that it shall mean anything, it is just her way of narrating stories that bring life to the recent past and see the good in people from different times of various groups.

History has it that frequent wars and insecurities mean that a woman must be fit for such life. The women from Kambata and Hadiya come as the first choice for this. When a young Hadiya marries a Wolaita man, she would be fast enough to learn and catch up with competing local beautiful girls and outsmart them and stand out so that her man stays with her the rest of his life. Her learning includes not just a household chore. No. A woman is more than a cook and someone who tends to children or milks the cows. She may demand the man to bring her a helper instead so that she can spare time and focus on some other important matters. The important key areas are learning about the art of trade, war, laws and history among others.

The older women of Wolaita teach the new members of the community about the history, of the wars won and those lost to the enemy. The war equipment, the hunting and her roles in a war must be altered to the point that she lives her life almost as a soldier whose temporary job is farming. This way the Oyate woman is raised into a fierce combatant, no Hadiya or Kambata or any other soldier would stand in her way. She is trained mentally and with all the war skills of attack and defence as well as the military intelligence of knowing her way around if a war breaks out, or if she gets a call of duty.

If her husband dies, this woman will never accept the reality that some other man with lesser social importance is going to inherit her household and take over her husband's role, or worse deciding over the fate of her and her children. She would rather die in the field avenging the soldier responsible for the death of her husband. It is this deep. The Oyate are not a class of just the beautiful women and men, nor is their girl a simple wife material. She has dignity and self-respect to the point that she lives with a man by choice, not by any form of coercion. She would know the death of her husband because the horses are trained to return home with the owner still at the back. It is the same if the horse comes home without the owner, he must have died in combat. She would pick the spears, sword and all other protective gears and gallop towards the war front to confront and avenge the soldier who killed the love of her life. If she is not lucky to get to him, the anger drives her to kill as many soldiers as she can before getting killed or caught as a captive.

A woman in Wolaita is way beyond what many would call 'she means a lot'. It was not so some time back with awful practices that eventually died out. But the significance and importance of women is clearly felt in Wolaita as compared to how they are in the northern part of Ethiopia. A woman is a soldier, but also a person entitled to accumulating wealth and rise to a social and political significance on her own, also equally like the men do.

Two main cultural practices are *dala* and *gimuwa*. *Dala* is when a woman, or a man for that matter, makes to own a thousand cattle. When she makes to a thousand cattle, there is a woman's appraisal ceremony, *Gimuwa*. *Gimuwa* is done with elaborate eating, drinking, dances and ululation to signify that the woman has now entered a new social class of wealthy people, men and women alike.

On this day, once the initiation party has begun with festivities attended by delegates from all places, it is the woman's time to show off and go to the marketplace to publicly present herself as the new rich lady. To show her unreserved collective honour, the market would split into two parts and to allow the passage of her caravan right through the middle. This is a social communication that a woman is celebrated by all belonging to such high social level. A woman would trade anything to ascend to such importance in our day. The modern way of life has not yet produced any better tradition, nor has it up held such feminine appreciation practice. These days, seeing women becoming wealthy and acquire high social significance is very rare and makes you wonder where it all went wrong.

A contrast to the way a woman is valued in Wolaita or even in the south, would be visible one day when people filled with a minibus arrived to Sodo town from Addis Ababa. It appeared that the assistant of the driver did not know much about Wolaita. Noticing his accent, he looked like he came from northern Ethiopia. He was exchanging harsh words with one of passengers.

He said, *"Ante ye set lij,"* meaning, you son of a woman. He seemed to have assumed that being born to a woman, a mother, is the same shameful expression like in the north of the country, only to be greeted with furious passengers all on his neck. He was collectively lectured that a woman is not an object of shame in Wolaita.

One of passengers said, *"Eza yelemedkibet semen hid ena techemalek, yih Wolaita new,"* meaning, take your bullies back to your north, this is Wolaita.

Even Today?

After a long while of my stay in Holozo and was working in my hometown in a American owned hospital, the ghosts of Holozo emerged again, through people's intense talks of cruelties and injustice that took place in Wolaita, also similar atrocities committed against people across Ethiopia.

I sat with my father and mother in an evening when we could hear the helper was preparing dinner, and as usual, my father was listening to the German radio Deutsche Welle, which he usually alternates with the Voice of America for news updates. My mother was telling the helper what to do and to check if the salt is not too much or if butter was added. Although it was not a common place when I grew up to have meat in the food, my mother told her to add it in the sauce (wat) which she instructed to be prepared with shiro and lentils.

I said to my mother that I had a question that I had been thinking to ask for long time. She asked 'what do you have in your mind?' I asked her 'why did your relatives torture people?' and she said 'what do you mean by that?' I responded saying 'they were chopping heads of people in Holozo and were rolling their heads down the hill on the mountain. Why would they do such a horrible thing to their own people?' and took out the air stuffed in my chest.

My father lowered the radio voice and stared at me with an awe of curiosity, as if he wrote 'where is this strong question coming from my son?' on his face though he just had bigger pupils and ears eager to follow where this conversation was to go.

My mother was quiet for a while and gazed at my father before saying anything. I am sure they were reading each other's reactions. She then said, 'ask your father about it.' And I responded saying 'I asked you' after brief silence continued 'I would like to hear from you.' From the look of it, she was doing two things with one attempt. Disarming my father and further restraining him from countering her arguments.

"'By now you must know that it was your father's and similar clans that orchestrated such sanctioned executions and the king had almost no power over this. You also know that if people feel threatened collectively, they can depose the king and reinstate if they feel like or regret their decision.' I was saying to myself, 'so to what are you setting me up?'"

I just wanted her to justify instead of sounding like distancing from the responsibility and pushing it to my father's side which means to the rest of the people than owning the mistake.

She asked me back, 'you know your great grandfather was a known judge all over the province and beyond?' And she was looking at me that now she has evidence in my DNA itself of how people are convicted of a crime and where this all process of legal drama started. My great grandfather was not just a highly respected judge of his time, and for his quality service, he received blessings from the public.

I learned about this because of an encounter I had when I accompanied an American Surgeon who was invited to preach at the church close to my father's village where I interpreted the preaching to the Wolaitic language. The people of Wolaita, especially the protestants believe that Americans, and other missionaries, brought gospel, freed them from superstitions and witchcraft, helped them abolish several harmful cultural practices and guided them create or adopt better practices.

In this day of seeing me with the American surgeon as interpreter of the preaching, and more so for my professional duties, some of elders came after the session. And they said to me that this day is a reminder of my great grandfather whom they blessed so that his children and all after them become a reason for blessing to our people.

By reminding me of this, my mother was not blaming my great grandfather in this sense as he held esteemed position or revered even after he passed away. She is implying that it was the legal system in which there was clear governance structure that prevents the king to conduct legal procedure without cases going through due process and that the judges decide to refer to him.

She perfectly pointed to the real owners of the whole practice and made her point guiding me conclude that every wake Wolaita of the time shares equal responsibility. And no single group bears special accountability. While this is most probably the case in the truest sense; it does not discount the truth that heinous practice took place in Holozo. My father did not even move except that when the talk went tense, he turned off the radio and quietly stood by mother's explanations. She told me the truth, and that Holozo is the failure of all Wolaita people.

Following this, I then sat with several individuals from different walks of life in Wolaita and tried to see if most people share this view. To this day, no informed and unbiased person stood against the idea of pronouncing Holozo as our collectively shared and inescapable truth. This is probably the absolute truth of the present day Wolaita people which we all need to embrace unequivocally.

Holozo in today's Ethiopia is just like every other beautiful mountain, of course only when we see it as a topographic reality in the country. Well bias apart, Holozo mountain is one of the most beautiful sceneries I have seen perhaps like those in Costa Rica, Brazil, Peru and Bolivia. Among mountains that I saw in Africa, perhaps Kenyan or Ugandan mountains may come close to it.

I wish it all ended here and this easy by talking about topographic contrasts. It does not. Here is why. If you see anyone from Wolaita collaborating with the state or going against — for any reason — there is this burden, they carry from this mountain. Knowingly or unknowingly, being driven by the thoughts of others or of own making, people are kept in captive exactly as one of the men to be executed at Holozo mountain. For the sake of a good read, let's say there are two perspectives of it.

The first group says, Holozo is just a reality of Wolaita history, it is quite the same as other situations in the country or elsewhere, and we must tell our children so that they know we made mistakes in our history and that this must be clear.

The second group would argue that no, this is a distinct cruelty that needs a punishment as a response. This group argues to harm this generation to set the historical score of the past.

This is today's Wolaita controversy summed up in the simplest reflection. In this you have a pro-republic group that thinks that once this kingdom is dismantled and has become part of Ethiopia, all must be taken from wider perspective. We are to take it as a learning as what I would say 'what not to do'. This group is usually filled with people who have biological ties with the royal families and people who accept their identity as Wolaita, the Amado's black, and for the most part would pride in themselves. This group also is open for overall Ethiopian and global wellbeing with building self-sustaining state that is geared towards shared wealth. This group has been repressed using state apparatus with an assumption that it would break away or would create a distinct ideology and a wide gulf.

This presumptuous and hate-driven discriminatory treatment has been counter-intuitive in a sense that the Meles driven government tapped into this, hurting people of this group using the counter arguing side as his errand boys. In this plot, he spared no one. He hurt both sides with different games and different rules.

Don't get me wrong here. I am not saying the republic is all well and that I see it as a heaven on earth, as I clearly see all its flaws and indescribable discrepancies. Yet, the way it is presented by the anti-republic group is not necessarily for its flaws, rather to get its access to hurt a group they hate, just like they did throughout the previous regime. The anti-republic group presents abuses and horrors of the kingdom, pressing on the wounds of local clans to its manipulation than solving the problem. The individuals in this group point fingers at the descendants of the royal family, and blame anyone who hails Wolaita identity and culture, and commit harm and deliberately hurt their children to set the scores of the past.

From divorces to business shutdowns, school firing to family collapse, from social humiliations to personalised persecutions, all have been done in broad daylight as a vengeance of the past. I still have my anger towards the state and unanswered questions that I still hope would be able to one day arrive at.

The anti-republic group sounds logical and are more towards pro-poor choices. Mostly filled with ideological eloquence and knowing the dark games of politics, looking naively, they sound as if they mean well. In complete honesty, I have never seen a very dubious, hateful and sadistic group as this.

This group was highly committed to Meles' Revolutionary Democracy as its directional ideology while its practices were so detrimental that when the game was over, they were nowhere close to getting anyone's sympathy.

As my Assyrian friend from Turkey stated that ideologies, religion and culture all failed his people, knowing that situations are quite volatile, risking failure for any static understanding of them, also as I have learnt for some time now, probably there may be a mix of ideas, and practices which also are supposed to be open for their own evolutions, may work for a country than a rigid definition of reality.

Present day Ethiopians who seem to exhibit fixation with the records of the past, which offers little chance to change its narration, and presents a closed door to change it, have already lost the possibility of utilizing this moment for progress.

We are yet to wake people up to consider that the future has more currency value than anything of the past. Besides, it all leads to Holozo in Wolaita, and the same spots of evil incidents across the country, that may recreate the demand for sustained attrition, assuming that in their turn it would not be done against the do-ers. As we are living history of our time, we all have now watched in our eyes, that we too are capable of unimaginable depth of cruelty, in what has been happening in the Tigray war.

Whether we see it or not, we stand in queues of life, and it better be that we create queues of good deeds than unending lines of vengeance, score setting and perpetual hate. For sure, we now know that we all have our turns sooner or later.

To me, without any level of risk for overstating, Holozo is a pivotal point of love and hate in Wolaita. I must say that both choices of love and hate are active and conscious decisions as a response to the past mistakes and good deeds, that are owned by everyone in Wolaita. Besides, the lived lives of the past are not stories of hell either. People lived side by side in love, respect and dignity, to highlight the least of good in the old days. Otherwise, there would not have been anyone left to tell the story.

This then calls us to think positive in the slightest way possible. Because our existence itself is a testimony of several good people in our lives, who do not deserve painting with the same brush of hate, have not set us up for our reciprocity with love. This is the least we can do in my view. In any context this can be a remedy, just like a tablet on a pharmacy shelf, or yemariam menged like our childhood, a way out as I would mention at a later chapter.

My verdict in this is that choosing hate is unacceptable regardless of perspectives and justifications. If it were wrong yesterday, it can never be right today, and we must see to it that it will never be presented as right tomorrow either. If one is concerned with its impact in today's generation, they must be working towards harmony, cohesion and healthy social transactions as a collective healing. Even for this, the push factor should be beaming from the idea that societies are advancing as of now and that the past should not be holding us back from marching together forward. In this sense, there is no reason to walk backwards!
While I was in Gondar, I had highly shocking moments to observe that I was watched and spied on by people I would never think doing it to me. To make it worse, very serious political debates would take place in my dormitory. In most of the debates, people wanted to know about my opinions, and I was freely sharing them.

You see, I was probably among few city guys who can relate to rural and urban students alike. I could get along with friends from Addis, Hawassa or Dire Dawa and Adama. Equally, the friends from villages from Wolaita, but as far as Wollega, Ginchi area or Assela also frequented my dorm to the point that one of my dorm mates had to complain and threaten to report it unless I start taking my friends to the student lounge.

I was trying to be less gravitational to the people that come to me, but it just did not work. It did not. At some point, my dormitory was chosen for me by people who wanted to live with me, where they all gathered from different rooms and created our own crib. There was unspoken communication among students regarding with whom they feel safe and protected. They would gather or bring their friends, tear apart government for its tyranny or criticise a professor or an officer. No one was to judge anyone for their perspectives or their backgrounds.

We would bring our foods and eat them together. Making some loud talks and the chaos of student fun was always there. I learnt after graduation that the fate of my life was decided up on based on my encounters in my dormitory than all other places combined. Here is the story. It was the year that late Meles and his party were in preparation for the infamous 2005 election. Dormitory talks were very crucial to the spies who would be roaming among dorms for anything they could extract. Normally students from Tigray and Wolaita would come and wait until others gathered.

Usually they would raise a topic and lead discussions with intrigues and provocations targeted ethnicity for most part of it.

Manta (Mr) Tadesse Boltena Zerihun

You see, my father is a soldier who fought the war with the Meles' party standing on the side of the Ethiopian government and the sovereign army. His argument was the same, 'These guys are all for divide and rule' and he would add they do it for their ethnicity. His argument was that the world is bigger than that. We must think and have a lifestyle with open mind towards others.

I literally took his perspective and did not hide it for most part of it. I still was aware of the ethnic based persecutions going on around. By then, two distinct groups were persecuted. Mostly the Amhara and the Oromos. In each of other ethnicities, family members of former royal groups were the primary target once some are recruited with vague responsibilities to suppress dissent.

To my awe, the Oromo were persecuted by some of the Amharas too, which made it a double hell. Presenting the Oromo as a threat, escalating by attaching their cause with Islamization seemed to get a buy in from many sides. While other ethnic groups were not framed this way, it is equally unfortunate that even the Wolaita, Sidama, Afar, Somali, Gambela, Gumuz and several groups were not spared from this systematic persecution.

My acquaintances from Wollega area, would pour their hearts as by then listening to them without judging was not a common place for many. I was trusted because I came from the South, also as I stood firm in my principles. The pain they had to go through was what struck me the most. It was that no one would listen to their cause, let alone understand them.

For most part of it, they were called names, were isolated and looked down on as some strange creatures. Right in the middle of our discussions, students from Tigray would press on this wound and get everyone over the roof. Heated debates would begin either condemning the Amhara and the 'Neftegna' system — an expression for the state of Ethiopia.

What is so strange in this thought is that those who are brainwashed to hate the 'Neftegna' system, did not realize that the urban people were collaterals of their political dichotomy that categorized anyone other than rural people as a defined enemy. Because of this, people who are born in cities are equally persecuted as people who are believed to have ties with the old 'neftegna' system. To this day, most people who were political cadres of the late Meles have not spit this out.

What I could not see in those conversations was that the then Meles's government was never to be blamed for anything. And that some localised incentives would be used to get you to speak something positive about the state. I had this feeling that I was being somehow followed upon and I did not know if I could bluntly ask around. I came up with a spontaneous idea.

One day, all were gathered, and a discussion was going on. A guy from Tigray, Angesom, asked me what I thought of the new university to be built in my hometown Sodo. We all saw in the news that the Minister of Education was there for the ground-breaking ceremony. The guy even quoted Meles where he said "A beehive is placed where there are bees" to strengthen his demanding tone that I must breathe something supportive to the state. I felt the manipulative manoeuvres he was using without even saying a word.

During his talk about the developments in my hometown though, somehow, I had a gut feeling that he did not come to my dorm for the sake of intellectual debate. He came for something more. I just did not know what it was. Later, I discovered that my conversations in my own dorm would follow me even to this day and were used as a justification to harm my life so deeply.

As an attempt to find out what was going on in my dorm, and trying to understand who was following me, and to what end, I uttered some positive reflections to Angesom's ego, which I was to use as a tool to find an answer to my question to identify the informants that frequented my dorm and the level to which their reports ascend.

I knew that everyone would talk once he left and if he would know what I or any other person would say contrary to the remarks they made, then we have someone else who feeds him information. This way I would be sure there were at least two people who collaborated in this.

As soon as he left, some students mocked him as usual. I expressed my contempt at the government and that I was not happy with almost extorting good words from my mouth using the new university as a leverage. Guess what, two years later we ended up in a debate almost close to a fight.

We were staying at Addis Ababa University dorms to do our internship. I remember that we walked from Addis Ababa University entrance all way to Lideta Campus where we stayed for two months. It can be an hour walk.

I argued that Meles was not supposed to kill the people to make his case. As it was known that he would win in rural areas that make up the majority of the constituents in the country, and of all the people how come he did this — was my argument. Cities were equally important.

Clearly, I had high regards for Meles even if I hated his politics. First, I got a humbling lesson that, Angesom was informed in the day that blamed the state as soon as he left the dormitory, following his question about my impressions about the planed university in my home town. He came to my dorm on a mission and recalled every bit of the occurrences. He was making me aware that they could hear almost everything at any time and place.

This followed me even up till late life that this was reported to some ranks. From our discussion he realised that I did not represent any party or was not a member anywhere.

I learnt that my name was passed among students to be jailed and tortured. I was notified for the third time with the list of students that were already kidnapped and that I could be next any time. We all were terrified that almost all of us wanted to leave the university compound and return when all calms down.

I left the university and hid at a friend's place for about three weeks until the political dust settled. At this point of my life, it was the Gondarians who saved my life by passing timely information for my protection.

In our heated talks, Angesom told me that I was their target in their fear of supporting Kinijit party (Coalition of Unity and Democracy CUD), a popular one that was led by Professor Berhanu Nega and famous engineers, lawyers, journalists and intellectuals.

By the time I was listed and treated as enemy of the state, the informants from my dorm had thrown me under the bus before my adult life even begun.

This gave me a sense of how organised the surveillance and intelligence were. Later, I contacted an intelligence officer, a trusted lady, and said to her that I wanted to know who the informant was who had sat in my dorm back in the day staining my name.

Ayimalo, the person responsible for this, came to my parent's home during my visit in 2017 and confessed that he was passing information. He said 'ne hewode kinijite gidiki?' Ayimalo asked me if I were not a CUD member. As if the torture was justifiable, and as if I did not have the freedom to work with any party of my choice.

He would argue fiercely to convince me that it was my fault. He did not want to hear my side of the story.

At some point I wanted to chock him and throw him off my father's sofa where he was sitting. He looked like the demons hurting my cousin in Holozo. He did not even have the slightest clue about what was going on in my mind, because I was calm and composed. The truth is, I was boiling inside. He was unaware that I pictured him as a man who had also contributed to the government's decision to throw me out of the country to live in exile.

By the time he sat with me, he held a political position which was probably given to him as a reward for ruining several other lives. This triggered the question as to whether the country was poor or if this was about the way people treat each other and the beliefs they dearly held in their hearts.

Clearly, Ayimalo's cruelty did not go without bearing a cost in the personal level in my life. With Holozo's verdict added, it made the government intelligence unit think of me as an enemy of the state. What was disgusting was that Ayimalo and people like him assumed that we still shared the same views of religion and social values. They chose a religion, of torturing people and harming their lives for little gain with the power they were supposed to use to make the world a better place.

This is more hurtful than the Holozo level of cruelty, I would say, considering the horror and heinous spiral of killings to change it all.

What started as a local friction had taken up the shape of a man finding himself caught up in the crossfire of a countrywide struggle. This meant that I was not alone. There must be countless others whose local intricacies set them up for much bigger fights, at times questionable if these were worth it.

Because my father repeatedly said 'awa worida boray na'ay woqa gidide ges' meaning the bull that killed the father visits his son until he is old enough. My father made it clear to me that the people who hurt him would not spare me. They are merciless and beastly individuals void of reasoning and humanity.

My fear was right; I was persecuted by the same body, not because of my character or my past mistakes, or the type of people I was connected to but because one I was from Wolaita, and two, because of who my parents are in Wolaita.

Several Holozo sites

I would learn the needle edges I was to walk through in my later life as my concerns and fears were real and that I was correct in suspecting that I was being seriously followed. When I was a high school student, I wanted to open a humanitarian organisation that would help women and children.

This was not because of a childhood fantasy. I grew up in a family that was repeatedly beaten up by government operatives that pay a visit whenever they feel like having the fun of hurting people. My mother is born from a royal family, a curse in Wolaita if not all over Ethiopia. The state hated it. Meles hated it. Local politicians hated it. Because of this and because Ethiopia is a low-income country, we had severe poverty as I believe. Several people would dispute against my views of poverty saying that we were among many poor people, even the whole country is so. But for me, I believe that a shared poverty, and imposed one on top of it, hurt twice.

Not that my mother considers her royalty as something important. She lived most part of her life distancing herself from such views. She would say, *"I did not earn it through a hard work. I am just born in it."* She was part of the social movement back in the day that taught them of human equality. She is probably the calmest quiet and observant person I know in my entire life.

She is very reserved to say something. Unless she is hard-pressed, she would remain quiet until talks are wrapped, and she would just greet for a goodbye. From how I see it today, she must have been deeply hurt by the double harm. She suffered from the social injustice like everyone else. Added to this she experiences more pain for who she was.

You see, the people mobilizing the social movements used it as a tool to harm and subjugate people like her. They promoted equality to get to power and used it to do worse than what we learnt in history. Then came Eihadig with its hell to my family. For those who do not know, Ehadig is a slang for the former government of Meles also abbreviated in Amharic to its equivalent, but people twisted it a bit.

My father was the Dergue army member for whom the Meles government had extreme sense of vengeance and hate. To make it worse, he would argue about the divide and rule policy they have and denounce ethnic divisions as acts of people with little intelligence. He would sit almost with everyone who opened a debate line. He was surely the enemy of the state, not that he considered to be one, it is that he was profile to be so. The intelligence community had list of families in every township and village. My father knew that they were hurting him for his political views. He had no choice other than living with the pain of it.

My parents' house was the Holozo site of the Wolaita punishment for which the powers and mandates of the federal and local government were also employed for legitimacy of present-day verdict. It is also a known fact that ex-Dergue soldiers and political mobilizers also their family members were exposed to a deliberate harm.

It became known to most people that more homes became several Holozo sites. Instead of going to Holozo for punishment, this time around, it came to everyone's home. This reversed direction took place in this generation. Instead of erasing Holozo from people's memory, and keeping it only in history records, murky hearts brought it into people's living rooms. They managed to perfect this by using the security apparatus as a clandestine tool of their clans.

Among family members, I grew up with uncles and aunties who go to a monotheist faith, evangelical/ protestant, Orthodox, Catholic and Adventist faith centres. While my father was a converted anti-communist, particularly the Albanian brushed doctrine of Meles, a few of his relatives were fond of it. Even if the talks were dominated by culture equality, solidarity and a universalist approach to social and economic life aspects, there were relatives who believed that without Capitalism societies would stagnate sooner or later, depending on their thresholds, they would inevitably collapse just like previous civilizations.

This all just made me realise in my young life that there is more to people than religious ethnic, social, economic or political fences around us. At the same time, I have had the chance to learn as much as diversity may enrich tolerance, it also may mean a risk to lack of coherence and consensus over simple matters if issues get in the way.

Pour Me the Black Milk

Situations demanded that I perform as the first son as my older brother never liked responsibility. He is a free-spirited person who would never abdicate this for a socially designed unwritten and unclear role. He chose his role, being absent from any age-related contributions. He lived free!

This was how I learned that his freedom may mean my burden, in such a situation where roles are misplaced. It does not matter if the roles were rightful or not in the first place. I had to pay for it.

I am the second child and my father knew that I was good at coordinating and talking to people, managing issues and handling pretty much everything even in the absence of my parents. I was good with money too.

I had to mature much younger which was not fun as my friends would be playing while I always had something important to do.

I refused my father's idea of studying social sciences specially leadership and management, but I had to pay for it by chasing and escaping from the profession the rest of my life. It purely is his Karma that remained inescapable until recently.

It was after I had worked with social movements that I understood the purpose he had in mind when wanting me to study social streams. He wanted me to fill the family gap by playing a public role which he did not get the chance to do himself. But he knew I was born with the gift and the drive to perform the expected duties.

I grew up helping my mother as our little sister was not old enough yet, my older brother was so proud to even touch anything and against all the culturally appropriate belief of not going to the kitchen, I would go in, put on some separate cloth and do almost everything.

From baking injera to fetching water (as we did not have water tap until I was at high school), washing clothes, making coffee to cleaning the house, collecting firewood to going to the open market — I did it all. I even carried enset, fresh maize, potatoes and sweet potatoes from my father's or mother's village as my parents' finances were in a very bad shape. There was even a time when I went to the bushes with friends and ate fruits from the bush trees. We did this for fun of doing our own stuff than staying home as sweet boys.

Even if I would make coffee for everyone, I had a health problem when I drank it, especially my heart would be racing as if it just wanted to fly out of my mouth. It was not until after college that my body got used to it. But every time I make coffee, I would never forget what she said one day. While I was serving coffee, she said to me, 'my son, pour me the black milk.'

One thing I noticed with coffee was that you get the chance to hear stories, and later in life, you either read a book, listen to a song about it or others may tell you even deeper than how much you know. Coffee tables are the best for this as many of the best stories are shared here, as many would be trying to pour the best of what they have read, learned or listened to. Now such places are either at a lounge, cafes, sidewalks, school backyards, bed rooms or a plane seat.

What sounded like a fable happens to be verified by historians even by some American and other archaeologists performing research on some sites close to my hometown. One of the stories I heard strikes me the most.

In ancient empire of the Damot, 3000 BC, there lived a widely revered prophet whom people called Hiragawa. The empire ruled over eighty-five per cent of present-day Ethiopia, northern part of Kenya, all way to Turkana and beyond to the shores. His name came from the idea of Hiragawa — the prophecy man. He was born in an exceptional midnight full moon when a small needle could be seen on the ground and darkness was never to be seen even until the morning. His mother, Buchamo Aye, whose reputation was secretly immolated by a woman in recent years, was a medicine woman and knew a lot about the signs of the mysterious works of the deity and the highest.

As per the advice she forwarded, her husband Ayikalo and her dedicated their son to the most-high, raising him for the tasks of divine mission without toiling the soil or raising cattle, as all his needs were served while he was watchfully learning about the voices of heaven, messages of the holy and instructions of the angels. As their son grew older and wiser, people would travel for wisdom and revelation all the way from the shores of Turkana also Afriqa Gita Abba which is today's Indian Ocean and the mountains of Bale, from the waters of Baro and the savannas of the rift valley area. He soon started to tell the visions, of what would happen in ten or twenty-five, fifty, a hundred and a thousand years as milestones of time for easier following of the realisation of his prophecies.

Many kings lost wars when they went against his directions of not engaging weaker kingdoms at their desperation, some restored their crowns after long sufferings and testing character once they erred, they would find roots and herbs for medicating during cattle plagues and found township locations withstanding wars, flooding, landslides and water shortages.

The Hiragawa, who was also called the messenger a few times, became the go-to-man at as early as the age of twenty-five. The communal courts adjourned with justice, the traders never cheated on scales, distant merchants would get the genuine currency of Marchuwa, the forest police would guard the security of wild animals, vegetations and wonderers; the messenger had proven to be the perfect guide of the Wolaita and its siblings who had faced disruption of their ways of life due to change of governance from being led by wise queens to the new arrogant and less consulting men who started calling themselves the emperors of the Damot Empire.

This created societal panic from kingdom to kingdom which exposed the vacant space of independent guidance and the perfection of keeping a social balance.

In place of the widely practiced concept of shared wealth and the insurance of the much- celebrated social capital, the men who started calling themselves emperors started demanding that they would be given new and virgin girls and lands that were not ploughed by common men nor seen the face of any cattle around it.

As the custom demanded, the communal judges gathered and called the public to allot new land slots for the kingdoms and that this would be the law of practice across all the lands of the Damot Empire. The people, who saw wealth and upper life as the norm for the most able and working, found this request as an intolerable demand and unacceptable even if it came from the emperor, whom they had appointed from among themselves, and saw no reason of the emperor getting anything more and different from what the queens had been blessed with.

This created serious instability, sporadic clashes between the king's guards and the groups of the people's police that guard the most parts of the land. It soon erupted into internal war where the emperor was secretly moved to a safer location across the border of the neighbouring Borana tribes. While the war was devastating farmlands, killing cattle and burning houses, the ruler of Borana requested the king to consult the matter with the Hiragawa, who solved the mysteries of his dynasty and set forth clear path that had not only enabled him to rule in peace for the past ten years, it also created trust and cooperation between his lower ranks and families that demanded an heir should be selected from their sons. After stubborn and deflecting refusal of the council, the emperor gave in to the idea as his Ganna, the diplomatic negotiators, sided with the ruler of the Borana in the idea and threatened that they would leave him there and return to the motherland to elect a new emperor and accept the fate with the rest of the people. The emperor accepted the offer.

On the arrival of the emperor, chacha zayiya, karabiya (drums) and several other full lines of orchestra were played while troops of dancers, theatrical shows men, acrobatics and horse riders performed a grand welcome back to the throne. Once people took seats and silence reigned, the emperor stood and held a stoically measured, articulate and focused speech on the new member of his minister's council who was gifted in guiding future plans and forecasting the coming situations that would soon become the normal day-to-day life of the partakers in his empire. As the tradition demanded it, the emperor then gave the floor to three wise men of the communities to express their validation and acceptance of the proposed new post of Hiragawa and the return of the leader back to his throne.

The first old man took the stage, called for calm and silence and started to clear his throat just before speaking very loudly. And he said:

"My beloved emperor returnee, his noble family members, all my sons and daughters, sisters and brothers, all the lovers of our emperor and the protectors of our land, may all of you receive heavenly blessings with abundance and excess of the most-high. I was breastfed and raised amongst you; played, erred and sharpened in your hands; was married and gave birth to children who are sitting with you here and now.

My people listen to me now. The emperor's reinstating to power and the appointment of the Hiragawa to his council of ministers, moconata as the Wolaita call them, is a blessing and the indication of a new era of hope at our doorsteps. We shall welcome them both, and the families of each, to the seats of the empire and shall listen, obey and provide our tax proceedings accordingly. My speech is completed."

Once he said this, he lifted both of his hands up, waved them towards all sides where people sat and gave the floor back to the stage conductor. The two wise men also validated, blessed and sat, respectively.

The Ethiopian Prophet (Hiragawa)

Once the Hiragawa was ushered to stand at the twenty centimetres' higher stage on which the ministers stood and spoke, mostly after the opening speeches of the emperor, he waved to the people with both of his hands and all the people stood on their feet, clapping, cheering and beating drums.

He was dressed in a milk white free dress that hung by the mid shaft of his lower leg, halfway below his knees. The dress had two lines of black stripes from the middle of both shoulders all the way to the edges of his dress. He also had two more stripes each on the right and left sides of his arms, also from his shoulders all the way to his wrists. The white line created between these two black stripes and resting on his chest represent the straight path up to the heavenly seats of the most-high. The stripe lines of the arms and the chest cross each other midway, making a cross on his shoulders. These also create a white line, indicating the path to the wonders and searches of human wisdom and the purity of the intent to guide in truth, sincerity, loyalty and seeking heavenly counsel as it also intersects with the lines of the heavenly wisdom right on the top of his shoulders. On the top of intersection, that makes the cross, the spot is attached with conical black cup made of pigeon's feathers and its sharp end is pointed towards the sky. This makes the cross the junction of heavenly path and human wisdom while the cup represents pointing towards the most-high signifying the ultimate human curiosity and will in the end point towards the heavens. He also wore a pair of trousers underneath, which were made in the empire's favourite colour mixes of black, yellow and red.

The Hiragawa looked very commanding with imperial authority and the blessings of the wise men, and everyone looked towards the black cone, implying the highest enlightenment of the messenger and of the importance of pointing to the heaven. Elders would stare at the sky every now and then, mostly followed by the younger ones more with curiosity of anything particular to be seen on the sky.

All went into complete silence and total immobility, no one even coughed or stretched their arms for the slightest movement. He opened his speech and said:

"The Empire of the Great Damot, the people of the Wolaita and all siblings, today I stand before our beloved emperor and all of you to tell you two prophecies and a new direction for our empire's stability, our shared growth, holistic prosperity and accumulating wealth abundant for generations to come.

We are the people who may engage in discontent and inflicting suffering to each other, but when we learn and stop it, we also know better than many about the ways of toiling the soil, breeding cattle, melting the iron, mining gold and stones, trades and merchandise, the methods of war and sharing spoils too. We are not like savages of the unenlightened who live in the darkness and lack of wisdom and direction. The savages envy our sharpness and are ashamed of their inequities. We are people of high moral, children of the light, a family of the wise and a community of the learning. We win because one of us wins. And we conquer because all of us are victorious. We may be pushing our emperor to exile, but his absence makes us see what is missing, and his presence makes us complete. While the emperor was away, he saw how empty a man is without his people and he too followed the lights of truth that teaches us that people without a leader are exactly like cattle scattered in the lion's den.

Here are the messages we all shall keep close to our hearts, hold in our palms, sing in our songs, play with children, write on our walls, carve on the wood and inscribe on the stones for the coming generation shall see what has been foretold and plans were made to prepare our lands for them.

Behold, the people of the Great Empire of the Damot.

Today, on the day of his re-ascension to this empire, we shall reinstate the emperor to his throne. All able people shall obey his commands, defend his will and protect this land from the enemies from outside and from within. By obeying this message, our land will enter the epoch of being led by the enlightened, counselled by the wise, protected by the strongest and promoted by the eloquent. The farms will yield twice the crop size, the cattle will breed without plagues, the children will be born without miscarriage, the toddlers will grow without illness, daughters will marry good men, men will profit from their trade, the mothers will care for honourable family, fathers will bring pride to their homes, wealth will be at the gate of all and happiness will be in all backyards, the sound of the birds will resume, and they too will start singing, for our singers will envy them and sing even better, the drums will be deep, our flutes will get perfect tunes, girls will sway men's hearts and men will steal the soul of their love. The people of the most-high, and our blessed emperor, blessed days are here for we all listen to each other and to the most-high.

Here are the prophecies I saw:

Our men and women will fly to the stars the moon and the wisest of all will land on the surface of the sun. They will bring lights of the sun in their hands, wrap soils of the sky in their leather chests. For when they return, they will look darker in their colour and slow to talk. They will bring the future close to us and the life of tomorrow to our gates. They will see the earth and all in it through a thin sheet of heat-baked sand.

In those years, our children will teach each other about our territory on the surface of the sun and its inner hells will be like the melting stones red and jelly-like. Those who believe will flock to the moon and the stars, but only the children of the Damot will make it to the sun and return to tell the story. For we are the blessed and sacred people, the sanctity of heavens will shield us through the garment made to withstand any heat and fire.

Hear me, my children, as people who have the territory on the sun, our great, great grandchildren will have two laws for land issues. The first law will allot abundant land on the plateaus of the sun for each family according to how much they ask from the emperor's registry permits. The second law demarcates among the land properties of the people, the emperor, his ministers (moconas), soldiers and craftsmen.

For the people who can agree about their land acquisitions on the territory of the sun, they will be wiser to create harmony about the common blessed land here on the earth. For if the man can have a colony on the sun, he can have the whole world for himself without hindering others from having the exact same abundance he once wanted for himself. This is the law of the sun on the Earth.

The law of the sun on the Earth is the rule of peace, the order of harmony, the dominance of high moral thoughts and ways of life. As perfectly flawless, this law is a dictating scroll across the farthest of the Earth's globe and the deepest of the waters and the wealth that is in its chest.

The law of the sun on the Earth is observed by people of the high spirituality and those whose sights can see the inner worlds of the soul while they can tend to the surrounding environment.

The observants of the laws of the sun on Earth would grow trees, care for vegetations, water plants and weed flowers. They will never fail short of fruits in their gardens and will always have more to give to others.

The observants of the laws of the sun on Earth will know abundant wealth, created by prospering many than by keeping them poor like the wicked. For the ways of wealth know no light in greed that has no end. The generational abundance of prosperous life comes to those who dream to be stewards of the Earth's blessings than the self-gratifying.

The observants of the laws of the sun on the Earth keep their weakest, support their strongest and defend their youth. For when they are around, no one will be oppressed. They know no war for disputes and no harms for disagreement. They talk their ways away from wars and sing the melodies of love to their adversaries. For they grow powerful, no one shall harm them and live to see the scent of their grandchildren. For their pain calls for floods, drops of their tears dry up the lands, their anger wipes cattle and their fury barrens the grass. They will be called conquerors of the sun. For they will own and preside over territories on the sun.

My children, for as long as you shall live, you must observe the laws of the sun on Earth. Behold, the people of the Great Empire of the Damot! In the years to come, when you walk away from the law of the sun on the Earth, you will have black milk that will wake you but will never grow your bones strong. You will drink the black milk that will not nourish your little children, nor your pregnant will get strength out of it. For the black milk will be poured from a black pot, nothing white will come out of it. On these days, you will know you will have too many children raised without wisdom. Your children will be woken by the black milk and will become weary of it.

There will be the strange years to come, for by then you will till the soil more for less crops. And your cattle will grow to be less and less in numbers and size. Their milk will start withering away until strange cows are brought from the Pharoah's shores of the north and the waters of the east covering the coastal lines of the big mother land, Afirqa. Your cows will breed less, and the far land cows will be the grazers of your grass. Behold your children will have less cattle and will slaughter goats, sheep and unpopular animals in the dark.

People will visit you from far places and will bring you the iron bars, the herbs men will be one amongst you. The great empire of the Damot shall hold steadfast to the laws of the sun on Earth and retain the cow's milk for its children and the meat and its cheese for the market, the black milk will be for foreigners who own cows with excess milk, for by then you shall seek wisdom to the ways of your world with them."

The elders of the Wolaita and its siblings would tell the history of coffee to their children and grandchildren while the evening coffee was being prepared. Once upon the time, the merchants of the Kaffa brought with them sidling of a special-quality coffee plant which the Wolaita call tukiya. The Kaffa people back in the day used to boil the red coffee beans, filtered the waste and drunk the freshly squeezed coffee, which the Latin American side of the world calls cascara. The cascara, though, is made from dried coffee bean cover leftovers while the Kaffa would throw the beans to keep their animals happy and alert. It helped them breed the finest beef that were shipped to many close by areas and across the shores as far as the Mesopotamia and Arabia.

While the Wolaita cultivate Tukiya plant, coffee, around their houses, making the final line after crops and mostly before false banana plants to protect from the wind, birds and animals rushing towards children that make their way to the cottage houses. The Kaffa were so bright in being the first to declare as discoverers of coffee, the people of Omo pressing for cascara, the Wolaita pride to have invented the present-day technology of coffee processing. The skilled Wolaita families in pottery created a special pot for coffee making unlike the far north Tigraway and others alike. The type of coffee maker commonly made by the Wolaita is a ball-shaped, medium-sized clay pot with a long neck that is attached to a curved handle. The curved handle is attached with the back-side neck of the coffee maker pot in one end and the middle of the back side of the pot's belly. A nose-like tube that is protruding from a little above the middle of the front side is used to pour the hot coffee, with two main purposes. The first purpose is to correctly pour the coffee in the cups, while the second reason is both to avoid the coffee from dropping on the ground while pouring, also to avoid burns from the hot coffee that can occur during pouring it. The Tigraway coffee pot can be made both from clay and metal sheet, while the difference is that it mostly does not have the nose the Wolaita coffee maker pot has. While pouring, the steam of the coffee may burn the hands and because of which, it has not become that popular across Ethiopia.

The Wolaita prepare coffee in four different traditional ways and drink them depending on the hour of the day. In the mornings, mature and orange-coloured coffee leaves are collected from the backyard; washed, smashed and boiled in a very hot water. While the coffee is boiling, herbs, spices, ginger, garlic and salt are mixed and meshed in a wooden crusher or on a large stone-made mesher.

Once the smashed coffee leaves are boiled enough, they turn into deep red wine looking liquid. The liquid is separated from the leaf waste that is to be thrown back at the farm. The filtered liquid is poured through the neck of the coffee-making pot, Jebena, and is put back on fire. Then the smashed spice-herb mix is dropped in the Jebena to cook very well. The Wolaita call this Hayita Tukia, meaning Leaf Coffee. Once the Leaf Coffee is ready, it is usually taken out of the fire, and it rested for some minutes before serving with the clay cups which are now totally replaced by ceramic. The Leaf Coffee is also mixed with fresh butter for smoother stomach and avoiding constipation. This is called Oyisa Hayita Tukiya, leaf coffee with butter and is preferred by older people.

Other than the many in the Oomo valley that came up with the cascara, the Wolaita dried the beans, fried and crushed them and boiled the dark brown powder to make the coffee we use today. The Wolaita refer to the regular coffee as Ayipe Tukiya. In addition to drinking the dark brown coffee, the Wolaita add butter on it to call it oyisa tukiya, meaning coffee with butter.

In addition to the Wolaita, groups like the Gurage, the Kambata, the Hadiya, Sidama and many others may also add butter and may also have nuances of their specialties, but much of the regular coffee-making is done similarly all over the country.

In recent years, coffee defied the old tradition of confining women in the kitchen and helped them open Jebena Buna, traditional coffee brewery spots in all streets of townships in the entire country. Elders that know about the history of Coffee in Wolaita would sit at the street side local Coffee Bars and say — pour me the black milk. They mean pour me black coffee. Coffee is now the main employment of the Ethiopian women and has started to be the influencing factor for men to either find a job, work hard and show for it.

Chapter Two

The Walk to Asmara

I was about a five-year-old boy when they sent my father to the senseless war between the Dergue communist government and rebel groups up in the north. I was so attached to my father that I could not bear the feeling of missing him like super crazy.

When I realised that no one would take me to Asmara, I decided to walk 1470 kilometres, all on foot. Can you imagine that? When I realised that my father was nowhere close to coming back anytime soon, I started a plot of sneaking out of my parent's house and start my journey to find my father and bring him home.

There was no financial, material or any other plan, it was the simplest of any plans in the whole world a five-year-old boy could ever think of. Waiting for my mother to step her feet out of our house and start my long trip, that is pretty much about it.

On one of the longest days of missing my father, my mother went out of the house to visit a relative, if I recall it right. After ensuring that she would not return for reasons of forgetting a key or anything she had to take with herself, I went out and started my journey. Two main highways would get me from my hometown to Addis Ababa back in the day, either through Shashemene, the Ras Tafarian heaven city or an alternative route through Hossana. Now we have four choices. I chose the Hossana — Butajira — Addis Ababa — Asmara road.

After I walked some ten kilometres from Sodo town, I reached to a small village marketplace. Horses, mules, donkeys, cattle, goats and sheep were tied to trees or benches. People were buying and selling different items, among which soap, kerosene, clothes and powders were from cities while bananas, mangos, passion fruits, cereals, crops, potatoes, yam, cassava and sweet potatoes were commonly purchased. When I was getting close to the market, the buying-selling loud talks make it appear like it was the hot hour of the day.

While I was noticing what was going on in the rural business transaction chanting, I followed the mud road that is now a fully covered asphalt road. Soon after I passed the market, a woman started calling me, not by my name but saying, *"La na'awu awu bay?"* and *"La ne o na'e?"* meaning, 'You little boy, where are you going and whose son are you?'

I could tell she was worried about me. Very worried. In my heart, I was saying to her, 'Lady, just shut up and leave me alone. I have an important business to attend to. As you also must mind your business.' She kept insisting and would not stop trying to get my attention. At one point, she touched my shoulder and poked me. After several attempts, I told her about my father, with a pride towards in his commitment to the war and with his achievement as a teacher. She did not even recognise him as a teacher, let alone as a soldier. I was mad at her. But I kept it to myself.

She then asked me about my mother; I told her about her name and her parents, just like I did when I told her about my father. She started hitting her own chest with her fist and said, *"Xoso ta na'aw tana mo, tana lamotayi xugo, tassi gido. Tana awu tana ha mishoyi mo,"* meaning, 'May your hurt of missing your father be mine. May I suffer your pain. May it be for me.' She recognised my mother's parents, all of my uncles and aunties. She then insisted that she would take me to them instead of letting me keep going to Asmara. She said once the night falls, the hyenas would be all over the road and they would hurt me. The sun was setting, and the dark was taking over, we could barely see each other clearly. Eventually, she convinced me that if I wanted to continue my journey, I may have to sleep over at my grandparents' and get their permission.

My grandparents have a very wide field space left for animal grazing, while a line of trees protect the higher grass that is cut for evening-time food for the cattle. At the two junctions of the lined-up trees, there is the front of the cottage where different activities take place or just people sit for evening talks or jokes while waiting for dinner. The cottage is round and used to be mud-covered with the grass roofing. This is now changed with metal sheet when rectangular urban-shaped houses took over the traditional cottages.

Behind the cottage, the cabbages, tomatoes, pumpkins and herbs are grown. The second line is covered with false banana or enset and banana leaves. The next and third line is made by coffee trees. The rest is layers of sweet potatoes and potatoes, crops such as maize, wheat and teff.

The woman who brought me from the market was served with maze bread and yoghurt while my grandmother started making coffee for her, the family and me. After finishing her yoghurt, she rose up and said that she would miss out a lot in the market and excused before rushing back. After we had coffee, it was soon time for late dinner. I was then given a place to sleep and take some rest after walking a long distance.

The night I was lost, the whole of my hometown went out looking for me. The police, soldiers and volunteers all were looking for me at schools, churches, rivers, water streams, gathering places and even under bridges, anticipating that I may have fallen while playing around it. They had a megaphone shouting for my name and telling me that my mother is worried about me. And that I had to come home.

"Lij Andualem Tadesse — Son Andualem Tadesse

You are kindly requested to return home if you hear us.

Your mother and all your family members are looking for you.

Come to us now."

Street to street, block to block, they would do the same.

I was nowhere to be found. They thought that I was kidnapped and taken to other cities. There is a tribe in a neighbouring ethnic group that steals children for rituals such as cutting off male parts as a display of manhood and proving it to their bride-to-be. There were so many speculations and wild guesses that just made my mother cry even more.

The next morning, little before the birds sing, my grandparents' house was knocked like crazy. My late grandfather called for my uncle Abraham and told him to open the door. I thought if it were thieves, Amaha, one of the four soldiers in the house would have been told to open it. We all woke up and thought something had happened to the neighbours. It was my mother instead, followed by five people.

As soon as she stepped into the cottage, she shouted, "Is Andualem in this house?" and added "Are you here, Andualem?" with a fainting sound of losing hope.

My grandfather got up from his bed, greeted and welcomed everyone in. I was sweating like a pig and shivering out of fear. I was guilty as charged and look what I had caused! But what did I actually do? I just missed my father and wanted to bring him home. It was just that old lady who caused this detour from my way and trapped me to see this. I thought if I saw the woman again, I would tell her to never do such things to children at all.

While I was thinking of this, my grandfather said to my mother, "God has spared you from double harm. One is losing your son, and another is answering to your husband when he comes back from the war."

When my grandfather hinted that I was in his house, my mother rose up and started yelling, "Come here, let me see you, Andualem," and was searching for a stick or something to beat me with.

My grandfather got up and told my mother to sit down. It was one hell of a drama going on. He said, "No one is beating anyone in this house. My son missed his father who is participating in this senseless war. This war is the work of mad men who do not know how to sit and talk through their differences. It is them that need punishment! They are tearing families apart and causing pain to little children's heart."

When he stopped talking, my mother was sobbing. All the people that came with her stood up and held her tight and tried to calm her down. They tried to help her to sit on the three-legged wooden chair. She was not listening to them, let alone calming down or realizing what the situation had developed into.

I was still sweating the type of sweat where your armpits, back, feet, hands and even your hair gets soaked I ran out to my mother who hugged me and cried so much so that she would not listen to everyone's begging to stop her. She realised as I was a little boy, there was nothing she could do other than understanding my situation.

My father would tell us a bit of a teaser about their efforts of hiding propaganda pamphlets under false banana tree roots or carrying required equipment to places where it was needed. They would work with their comrades from the rest of the country all the way from Eritrea to Jinka.

One thing is for sure, that for every prominent profile to come out distinctly popularised and highly influencing the country-level progress, there are thousands of brightest men and women who labour underneath to make it all work. And it is the stories of such people that truly attracts me the most, knowing that most of them were by far the greatest and coolest personalities who would prioritise the collective progress, turning incompetent men and women into a formidable force and yet live a very humble social life; some of whom took it too far.

My father was among those people who wanted to lead by example, sacrificing the best of his days for what we would call progress. But what is progress if you are not in it? What if you are taken as a loyalty machine and production line worker who serves without a check, a recognition or even to be sold out whenever a shakeup takes place and that you come the first on the list of sacrifices to make it work? Just give me a break! Progress itself also needs to progress, or rather the practice of it has to be seen differently at times.

It Is All in the Names

"You are blessed or cursed based on obeying and changing them or refusing and keeping them."

One day in late 2020, I was deeply consumed by a thought while going to someplace in the Stockholm city metro. I woke up to realise that I had passed the train station I planned to exit and went five stops without noticing it. So, where was I? I walked about half an hour from my place and jumped in a metro travelling from a station called Telefonplan and to headed towards the Central Station and beyond.

We were waiting the train for about seven minutes. This is when you get impatient as the mid-November evening weather is telling you that winter is here, and you have to check your wardrobes and make changes to something warmer and thicker. As the Swedes say, no weather is too cold except the cloth being warm or cold.

While the minutes were getting closer, I saw two ladies passing by me, then a pretty girl that stood next to me, and went on after a guy who was also standing. They both kept walking to the last line of the train stop swearing at each other, throwing 'I hate you-s', 'ugly bitch-s', and 'fu*k you-s' at each other as if no one else was around. They both seemed super drunk with the way they walked and mumblings of words when they spoke. It is rather a less common place to see such incidents in Stockholm, especially towards the winter start when people save energy and behave reservedly for most part of it.

With this said, though, few people do the same even when they are not as much drunk but just when they are in the mood to party and are on their way to some place; be it a bar, pub or a club. In this case though, it is mostly teenagers and young adults that are full grown up and of the age the two ladies seemed to have. They looked something like forty-five and had features being in the same age group. People were either fidgeting, some walking here and there, some on their phones while others were surfing, the two ladies were almost forgotten except when we all turned towards a loud cry.

The first woman shouted, *"Är jag en hora?"* — 'Am I a whore to you?' and started to cry. She would repeat this over and over again.

Her friend took after her and said, *"Ja. Jag säger det!"* — 'Yes. I am saying so!'

And then literally everything changed.

The first woman continued, *"Jag visar dig hur en höra ser ut som en person."* — 'I will show you what a whore looks like.' And started to undress herself.

The men including myself turned away. I was hoping, a lot less expecting, that she would stop it there.

Four police members showed up as someone called the security, and by now the woman took off all her clothes and stood completely naked. They insulted each other crazily. At some point, the other woman took out milk and poured it on the naked friend of hers, and that was when I realised she had milk in her bag. Well, how would I know that she was fully naked unless a female member of the police said, *"Jesus, hon är helt naken!"* — 'Oh Jesus, she is totally naked!' And one of her male staffers said, "Ojojoj!" — 'S*it!'

Our train was ordered to pass us without taking any of us in, and we were stuck with two drunk women and four police force members who called for more support. With more help, they started to cover the woman's naked body and walked them both outside the station. I was walking partly on flashbacks and on the rest wrestling with myself from thinking about the deep scars and wounds name-calling can give people. Because for the naked woman, it was all about name-calling and she lost it all, exacerbated by considerably the excess alcohol she had poured in her blood. It was both her situation and the memory of what a popular engineer from my hometown told us that carried me away to forget my train station and brought me all the way to the fifth exit.

Of course, there is more to the story of name dismissal and forcibly giving a new Christianised, or Amharanised names, which triggered me to pay closer attention to what was happening at the Metro station. The encounters I had about this happened in my hometown and Addis Ababa.

On my vacation after the first-year studies of college, I went to see my parents, meet up with school mates to hear their stories of what took place during their studies of the year. One day, we sat at a rather popular hotel in Sodo, also across Ethiopia, Bekele Mola Hotel. It is frequented by the French, the Americans the Dutch and Germans, the Brits and many Italians. Most of us were returnees from campus year and a few were still at high school, but we all were buddies that hung around together.

With what can rather be taken as youthful naughty talk, we started mocking each other's fathers, mothers and almost every significant member of the city we grew up in. It was not that kind of the swear and slur words though, no! Not at all. It was questioning one thing. Why we were given Amharic names and not called with the local Wolaita names. We then started giving local names to each other. Once this exercise was over, we then moved on editing our father's names and replacing them with local names again, and some frenzy of laughter when meanings were mismatched and why the sneaky choice of a particular name was important would just wreck our laughter to the hell out of us. Without any reservation, we were spending the youthful freest moments of our lives to the point that everyone was allowed to mock at anything and anyone to the height they chose to realise that the jokes did not have to go all the way for some loose laughter to occupy the air. We were loud and occupied the entire hotel veranda as if no one else was around or watching us.

We were not as unwatched as I thought though. A known townsman, and an engineer by profession was listening to all our jokes and mockeries of our parents, ourselves and almost everything one of us would pick. What was emotionally and intellectually important to him was the one part where we joked about the names of our parents and that of ours. He just passed away recently, may he rest in power!

The engineer, Engineer Yacob Gebeto, built two of my former offices of both hospitals I worked at. A very disciplined, quality-oriented, value-driven and down-to-earth man against all the great things he had done in his life, for his family, loved ones and the country. We all not just respected him and his family (as the rest were also highly esteemed individuals), but also saw them as role models.

We barely noticed when we were having our youthful moments and Engineer Yacob graciously excused us and asked us if he could join our conversations. We were both shy and happy at the same time. I said, "Of course, Engineer!" And he dragged his table and joined our table. We were Chuye (Ephrem Daniel, whose uncle fought side by side with Meles and was killed on the final moments of victory on what appeared to be an obscure end-time betrayal), Eme (Behailu Fanta whom I trained for swimming), Degu (son of a late trader), Tarekegn (a mixed guy of Wolaita father and Oromo mother, a free-spirited man because of growing up in Harar) and me (son of a soldier, political play maker and teacher); five gangsters. Engineer Yacob became the sixth member on the table.

"You see, my children, when we were at your age, this city was not the way it looks like today. Even our villages were fully controlled, surveyed and those people in the power circle did as they wished and got away with it. We had less freedom than what you all have today. These people would come and plunder farms, snatch cattle or demand payments. They would kill stand or break legs or arms as easy as chasing mosquitoes away. They saw townships as if they were their properties. People were considered like personal toys and were treated worse than how animals are treated.

If you go to the churches, they silently supported them, they are in the police, the army, civil service and all service sectors in the town. Even the smallest of all, the postal office, was their own backyard. We had nowhere else to go or had much to do about it. They controlled and monitored all superstructures too and subjugated them to their gains and all we had were brains, literally ourselves as individuals. We were not allowed to do anything in groups or as a people with any sense of common identity or shared views. And values."

After telling us something, every few moments he would pause for a thought and would stare at the table deeply with stiff muscles of his neck and wrinkled his forehead making three horizontal lines on both right and left sides and two in the middle above his nose. He sounded all genuine and seemed to share it all with real sincerity. He looked like he was swallowing so much of anger and was seen struggling to contain his tears. He was in a deep emotional pain in just explaining about it to us, that he just said, "You have it too easy for yourselves now, all too well. You must feel grateful about what you have to work to get it even better.

"My children," he said, "there was a time when recruitments were to take place for the security and high-ranking officer jobs at Hurso academy. Emperor Haile Selassie sent out letter to all *awurajas* — 'provinces' except the Wolaita awuraja; let's call it 'Wolaita Province'. He sent strict verbal orders that this is not to be shared with anyone in Wolaita and that none of their students should be admitted at the academy. We heard of this several months later after recruitments and admissions were already completed and studies had begun.

After hearing the news of this, we went to our villages and met each other on our way of going to the open marketplace and started to come up with a way of bypassing this glass ceiling imposed over us. While many solutions were suggested, the dominant one was to change our full names to Amhara names and register in other *awurajas* than our own. This did not only become a widely accepted secretive move, but it also even proved itself to be highly effective for all of us. We all went to neighbouring and even far-away *awurajas* (provinces) such as Gamo-Gofa, Jima, Sidama, Shoa and a few went to Addis Ababa. Most managed to change their names in one of the provinces and found employments and admissions at academies and better access to economy.

Most of us performed greatly and built names for ourselves. Even many managed to excel and get known in their townships, provinces and were invited to higher studies. This then became a problem, as when the emperor came to the Hurso Academy and even other colleges to give medals, some Wolaita students managed to become medallists that caused alarms and severed our chances for later. We all yelled — 'why?'"

Then the engineer continued, "You see, to give higher positions, they needed to do background checks of students, as simple questions as where they come from, where their close ones live and so on. This somehow exposed many of our own and things started to get bad again. Excelling in the studies did not buy us mercy or the goodwill of the monarchy to continue our studies and do something good with it. Because we were exactly like unwanted children of the country.

"We were denied of our existence as a people group. We were cast out and cursed upon. There was a very systematic campaign to get us hated, fall under suspicion and get ill treatments by individuals if they wished to be bad to us. We were also to be slowed up on, get delayed decisions, even got many of our dossiers shelved if we submitted a request for services others get very quickly and without any major problem. We were not just discriminated and hated, we were hunted and targeted. It was daily bread and water to be stepped up on.

"By then, the only one who would listen to us without judging was God. But even God was deeply silent and we had no one to turn to here on Earth. My children, what we went through was a real hell that I wish to happen to no one, even to the worst of my enemies, I would not curse it to fall upon them. My children, Ethiopian-ness was not for us. We were not trusted, and people were told to never trust us at all. The controversy of all of this is that most of governors of the National Bank (which one can arguably call the treasury of the country) was mostly managed by people of Wolaita as records show. It is an obvious psychological warfare.

We were painted to be perceived as evil and beastly that people were advised to stay away for their own safety. And this all was supported by the state institutions. While all the others were enjoying their advantages of being related to the state or those in positions, we were met with disincentives instead. This was so that others would advance in life, leaving us behind so that we would be kept poor and unable to pay to send our children to schools or even just make sure they may eat food for their dinner. My children, the growing number of poor people and the mass poverty we see today is the result of man-made barrier to hold our people back and to starve us one by one. Poverty is man-made, my children. It does not happen out of the blue.

"I beg you all to not pay this back to any of their children or their grandchildren. The reason why I am telling you this is for you all to know how we have got here, what our people went through and why it is important that you all have the awareness to prevent its return in case the tides go against us once again."

"Why are you worried? We will fight if we have to," said one of my friends.

My fear is that these bad days may befall upon us again, and you all must know what this means in the real sense. He then took out a tissue paper and wiped his tears.

We all looked at each other, then at him and silence reigned among us.

He said, "Most of our generation that had to do the things I told you only for the sake of employment, access to economy and improved social status all carried a deep sense of guilt, as we all have this feeling of identity loss, partially for some of us who just changed our full names, but also more to those who went on marrying Amhara wives and denying their identity. Please, my children, I understand if you are angry at us, but I must beg you to not judge us for just trying to survive in the fenced system unlocking which was only through burying our identities and carrying on a new identity from the Amhara. We were subject to forceful cultural prescription."

Still having some troubled feelings from the engineer's stories, I went home and hit my bed only to turn left and right, staring at the roof, getting up trying to read a book, and playing music, all failing to arrest my impatience and bringing any little feeling to fall asleep. I was battling with the idea of Ethiopians imposing some way of 'Ethiopian-ness' on others who just have their natural 'Ethiopian-ness' that was just to be embraced then deleted. Only God knows what else they did, which this man did not telling us or may not have been informed of. I was asking myself if the story should have stopped here, or if they should have fought it systematically in response. I did not know what I had to think, but I was attempting to pick and drop all sorts of ideas.

This sounded a lot more like what Dima Negewo, Oromo leader, said in a long conversation I had with him, where part of the talk included explanations about the sacrifices made by the Oromo sons and daughter (Qeerroo and Qarree) that they realised that identity reclaiming was an important step in taking back what was theirs. I remember we sat at the Sheraton Hotel in Addis Ababa, where our discussion was more of healing the Oromo—Wolaita relations, but also fixing and improving the political gaps created at the country level. He was great to listen to. And he is a great listener himself and one can see experience really pays off with his level of endurance that most young people lose because of being impatient and oversensitive to time, to the point where the main issue gets ambushed. In this theme, they changed their forcefully imposed Amharic names back to Oromo names. Many of political leaders, intellectuals, the academia and traders who are mostly in the diaspora changed their names at the courts to reclaim Oromo-ness.

Luckily for the Oromos, the Germans and Scandinavians deployed for missions did not limit their assistance only at sharing spiritual views, but also extended the practice of rights awareness, facilitated education, travels overseas and trained and enabled them to engage in political movements, parties and even facilitated or supplied what was needed for armed struggle. This gave them to change their names back to Oromo names and claim their original identities. And this is the tip of the iceberg in addition to taking over the country's politics. For every systematic discrimination and harassment they faced, they used international access to de-condition themselves, and freed themselves from the enforced 'Ethiopian-ness' and re-oriented and took control of their sense of self.

It is not clear to me yet as to why the Americans that lived in Wolaita for almost 100 years have not paid enough attention to the visible social issues, the slightest of what is visible in the partnerships of the Germans, the Scandinavians, the Norwegians and the Irish with their counter parts in Ethiopia. The humanitarian imperative appeals to the good conscience of nations to partner for improved human rights, better development and positive social progress. Or maybe I am missing out something here.

Wrapping up the stories though, whether it was the naked woman at the train station, the engineer's batches of students or the Oromos all witnessed people get under their skins. All that happened was to be given names, in place of the names their minds were at peace with and emotions were at their healthy levels. For all the three types of people here, it is all about names than whether they meant anything in real life. It was the dishonouring an individual's dignity or disrespecting a group that got all the three naked publicly and stand with their skins visible to all.

Yes, the woman's body was naked, but wasn't it getting naked when an identity is skinned away from a person or a group and a new skin was grafted in its place? Isn't it equally shameful to be told that you are not who you say you are? Why can't a person be themselves and a contributing member of the society? And some people go to the distance of saying what your parents were telling you since childhood does not represent your identity. Here you have a new identity. Take it or leave it, it is up to you. But on the occasion of refusing to take, do not assume that you will get a job, income or any social services. The social services, employment, academic admissions and obtaining income are not arranged for the likes of you who do not look like us. You are not one of us. And to be one of us is to be called like us and start believing that you are not yourself any more until you join us on this side of the world than your miserably hated cage we have made for you.

Identity denial and taking it off of someone is undressing them of what they feel they identify themselves with in a forcible manner so much so that they feel ashamed for going through such situations. The guilt and sense of powerlessness meant that they kill the inner self and put on the new hat of external cover. Dishonouring the will of people and giving them new identities, acceptable behaviours and newly lucrative virtues are the acts of social engineering to wash away pre-existing collective sense of togetherness and disrupt the people's accustomed way of life to the disadvantage of the targeted.

"What a shame!" I said to myself, while the talk was slowly changing from politics to telling what we study, our encounters at campus and so on as the engineer was asking us one by one. After a little while of less tense talks and light jokes, the engineer loosened up a little bit and excused us once again, went to his pickup field car, got in and left us while waving away.

Highly Personalised Hostilities

I experienced my first assassination attempt in my hometown while I was in a car with a friend of mine in 2007. I used to drive a car and park it at a closely hotel as my parents did not have a proper parking as we have today. On a weekend my friend Anjo and I took off to a nearby place to chill and discuss issues of business. After several hours of spending time, we started heading back to the town.

Just before we drove some five kilometres all the four tyres started sounding funny. We stopped the car and realized that all the lug nuts were loosened. We took the car to a mechanic friend for his inspection, and who said in his conclusion — "it was done by someone who assumed you would drive at fast speed, one or more of the tyres would fly, you would instantly lose your balance, and then your car rolls over for a fatal crash.

Such clandestine incidents are not usual, but they happen to few people who caught attention of evil people. You must have a real enemy that wants you dead without a trace of its cause. If I must tell you, it is not anyone other than intelligence personnel that are instructed to target you. God wants you to live and tell the story."

While I was at high school, I shared with my friends my idea of wanting to build a humanitarian organisation, companies and organisations. On my college study front, I gauged my results and would put more time if I saw it is going too low. I was not aiming at becoming an A-grade student. Not that it was impossible, I had already made up my mind before I set my feet at the university gate. I would spend more time on the issues I wanted to focus on than chasing after grades and graduate empty headed with just a degree and no clear purpose in life other than to become like every other employee.

While I was working at Sodo Christian Hospital, I was setting up the office for the new humanitarian organization I had been working since high school and was putting things together. At the same time, two things started to slip away from me. And I was not in control at all.

At this point my haters stepped up the war. They threatened my American partners that they would get shot at if they would not leave Ethiopia; created a story and tricked a woman who agreed to rent out an office space and made her lie against the organization. The Americans left Ethiopia having serious doubts that things would work out later.

It took me almost a year to bring back my donor and his team. Seven people came, we signed a Memorandum of Understanding and that the deliverables were clear, and my roles were laid out.

I relocated to Hossana town, got a room, settled in and started focusing on building the organisation. Our financier was a very kind man, gifted in listening and discerning a younger me seeing through a possibility of setting up the humanitarian organisation. I hired nineteen staff members, built the working process, put up financial and other important policies partially from my studies where a Nigerian professor, who was also a common friend of Melkamu and myself, helped me with it. Partly because of Bridge Ethiopia, an Israeli humanitarian organisation where the manager used to coach me shared a few documents I needed to have a look at. I also was helped by my Australian professor, and three professors from The Netherlands.

As soon as smooth work process was set up, and that people were oriented, trained and equipped to deliver on their roles, something came up. A policewoman, top officer, a politician and two other government workers were sent to arrest me. Whatever they were told, the meeting with me proved that they were lied to and that the policewoman broke into tears seeing that we were there to help their community.

The personal pressure against me started coming back one by one. At some point, I realised that they wanted to control the humanitarian organisation and I was in their way. Now from this aspiring young man who just wanted to do good, I had become an unwanted person because of the very good thing in me. For worse of it, I was just starting but they wanted to see the end of it, NOW. What complicated it was that one of my drivers seemed to have some sort of affair with my American colleague who listened to his gossip and went against the choices of the board and the donor that wanted to stand on my side.

All attempts were made, clearly all doors were closed, and I sat with two of my colleagues trying to convince them that my resignation would buy them time. After intense talks, heated arguments and some taping, we all agreed to give a try to my resignation. I handed it in but made sure that it was audited that they would not confiscate receipts or important documents to implicate me with something.

A decade later they jailed the person they planted in my organisation for charges that are not clear to me apart from his role to transport weapons and his participation to overthrow a zonal government. What I know is that they used the organisations license to amass money and illegally smuggle children into the USA in the name of adoption. I worked over sixty-five cases of children who were adopted but had to pass the final stages of the process as I was under immense pressure to get anything done. Much was done after that with improper identifications, recruitment, foster care, documentations and legal procedures.

Opening a New Clinic

After a while of staying low, I went to this clinic to see if I could work for a while. It was led by a woman, possibly in her fifties. She called for an interview and it went pretty much well. We had one of those moments where they ask you subtle questions, often private and tense. She walked with me out of her office and stood for what sounded like a chitchat. She then asked me a question, "What is your ethnicity?" to my shock! I asked her if it was relevant for clinical work.

Listening to her, I was stunned to be asked this question in the middle of Addis Ababa, that boasts to be the capital of Africa. I told her I didn't want the job and that I wished her success. How come we have such a city where I can be asked such question at a professional working place? This went against my perception that it did not matter where people were born or what background they had for as long as they mean well. No, it did not work that way!

Not long after this, I went straight to Bethel Teaching Hospital and met with my friend the late Dr Yigeremu. Dr Yigeremu and I have something in common, we both know hardships and are gifted in imagining something and making it happen. He built a medical school, two hospitals, clinics after clinics, an orphanage, a chapel and so on. He was a highly gentle and very playful man if you managed to take the professional layers away. He would laugh at any situation and shrug it off and say yes if you proposed a solution. His hospital did not have a physiotherapy clinic and I proposed to him that he shall give me a space, staff and some finance to set it up as business expansion. He liked the idea, and ushered finance and technical staff at my disposal.

It is to my shame and awe while my college mate oversaw the physiotherapy clients as his part-time job, he did not come up with any idea that matched the need of the hospital. By the time we agreed to open the clinic there, he was pursuing his studies to become a dentist. The test of all of it was that Dr Yigeremu's father had stroke and was bedridden at the hospital for quite long time. My college mate was his therapist. The contrast was that in a few weeks, his father was standing with walking aid support and would walk a bit a few times a day. I was surely making the nurses and supporting staff busier but this change in his father's progress meant that I mean serious business and there was no joking around. Most liked it, some were not sure of what I was doing as it was a new profession to the country. My work appetite was such that I was working full time at the hospital and was teaching at Central University College at two different campuses. This was also my hiding place from the roughness of taking my first-brain-child, the humanitarian organisation, from my hands and I could not allow grief, anger or any other emotion at this point.

For most part of it, I had a hard time to say Addis Ababa is a place to feel like home. I do like the city and always wanted to buy a house or an apartment, but I still feel the same. You go to work at three different locations and making to each of them on time means life is not just hard, it is almost unbearable. For me, if I didn't work hard and saved some money, there might have been a day where I had to run away and may not even have made it. So, I had no choice. The contrast is that instead of going around with my driver in the previous work, now I need to either stand on queues for a taxi or pay a lot more for private service. Since time was more important, and my work was also a healing, I would pay whatever they asked. I would work so hard that, after all duties were completed at the hospital, and I was teaching during day, evening and weekends meant the only free time I had was Sunday afternoon. This was mostly my sacred time of rest; I used it to go to cinema or somewhere quieter to really meditate, contemplate and make peace with myself and God. I was a stranger in a city where I spoke the language and had many friends. My needs, aspirations and challenges are distinctly not Shagarean (dwellers of Addis Ababa are alternatively called Shagareans) that I knew I was out of my place. It was the same when I was in Sodo too. I was running a humanitarian organisation while working full-time. This was in addition to establishing a university student's fellowship for the newly opened university in my hometown. I would have several meetings with university staff, students, faith leaders and other people. We worked ahead of the study starting dates, preparing almost everything, so that when students came, they would have a place to go to. As our last activity, we gathered some money, bought several books, arranged musical instruments, sound systems and all other things they would need. We facilitated so that they would elect their leaders and committees before handing over responsibilities. I still visit the university sometimes and check out the fellowship. They have thousands of members now and almost no one knows me there. Things do change.

One of the challenging moments working with university students was the moment of Oromo disappointments that were partly genuine issues of language barriers and a mix of hate and politics. Several Oromo students, especially those from the Wollega and other areas, did not speak Amharic. But they wanted to participate in activities, and it would hinder them from doing that. I observed three different views in the making, a bit different from what happened when I was in Gondar. The Oromos were not as loud in Gondar as they were in Wolaita Sodo. Perhaps it is because people in Sodo are more tolerant and accommodating.

A group of students, mostly from Addis Ababa and other main cities, felt offended by the very idea that the Oromos were asking for Afan Oromo service. We had genuine talks where people needed to understand each other in a way that would be acceptable if it were to be done five years later. That co-existence meant we accommodate each other instead of tagging or labelling each other. The Oromos are large in number and majority of which were asking this question and we could not ignore it away. All of a sudden, they created a situation where the students from cities felt bothered by a group that was saying they were left out through language barrier. The concern of students mostly from cities was the worry of divisions and potential hate. Fair and square.

A few Oromos and some others joined the student group that refused to even talk about the question and that they were creating rough situations. This is more dangerous than the group asking the question and the group that is fearful of consequences. This is the group that could actually divide the whole fellowship and create a havoc. Then there is a silently loud group that exerts subtle influence, at times making you say the words — the Amhara students. The Amhara students don't show it, but they somehow would want me to side with the Addis-city students and call off anything that has to do with language issues. At the surface, it was a concern for divisions, but looking closer, one could tell there is a rift going on between the two groups. It was an attempt at using me as an instrument to be gentle to silence the Oromo into accepting the dominance of the Amhara students and that this is good for all involved. It was little things they do that carry more meaning than the sentimentally obvious gestures or talks of unity and strength. Sneaky, I would say, but hey I was not to judge, I was to ensure smooth ending where amicable situation could be created.

After proposals of interpreted sessions, or having a separate program, the Oromo group won the voice and went on creating their own chapel. It was here I realised that this was an issue of Oromo justice and would catch us up and shake the whole country except that I was not sure when. This fun was not meant to last long. I had this feeling that my life would not be a life of a settled urbanist that lives a still life. I was not afforded this possibility by the very people I wanted to serve, and that I was not allowed to afford it on my own either — as some people would like to believe so. It is that kind of situation where the grey zone takes over the light regardless of the intensity of rays coming out of it.

Ethiopians Getting Tormented

In the 2017—2018 time period, I was very close to the violent shakeups and scary political tectonic movements happening underneath the surface of smiling faces and spirits of people who were still trying holding on. Because government change was taking places, which also translates into few people losing their status, wealth and perhaps fleeing the country.

I was also aware that it hurts the feeling of many if I speak up what I truly believe in and I had no energy to apologetically explain and have elaborate moments of informing people. Besides, I grew up hating the idea of organising ethnic lines which eventually may end up being religious grouping whenever sound policies are depleted due to bending the contextual grounds that we do every often.

Meanwhile, lootings, burnings, killings, sporadic but organised attacks and heinous atrocities were being conducted in what appears as theatrical and graphic display of brutality openly on Facebook and YouTube to the point that it was clearly a strategically calculated manoeuvre of shock tactics to get a message across. A new political force was rising, and it was making clear that it was to be feared like hell for a later assumed respect that may come with it; if people were to buy it, that is.

This is typical Old Guards' era method was repeated by people, delaying, weakening, frustrating and sending back the diaspora and stealing all the ideas and opening their own new company instead.

This was when I said to myself that my decision to leave to Uganda was not just right, it was as if in a movie act somehow my soul was holding back. Except that my sincerely great and humble friend is the one who asked for it. I wish it were someone else. I really do.

I may be a simple graduate and there can be many with similar competencies, but a good punishment to a brutal and beastly regime is by taking yourself away and not avail for any good reason at all. I mean at government level. I may not have thought of it clearly this way at the time. But in reality, this is what I have actually done. I realised that sometimes it is not your presence that matters, it is your absence as it affects the most. When I came back to try once again, I was aware that hurting my plans can be applied just like before, but I took the risk knowing this all along.

Deep down in my heart I knew that the country was left with a few years of horror and unbearable painful seasons. Some weekday, my friend Yadesa invited me to listen to a *song about people's nature of being crazy*. He had a thought. I refrained from involving in the politics of the ongoing crisis, even while people from the area I came from were dying, some rapes and tyrannical butcheries were reported, I just focused on trying out business. Breathing is Yadesa's moto. Thankfulness is his repeated word. Environment, planting trees, Africanism, oneness, togetherness and then that snap sound of y'iay occasionally if you entice him with a good talk. I got shocked when I saw on the news that the forty-six-years-old American hip-hop artist George Floyd was kept on the ground for over eternity of eight minutes and forty-six seconds, kneeling at the back of his neck, pinning him down on the ground. His words of 'I can't breathe' shook the entire world as we know it. It caused firing all four officers and shook the entire world as it added to the global COVID-19 pandemic that highly distressed the entire planet. The Black Lives Matter signs flooded social media timelines with condolences, frustrations and anger set cities ablaze that law and order was tested in the entire United States of Africa, oh I mean, America. Comedian David Chapelle held a speech in memory of George Floyd, he even stated that he was born at 8:46 and that it was his birthday, this man's death got to his core. This reminded me about Yadesa.

Yadesa and I used to sit at the Hilton Hotel, order Scotch and sip until the old man would feel tipsy and say, now I am done. We would talk about our wives, friends and pretty much everything under the sun. And then he would come with some elegant beauties of Addis, pass them in front of me and do some sneaky smile on my face. He may introduce them to me and flatter them with some compliments that are half flirt, half admiration; they even stunningly roll their eyes often. All this was while a war was going on in the country.

One afternoon, we sat and had some whisky and peanuts also with some barley in a very Ethiopian way. This is one of the coolest things at the Hilton bars. You do feel the people around you knew etiquette unlike many hotels in the city. Looking around the bar, the gestures knife and fork clutching or mixing sugar with tea or coffee can give some variety to a quietly toned sound. The wide tables, chairs, the high-rise roof, the wide windows and tall doors make you feel like you are at a place to sit for a while. We talked of this and that and just before we were to wind up our afternoon, going to some place was suggested. We went straight to Bole and had something to eat before changing the place where we could have a drink.

After a while, at some bar close to Bole Medhanialem, it started getting packed with all sorts of people. One thing that bothers me at some of the bars in Addis is that you have commercial sex workers at times a lot more than paying customers. They make it so obvious that you want to puke. It gets worse if you bring a senior friend or foreigners as the contest to draw attention, some body languages and excessively generous smiles hint at you. One-third of the tables can be occupied by such people. But then this is what pulls most from other African countries to have the taste of Ethiopia. In the middle of all this going on, a common younger friend, also my assistant, whispered, "Andualem-*n netib enastilew*." I heard him saying let's set him up with some guy who showed up. I felt betrayed, thrown out of the window and belittled. He then approached me and started to say provocative words that hinted something was already going down behind my back. It had to do with the intelligence community condoning to destroy my presence in Ethiopia. Putting it all together, I realised that I was being played at and that this had been a planned move. I then told him to stop harassing and misbehaving. He was determined. Worse, we sat at a VIP area where they could see and hear you through the cameras. Clearly, he fired himself, but equally clear that I was played at with people of power.

What I realised was that even the bartender and some of the people sitting around us were all impersonators. I was clearly being setting up, but to what end was my question. Yadesa said he wanted to leave, and I called for the bill. I took the bill, paid it all and left some tips for the bar tenders. Right before I was to hint we could leave, the bartender came back and asked for over a hundred dollars saying it was too little. I was so sure I had paid properly and left tips! She started to argue, and my assistant came poking me and throwing words. This was not a situation where people were tipsy, and things got off the edge. No. It was a drama to just make me lose my cool and as they expected no consequences. I was already tested with office visitations, serial appointments, empty promises, fake delegates and a number of preying women to drain out my money. Now I saw my assistant was cooperating with bad people and he thought I wouldn't realise what was happening.

They thought they were playing a blindfolded man cognisant to nothing of what was going on. I gave a warning; when I got almost the same eye-rolling action from three people nodding at each other, I took the hardcovered bill holder and sent it circling on to the open space. It had sharp metal lining around all the edges.

What happened afterwards was that some vodka, whisky and a few other bottles were cut in half. The whole house changed into that moment where music was quiet, people confused and the old man pulling his nerves in shock that I could do this in front of him. The guards came, and we got a situation. The manager knew me and when he came, he did not know what to do or say. He told the guards to ease up on me. By that time, I was on the roof as I did not care what was being said, what was happening and who was saying what. I knew that this was part of a bigger plot and people had already marked me and had been stalking me in the city. They wanted me to lose every drop of my money and leave in disgrace. There is a name to this. It is your country, or its guardians, regardless of their legitimacy, doing something personally harmful, arranging intelligence to drag you down.

This is betrayal, cruelty and heartless act committed by unfathomably belligerent people in the dark. I told myself, I was left to fight then leave the country. For whom? Smashing the bottles on the walls was a message that I would fight and that I would not get hurt quietly. It was to show defiance and paint the picture that I did not care about protocols, status or manners if this continued and that no social order or codes of conduct would be on my list. My dignity was stepped on and I would react and hit back where it hurt.

Yadesa was surely informed of what was happening, and it was clear he could do nothing about it. If he were not informed at the time, he would know that something serious was going on to harm me. This was where I really gave no nuts to a situation. When I am under attack, whether people see it or not, I react in the meanest way possible and ignore what others say. I was thinking, it is the government's operatives once again. We are at a smokeless war.

The good thing about it was that this was caught on the camera, and I was sure there were people who would watch it for their purposes. Now the message was sent; they wanted me, and I wanted them. They were driven by tribal hate. It was long ago that I decided hate would never have any business in my head. But I would not take being played around just like that.

The next morning, I discussed with the manager to settle compensations and could see that we were seeing things differently. He saw some manners being broken, I saw a man resisting systematic war waged against him. How could I tell him this? Who would be blamed? Who could I throw off the bus to prove it?

Never mind, I said to myself, it was better that the manager was left to decide however he felt like understanding it. For otherwise, he would feel I was hallucinating, or some weird stuff was going on in my mind. This is not the kind of chance you want to take doing elaborate and apologetic explanations to a situation you knowingly created and to the mess you stand to pay the cost. Bill was paid; one or two people said they saw all was paid but they did not know what happened after that, but it was a drama and what people saw or said did not matter.

I got a phone call to come to Sheraton and sit for a discussion with Yadesa and my assistant. When I got there, one of the girls from the evening was there. She was almost thrown at me as if to say, 'Ease yourself off, and if you need anything you may ask.' Nobody said it, but I could sense this was the gesture.

On the next table, a CEO of one of the biggest banks was sitting with someone and I knew I was seeing a staged situation once again. The CEO was one of the great and smart guys in town, he asked me who would be the owner of implementing a hospital project concept. His shock was evident when I said I would be the owner. I had said a taboo word. I realised that some people are not meant to own anything at all. They are just there to serve, pave way for others to get rich and live a lavish life. It was a clear message I was risking being one of these and I needed to decide if I still wanted to give it a try.

In the middle of the conversation, my mind was racing for answers and that this hurting would continue only God knows for how long. When someone is monitored, surveyed at and is sent a person to mimic their behaviours, way of speech and the like, it is meant that the identity is being stolen and an impersonator will take their ideas and concepts and pass it on. It is a mafia system, a real thug-life that is unbearable to my taste.

It is a grave mistake then to expect some elegance, the honour of respecting people's work of mind, their aspirations and dignity as an individual. But no, this does not work with these people. Yadesa woke me up from my other world, saying, "Do you know what a few of us said? Andualem should have smashed that bottle here at the Hilton for history's sake." He then had a loud and long laughter. He meant it.

What pissed me off, rather alarming thinking of the country as a whole, was that obviously my assistant was an informant for three different groups. His primary bosses were Tegaru, the second ones were Oromos due to his half side being Oromo, and the Wolaita as his father is from Wolaita.

It is such people tossing the dice and playing chess without even knowing enough about what deep impact it would have on individuals, groups and the country.

He was young, was rejected by the system and was fighting to make things work once again. In his attempt, he tried a project and seeing delays, he tried to throw me off the bus. For anything that could go wrong, the Amhara are the escape goat, among who some would take responsibility to take pride.

On the table though, only the Oromo, Wolaita and Tegaru are implicated; it then triggered a question in my mind. *Why should the Amhara be blamed if others are hurting me and my people?* and then had this feeling that many of the Amhara have not been discerning that people hurt each other and blame it on them. But then, they like to be called those who can ruin your life just to get the credit and appear powerful.

At the same time, if there is no innovation, culture of productivity, fair competition and creativity, the spiral will only continue even once this war is wrapped up. I just kept this to myself. But this time, it is the Tegaru that are on fire. They are burning the country and the fire is just catching their homes too. For once, I came as a businessman and aspiring entrepreneur, these things were meant to be off the table. But they keep coming one way or another.

The uprising is getting intense and I called Yadesa to have a talk and ask him a few questions.

I asked, "How do you feel about the atrocities and the war going on?"

He replied, "I am here to do good and good only."

I then asked, "How do the others take it?"

"As you usually call them, the club of the conditioned call me weak."

"There is going to be change of government obviously," I remarked.

"Well, you see it right," he said.

"What will happen to the country?" I asked.

He replied, "The country will continue."

"But...?"

He went on, "So sad that many people will get hurt."

This meant that the fate of the country's continuity will demand sacrifices to be made and many people are to be caught in between those who claim to save and those who are said to be dismantling.

My second incident was with a friend within the same circle who happens to be linked with Lema Megersa — former Oromia president — PM Dr Abiy, Abadula — former speaker of the parliament — and the likes of many. He sounded optimistic knowing that it was Oromo-dominated government and that almost all Oromos had gone through hell on earth to see the day a leader would sit at the Arat Killo Palace.

It was him who first came and said, "Andualem, meet your new Prime Minister PM," and took out his phone, told me about his portfolio and prior achievements. He is a married man, pretty decent, a protestant Christian, Muslim father, a Amhara Orthodox mother and a holder of PhD, and above all Oromo, very new to the country. It was stunning and mesmerising to have heard about him. This was about two months before the country knew the man existed and sworn in as Prime Minister of Ethiopia.

The day PM Dr Abiy was to be sworn in, I was in a rush fixing a few things and it was too late for a TV moment; well, I don't have TV at my place as much of what I do is on my laptop for so many years. I parked the car at the side parking lot by *La Paresiense Café* at Haile and Alem Building at Bole. I stayed in the car, turned on the radio and said to myself, instead of missing the moment, I would watch the video later. Some introduction of the parliament session was done and Abiy was ushered to the stage for his first speech.

The new PM had this captivating tone and the speed that makes people want to catch in contrary to most Ethiopian leaders pausing now and then to just follow their speech protocols. He was a winner for sure. No question about that. But then, I was like, would this man keep his words or is this just an intro euphoria that will change eventually and continue the crisis to an even deeper level. I kept thinking this while the news was being read. As happy as I was, I left with more questions than answers about what would come next. At some point, I invited my second younger brother to watch a movie titled *Crisis Is Our Brand* in an attempt to explain that the new power circle seemed to play by the rules of this movie.

I felt pity for the people in Addis Ababa who were terrified by what was going on, as well as people in other parts of the country alike. The new actors operated in a way that even the most cognizant of all would fall short of comprehending the daily episodes of crisis after crisis.

It is also synchronised with organized and programmed unleashing of distressing events. Telecommunications would make the internet slow, the calls would be cut or disrupted, electricity would fail ten times worse than the usual, roads would have unimportant check points in several spots that would coagulate the traffic flow and create huge congestion, tap water would disappear for weeks in a row, goods and commodities would be off the shelves, the police would not respond to crimes, banks would tell customers that they have a system failure, revenue authority officers would say system dysfunction, the traffic police would watch cars that would come from four directions and interlock each other, restaurants would serve tasteless food, schools would act funny, the media was broadcasting weird agendas, the radio would be playing something meaningless.

All while, horrible news kept flooding every few hours of the day and night to the point that people were drowning in information overload. All of these were happening with the speed of light.

The shock tactics were applied better than what the books said.

Three months after Dr Abiy became the prime minister of Ethiopia, the very friend who introduced me to his portfolio and said 'our untouchable and yet to be prime minister' started to complain with what looked like a sense of losing hope and disappointment. This is five months after I learned about PM Dr Abiy's existence. We sat for a dinner close to Moenco area in Bole where we usually grabbed something. He was furious about an incident in Moyale where several youths were killed. It shook men too for they killed a teenager with horrendous cruelty. As anyone who was emotionally moved, we were tossing words and venting out angry feelings.

He said, "We don't want this man, he is *'neftegna'*. He is a liar. He would lie to you and assume that you forget about it and lie to you again." He then started ranting and tarnishing his image, I was just sitting still, frozen like a stone. I would not hide that I was shocked and moved by his statements. He even did not care if other people were listening. I argued that we need to give him time and chance so that he could prove himself.

He said, *"Seteseqi yegezashatin qariya eyaleqesh tebeyatalesh,"* meaning, 'the pepper you bought smiling, you will eat it with tears'. It was very disturbing as he was highly irritated by every word I would say; if an Oromo started to feel this way this fast, how would the rest of the country feel throughout the whole regime?

I was highly terrified when I left for home. The stories he told me were very accurate and visualise the Ethiopia to come. It is a wakeup call to watch a horror series to unfold before our eyes. I did not sleep the night tossing myself or getting up, opening the laptop and pretending I was doing something before I would hit the bed again.

After a while, he left for Australia and dropped any little hope he had in the country and the prime minister. It was very fast and there was not enough time to process every incident properly. As information overload was part of their struggle tactics, people were held captive to the information released the whole day, much of which was horror after horror, one would wonder why we even had a new government at all. Both Yadesa and this other friend made it clear to me that the country would go through a difficult time and people would experience turbulent future.

These men were from Oromo group and hearing them say this meant surely hell was coming. But I was not this prepared to face it at a close range of personal level. Staying within neutral range and the shared space of humanity seemed to be working for a while.

Somewhere down the line, I found myself attempting to shape up the social movements into something up-to-date and assisting our youth that were trapped with the propaganda streamed by the Old Guards. From trimming social media contents to setting strategic lines of detaching the youth from the trap of standing underneath a falling tree.

Throughout this, I was more of a neutral to be honest, except wanting to assist them to stand for their cause, even if it meant that I would sound a staunch nationalist. Peaceful means were what people wanted as a choice for the struggle, and I facilitated it as much as I could. Deep down in my heart, I knew that the entertainers of the violence-philia, obsessed with aggression and information flooding would take the advantage, but in the long run, the Wolaita and its siblings would benefit from strategically calculated peaceful moves than vengeance and the works of darkness.

Assassination Threat

Since Ethiopia was going through a phase of gradual escalation towards war, and the sides of the waring two groups building up their armoury and showing off their arsenals, part of me was saying it was all military circus to either intimidate or display deterrence. My heart knew that, it was a matter of time, before it all would begin, with its horrible consequences.

But then, as a cloud gathering to rain death and destruction on innocent people; when few muscles, testosterones and adrenalin drive much of people's judgement abilities, anything can potentially happen anywhere, and that trying not to get entangled was the main thing any sane person would do.

As for me, though I had a chance back at the time, I saw that the people of Wolaita had no options left. This put me in a difficult position. In trying to detach people from the coming rain of fire, I was becoming embodiment of the struggle. After battling for a brief time, I was at peace with myself to accept it for the fact that much of the challenges were consequences of the past mishaps by our seniors, and that someone had to step in to clean up the mess.

I called for a friend who was well-linked with the top security players among the past and present actors, also the foreign political gamblers who were playing docile, innocent and harmless poor souls in town. We greeted and sat at a hotel porch as he would smoke now and then. The fresh air was soothing to the lungs as much as the soft wind rubbed the skin, it had this good feeling to sit outside on a good sunny day in Bole. But the state of the country was throbbing the blood so fast that the calmness was more because of getting used to pressure than how one would react to imminent crisis.

We started talking, touched on many things and had those moments of kicking the balls to each other till the ball dropped on the issue of the ongoing situation personal to both of us.

I said, "So conflict seems inevitable, right?"

He replied, "Sure, everyone is warming up."

I asked, "What do the people of Tigray want?"

He responded, "They have pretty much no options left."

I then asked, "Why is that?"

He explained, "If they step out, they get hurt at home. And if they stay loyal, they will get hurt by the federal state. Harm is inevitable, death is coming. And a lot of troubling things can happen."

"Why not negotiate?" I wondered.

"You know it," he said.

"Which part?"

He said, "the two majorities want to trash the role the house of federations plays and diminish influence of the minorities. This leaves us powerless while the fate of our children is decided by others."

I said, "I remember telling that the federalism does not have an institutional host and defender. It also needs to be led. I guess it is too late to fix anything now."

"Sure it is," he said.

"I would like to ask you a favour."

He asked, "What is it?"

"What does my security risk look like?"

He replied, "They may jail you."

"That does not hurt, I remarked.

He was laughing.

"What else?" I then asked.

They may escalate on you too," he replied.

That day, in less than an hour, he finished three cigarettes and was smoking so heavily; sucking the smokes to the last gasp he could, and his cheeks made wide holes. At times, he would close his eyes in what appeared like he was seeking some relief.

Later that week, I sat with another friend who knew his way around and was tied to some people. I started asking him some questions.

"Where are we now?"

He replied, "reaching the peak of crisis."

I then asked, "what are our chances?"

He said, "no, your chances!"

"What does that mean?"

He said, "you may get in trouble."

"How bad?" I asked.

"Can become really bad," he said.

"What does this include?"

"Attacks, attempts for assassination or at least scare you to get your silence" he said.

"What is the biggest of my condemnations?" I questioned.

"They cannot figure out what to do with you," he commented.

"What does that mean?"

"The talk is that you refused big money. And they know you need money. If they cannot buy you out, lure you with a political post or any of the incentives they have, this makes you a potential threat and a possible target."

"Why don't they answer questions so that we leave them alone then?"

"You know it does not work that way."

"Why?"

"Who will take the credit?" he asked.

"We will."

"As in?"

"The people who are in it."

"That is not what they want."

"What do they want?" I asked.

Their party to declare the victory."

"That will be a problem," he said.

I asked, "why is that a problem?"

"It is an ownership issue. People shall own the win, it is happening."

He replied, "regardless, you are being watched seriously."

"In this eye means contemplations are underway."

He replied, "yes."

"Little chance of staying safe," I commented.

He agreed. "yup."

"This is rough," I then said.

"Yes. It means they will have only few options."

"Now I get it."

"Yes. Be careful, man. At this time of the history, you don't want yourself to be found as a victim by mistake, while mistakes can be cover up words to the cruelty of dark-hearted and blood-thirsty bastards out there.

More and more people are becoming flesh eaters and blood suckers in a figurative speech. Many have turned out to be thoughtless than wild beasts or carnivore birds and vultures. A few are like those flies that sit on the knives the butchers are carrying on their way to the new bull to be slaughtered. Killing is now a common and accepted trend in this city. People just do not notice it as it is done differently now that how it used to be. Personal attacks are carried out smokeless and in silence and deep levels of secrecy you would not even know long after it happened. They seem to have mastered this quickly. They seem to learn of this quicker than what matters to the ways of making our lives better.

I received a phone call asking me to invite high-profile personalities of Oromia to hold a speech for the youth at the town hall in Sodo city. It was Kuleno who called me. Kuleno is one of key mobilisers in the city and beyond, rather known for unconventional approach of guiding social movements. He has no fear, patience or time if he decides to act. Though I did not agree with some of his tactics, I made sure to keep him close as we needed his presence for greater influence.

We had a long way to drive, over 320 kilometres from Addis Ababa headed towards the south. I sat with Bekele Gerba and Mulatu Gemechu in the usual 4x4 Toyota Landcruiser frequently used by African leaders for the most part. Elaborate talks took place as well as intense discussions. Mr Mulatu was among key individuals who sat with delegates of the then-fallen government in negotiations of power transfer to the new players among whom the incumbent Prime Minister Dr Abiy would be nominated and later sworn in to the highest helm of power in the country. This by far is history in bone and flesh, audible, visible and palpable in a close contact.

While Mulatu was talking about the sceneries of what took place back in the USA where he lived most of his life, I was switching between two sceneries. On the first, I was picturing his description of the meeting, on who said and did what, which rather felt to me as power abdication by the falling government and ascension of the newcomers. As we all know it, Ethiopia is not spared from the track records of Africa for being the most war-dependent and violence-attracting power-transfer practices. Though this power abdication was not totally free of violence; it just carried a sense of some normalcy in its eventualities. Especially now that I hear it from the horse's mouth, it makes much more sense in a way that the table they shared and the negotiations they conducted averted much more widespread bloodshed than how it appears today. We have at least some people who think and know what they are doing.

Yet again, I was seeing what would unfold to the rest of power block left in the power transfer, the strong hold of the previous leaders, Northern Ethiopia, Tigray in particular. This is because Mr Shiferaw Shigute and the late Asmelash sat for negotiations on behalf of the federal government, and there was no clear negotiation that took place between the newcomers and the Tigray regional power block in how things should look like on the aftermath of the conflict, and its subsequent power transfer that was taking place. Of course, there was some level of agreement, but it left much of key issues for later, that then would eventually deteriorate into the act of power grabbing by the side of the federal government against the will of the former movers and shakers. Many of the leaders are now dead, are in prison or those that managed arrests are subject to monitoring from their bunkers giving orders to the waring youth or are plotting political strategies in an attempt of paying back to the new players that just unseated them from their throne.

The deal took place in Seattle, the United States of America. These were the times when many layers of acting were taking place at party-to-party, group-to-group and government-to-government.

It is in this overall eve of new context building that Mr Asmelash, the late veteran, and Shiferaw Shigute, the party secretary, were among the delegates on the side of the government who flew to Seattle for the talks. For Mr Shiferaw, it was just party mission and he was to get it done and report back. For Asmelash though, it was about letting go of the power, his side of the government fought for, and tended to for decades. It is unfortunate that the inevitable war claimed the man who was devoted for a cause he believed in even though he managed to outlive two wars before this. In both wars, in the one he lost his arm and in the other his eyes; he gave it all without sparing his life. News of former minister of foreign affairs, and late ambassador to China, Mr Mesfin Siyoum was said to have bombed himself in refusal to surrender and face jail-time or worse. So much sacrifice at personal, family and collective level means the former leadership remained loyal to its beliefs and ideological leniencies.

The side of the late Mr Asmelash, on their own took down the Dergue regime, known rather for its notorious Red Terror and bashing world powers, siding with Russia and threatening the West, including the USA. After the running away of former President Mengistu Hailemariam, in a CIA-arranged departure to Zimbabwe, the late veteran's power circle shook the entire Horn of Africa, reshaped how business is done in Africa, especially by creating a traction for business opportunities for the China—Africa relations and keeping everything back home within their grips meant letting this go must have hurt to the core.

The other side of the story has it that they posed as guardians of the minority rights in Ethiopia and their departure from the power arena would just expose the ill-organised group into a predictable submission to the power demands of the majoritarian ethnocracy power play. Beneath the surface though, the reality is that the minorities were disempowered on issues that matter and were over-prepped-up rather on issues of publicity stunt, and meaningless acts of sizing down their grievances into a once-in-a-year cultural dance. One can look at this from the perspective of the Oromo and the Amhara that had this and were demanding more. Looking at issues as an observant though, it appeared as if the duo-ethnocrats, OroMara, wanted it all for themselves and had no room left for any of the minorities.

Absence of the side of the late veteran's power block, with the fact that there is no replacing power balance, would mean that the minority will be further disenfranchised, and will be coerced into incoherence and lack of collective voice. This implies that the duo-ethnocratic group would find itself in unexpected situation of free reigning by taping shoulders and clapping for few individuals for the sake of showing to the public acts of inclusion and cooperation. In the political game of competitive cooperation, the country witnessed fierce competition, at times accompanies by armed skirmishes of localized brutalities, much more than gestural cooperation performed through public relation stunt. For this, one side leaned on the western power block, while the other depended much on Russia, it is only China whose role has been ambivalent, perhaps preferably positioned itself as neutral, since its motives in Ethiopia have so far been focused on investments.

In a truest form of presentation of this event, the power abdication by late Asmelash was not just the expected country-level handling of state affairs and executing what must be done for the overall majority of the citizens equally. It is rather overpowering and leveraging to demand and take power by the Oromo while the Tigray side stood at the losing end, giving it away with negotiations or forceful means is that it is a mix of violence, demonstrations and media campaigns that yielded this. There is a word for this, the call it victory.

These are the moments where you have to learn a lot, but also make your thoughts understood so that future actions may be aligned both at personal and collective levels towards shared progress. Sitting in this car means literally engaging with the power transfer facilitators, on what would become Africa's crucial, and yet the most grey-ish social development that would shake the entire Horn of Africa as it never happened before.

While Bekele is full of stories and idea of actionable scenarios, one can tell Mr Mulatu is more of man of wisdom and backdoor enhancer than front-liner who engages in the public mobilisations and intellectual debates. With all of this going on, I noticed that the driver was quiet and listened to almost all our talks and saved them like a sponge. I then wondered whether the car was not fit with audio recorder or remote access. I don't know why this crossed my mind except I just was noticing that he had a bit of half smiles or some sort of reactions to our discussions.

Stopping on the way, I noticed the deeply green fields and bushes, the cows and line of cattle on the side of the road, waving at kids running for 'highland, highland, asking for plastic water bottles'. We arrived in Sodo and made it a bit late during the day.

Once we checked in at the Lewi Resort Hotel located at the top hill of the Sodo city entry, a few youths led by Kuleno came to greet and welcome us. After brief talks regarding the event and dinner had been eaten, I was starting to get seriously worried as somethings were not adding up.

With less than a week apart from the deadline of the statehood quest, townhall talks are invited and some Oromo personalities are to speak, but the actors were trying to stage something dark behind the curtain and I wanted to know what it was. I had already started to question everything our youth was going through; starting from the federal level, on how the politics is conducted, why the bad face had turned to our youth and how all this had been played at both on personal and group levels.

Above all, knowing that the northern remote manipulators did not want our people to achieve what they were asking, and that they wanted to use it to instigate violent confrontations against the government and knowing who was behind it on the side of the Wolaita was my serious concern.

The next day, we ate our breakfast and a car came and picked us up. The cheerful youth were all on their feet clapping, whistling and making noise; it felt like a huge music festival where you have famous artists appearing on the stage for the first time. For once, in a normal setting, I usually don't indulge myself in celebratory mood, not when our questions are not answered yet.

Speeches were made. The cheering went on for almost three minutes; it felt like some were instructed or were given incentives to do it but looking at the youth, they were genuinely happy about the event where Mulatu made a measured speech and mentioned about the Oromo—Wolaita relationships. Bekele spoke about the Oromo struggle (that then had forced the former government to capitulate and hand over power), the sacrifices made, the commitments and the collective determination that was lenient on solidarity. He then talked about the methods their youth employed when one of their own was arrested.

In one of the towns, the police in Oromia arrested one and all the youth flooded the police station demanding that they also get arrested. It created panic around the police force who then were left with no other option than releasing the youth they accused of not following the law and order. He surely was communicating to the youth in a way we would not be forgiven for if we said so. But it looked like every one of the participants at the Gutara Hall took in everything Bekele said, perhaps except a point where he said Wolaita was an Oromo.

This part annoyed all of our seniors and a few youths that would not accept the idea of getting systematically engulfed. Whether Bekele wanted to wake the Wolaita out of the people so that it comes out as a reaction, which is what I thought as his personal tactical move, or really believed in the lie that Wolaita could be another ethnicity it was not was unclear; for me, it would just stimulate debates, curiosities and some would not know what to conclude, what to take and what to leave.

The following day, the guests requested that they go the church and talk to Bekele's college mate in the city. I decided to stay at my room and head to my parents as I was expected and just greet them and be back. We had a great day, all of us, and the guests were to stay over until Tuesday. We had the whole Sunday for us to visit a few places. We ate raw meet with almost seven types of red pepper, green pepper, garlic, greenest bile drops, and some more spices mixed with the inspiration of the chef. Some ordered grilled beef and others something else. A few townspeople came to greet us. The zonal president also came to have lunch with us and say a word or two. At this point, almost no one realised that I was building a picture of the whole scenario and what was to happen on the days to come.

On Monday morning, I made up my mind to stay in Sodo than returned to Addis with the guests and had to come up with tones of excuses. By then, I was very sure and that if no one would do anything about it, they may even get away with compromising the cause. Waving goodbyes to the guests, I went back to the room. Contemplated a few scenarios and pinned down the issue on the zonal president and the regional political representative for the purposeful gaps created for playing out the youth.

We wanted the statehood and it had to happen. We made several visits to the prime minister's office and held demonstrations after demonstrations, media debates and interviews, several articles suited for social media reader and some artists released songs. We were not to leave it in the hands of a select few who wanted to set up the youth and propel on political posts while others wanted the rewards all to themselves at the expense of all of us. I knew few people were to die and violent confrontation was inevitable. I would not trust anyone other than myself and would question my own moves every now and then. I knew the hotel I was staying at was bugged and that they had recordings (possibly visual too) and acting as if I did not know meant they would add to my advantage. I was to listen to no one except getting the questions answered and the rest of noise had to meet with deaf ears. My focus and strategy were pinned mostly to avoid conflicts, and if they happened, to make sure it would have nothing to do with the countrywide violent future that would break a war between the federal army and the Tigray regional forces. For me, these were separate matters than the Wolaita's long-standing questions. The Wolaita are asking for structural justice, which has no element of power rift with those that control the state.

On Tuesday, I was meeting with many people to check where things were at and what could be done to alter if the day was to fall under the hands of the regional political player who seemed to also play the zonal president. You see, the man in charge of the top regional and federal political appointment had a pact with Tegaru politicians. The zonal president also had a pact with the Tegaru politicians. But the regional political appointee wanted to win it all and kept a few matters from the zonal president. The zonal president in his turn also hid some issues from the unsuspecting youth and played like the sweetest, bravest and the people's man role. There was a man who was in close contact with the former rulers with the blessing of these two gentlemen, but he too was not completely aware of the overall plan the former rulers had the position they set for our youth. It was soon to catch up on everyone whether they saw it coming or not.

My intent was that if violence would be under a single strategy, whereby the federal government army would campaign in Tigray, and link it with the Wolaita, then our youth would be the real collateral. The Wolaita were completely unarmed and had no proper weapons other than a few AK 47-s and personal pistols that few business people and those with ties with security would be seen wearing and showing off at recreational areas as a sign of displaying power and intimidation at the time of fear of getting attacked. This would be a huge power mismatch between bare-handed marching youth and a mechanised army. Total butchery and bloodbath were intended to escalate it to the rest of the areas and bring it to Addis Ababa. It was a rather predictable precedence if the Wolaita youth were lured into this mess. A counter strategy was to instigate the conflict and shorten its commencing time. Though unpopular, the more we pressed to take the 'perceived extreme approaches' on our media engagements, not on the ground though, the youth started to distance from it one by one. I was sure it was working, that the youth would not get head on collision with the federal armed forces. I then realised that considerably, the youth had started to take orders in mass and perform them like a single body. It was so great. This meant, we were ready to manage campaigns together.

On the day of December 19, 2019, Wednesday that is, four of us, perhaps key plotters of all of this, sat at my hotel room and were planning what could be done, in which anything and everything was contemplated. Some much of intense brainstorming took place and we concluded with some plans and the meeting was completed. Deep down in my heart, it was going to be the silent and artistic one who would outperform the effort of all of us combined, for when a person is determined, nothing can stop them.

The city of Sodo and all people in Wolaita were nervous about what would happen the next day which, according to the law, was a deadline for the statehood request officially submitted. Several informal discussions were taking place contemplating about what people should do, and what the security forces were prepared to unleash. Towns talk had it that two generals were assigned, and heavy military was mobilised to the city on high alert.

Just before lunch, the three of us convened and talked about what to do while Nikola, the fourth guy in yesterday's meeting, said he would not show up. He was uneasy and was not breathing right when we talked over the phone. I was sure that something shocking would happen in the city, except that I did not know who, where and when. Some people would want me say word so that they unleash their wrath. This is when I was sure that words can mean the exact copy of actions and that any slightest Facebook post would end up in damaging something serious.

One of the nights I posted 'the regional quest is in danger' to check how people would feel if it happened actually. I shut the privacy after I received a hundred reactions on comments section while the rest were so furious, some getting angry with me, others questioning my judgement, but ninety-five of those who answered would not tolerate any mishap with the shared demand of the people. This meant, I communicated to whoever that was interested to know how people would react if things went wrong. Now that all was clear, tomorrow was when we were to see and measure to what level people were prepared to commit to achieve their goals.

In the afternoon, we sat again; discussions were happening, and the youth came from other districts to read us and check all was set. And I realised that high-level of secrecy meant that some of them were oriented so that all learn of the events at the last minute. It was, I was told, for the safety of all of us and that no harm was to be done to any of us because of our mistakes. It felt a no-error move. We had no choice as many groups in the country were manipulated to turn against our youth, the only way out we had at the time was to have a no-error as part of the strategy.

I went back to Lewi hotel with one of our guys on a motor bike and found the regional political appointee sitting with a local investor. His guards sat on a comfort sofa opposite of him. There was at least ten meters distance between him and the guards. I turned and saw few of our female mobilizers, some of whom were play-makers of activism, sat and were pretending as if they did not care, but I saw they were all over us, watching every micro inch of move we were making.

We approached the political plotter of the regional body and greeted him. I was almost impatient since he was dragging conversations and slowing us. I felt it was tactical than real character of the guy. At least, this was what my gut felt. I demanded that there would be a rally and that he was to lead the rally, soon after he told us that there were military generals and the arms had been already stationed. He said, he learnt of it himself after he came to the city of Sodo. There are those liars who are good at it, and there are those that lie and don't realise that you are noticing their lies and are just allowing them to say it all.

In the end, he asked me what I was going to do the next day.

"There will be a rally, and I will be going out with the people," I answered.

He said, "People will die in that case."

I asked him, "Why."

He said, "The army is ordered to shoot on site if anyone does a demonstration."

I said, "We will go out anyway."

He then said, "You will be shot at. And even get killed."

I said, "Do I look like someone who is afraid to die?"

He said, "You have a child. I told him yes but many of us also have a child or even three."

I left them there and rushed to my parents' place. I spoke with my mother and she knew we all were in serious trouble and could only say she would pray. I was being watched from every corner and people would pick their phones as soon as I passed. The whole city was infested by informants and people who were doing surveillance over us. Several actors serving various interest groups were roaming on the streets. Some of them were totally new faces and we did not know who worked for who in many instances; it all was smelling bad. I then went to the zonal political office only to find a secretary and a janitor who told me that it is better if I wait. I sat on the old, broken guest sofa and waited for a while.

I saw a handful people going in and coming out who were either greeting me, giving me morale or others staring as if I am in the wrong place at the wrong time, that was hard to tell. Once again after a very long time, I had this overwhelming feeling that something terrible was about to go down.

Between an Affair and a Responsibility

I remember the night the previous government officially, but secretly ceased to exist, and the city of Addis Ababa became a vulnerable place for security risks. I even recall that the dogs barked differently, the birds had a different pattern when they flew, the air got very thick to breathe and people's collective behaviour changed very much. It was as if everyone became Schizophrenic for an evening. It was one of several scary evenings whereby people were disorganized, disoriented and agitated all together. It was surely a collective madness.

The same overwhelming and scary sense of power I felt was also the morning when Engineer Simegnew of the GERD was killed. I was with my brother driving by Arat Killo passing through Meskel Square heading towards Bole. Right at Meskel Square, I told my brother, something heavy is going on, what is it? He asked me why I said it. I explained to him that everyone in their cars were scared to death and I could see that they were breathing heavily and are sweating in their cars, obviously many were shaking. We learnt that the engineer was killed and found in his car in the open square, very foreign to Ethiopians.

This day made me feel that I was left out of information and that I was not even given a slightest of hint to be careful. As I recall, many people are informed prior to such incidents. But I was not sure why it felt the same this very day in my hometown. I had this feeling that I cannot express in any way. While I was in this thought, not differentiating between the past and the reality of the moment, in no time, the office was set ablaze, I jumped out of the office and stood close to the flowers by the open space.

A policeman said, stop there and do not make any move."
I asked, "what is going on?"
The police said, "You will answer to the court."

"But tell me what is happening."

"You have broken the law," a police officer said.

I questioned, "Which law? What did I do?"

He took his AK 47, held it up and shot to the sky. There was no conversation, it looked like people had started to panic. Everyone came out of their offices, guards gathered, main entrance was opened, and the public started flooding in. I found myself surrounded by over fifty local police officers in less than three minutes. The smoke made the sky dark; all of the sudden, half of the city was there in no time. People filled the open space of the zonal political office and were standing outside and filled the street.

Several cars were rushing to drop more police force and drive back to bring more. The security guards seemed highly startled or behaved so. Most people seemed to be confused, others scared while some were carefully watching everything that was unfolding before their eyes.

Few minutes later, the fire fighters were deployed, the regional security surrounded us just before the federal forces from the military arrived. Those who appeared higher-ranking of the local police, the regional security and the federal army all were on their communication devices. Some people started to get anxious as this was a day before the deadline and to next day may either get bloody or people would be afraid and would stay home. The youth seemed unmoved and stood to watch and make sure that I would not get hurt.

A policeman instructed that I get in the police car. The car drove to the police station at the old city and dropped me with two of their staff before embarking back.

One of the policemen stared at me and said, "Is it you who is shaking the city? What have you done?"

He asked me countless questions, but I really was so mad that words would not come out of my mouth. I was totally quiet. They took my phones, wallet and belt and said I had to sit at one of the office spaces and could not move anywhere. I just sat there.

About two hours later, a car rushed into the police station and three men jumped out of it. They went to the policeman who was questioning me, said a few words, throwing their hands here and there. Then they came to me and said I would be moved to another police station close to the Mercato, open marketplace, where the sub-city, Mercato Sub city gets its name.

A policeman would ask me questions, and I would say something briefly and had this feeling that was like wanting to kick the door and crush it to the ground. I was angry with all the drama to just set the youth up and that if it were any of the regular ones, not so many may campaign and that their stories may not even be noticed. And it is to this that they were preparing the youth for, and there would be a conflict to claim lives.

I was a leading force for the peaceful struggle embraced by artists, musicians, engineers, politicians, activists, nurses, doctors, teachers, carpenters, farmers and soldiers, urbane, villagers, women and men alike.

One thing must be crystal clear about this. Nothing made me happier than this which is priceless to stand there watch in my own eyes the political office getting destroyed and burned down, a place that paralyzed our political culture to the point where we were left defenceless in cities and farms across the country whereby killing, rape, mutilations and harassments were done against our people under the watch of the police and the military, several special forces committing crimes in civil clothes regardless of this being state sanctioned or not. It ended a political chapter of Wolaita to open a brand-new culture of social movements for the people, it was of such significance.

This is the office where they conspired to jail my father countless times, abuse my mother, confiscate money, open court cases one after the other, charge me and my siblings for 'suspected violation of the law' even while I was out of the country, that harassed my family, harmed several families, impoverished people and walked over their dignities and basic rights.

I was ushered by two policemen to follow them. One was beside me while the other one was behind us. I was shown a door. Before it was opened, the policeman behind us said, "No, he can't be here. Take him to the next one."

The door was opened, and I went into the cell I would stay in. There were eight people stashed in less than somewhat a three-by-three room. There were holes everywhere; you could see outside, to the room I was told to go in first. Thank God, I was not there. It was almost forty people in a room a little bigger than where I was staying at. It was chaotic, with so much noise, fights and pushing happening every now and then. I would just puke to be in it.

Surprisingly, there was some sort of order and way of communicating to both rooms. After I introduced who I was and told them what I was accused of, one of the guys stood up and said, "I know this man, Andualem; he is the people's man. Even his haters would want to be like him. He inspires our youth and is a real man of character. We saw him grow up as a disciplined man, and if he said, did or believed in anything, it is not for himself. It is for our people. For all of us. We do not listen to the officials trying to paint him dark. We see him, we know him and that is what we believe about him. I am your fan, Andualem, and I will make sure you are safe in this room that no one raises a tone on you."

I realised that they had already heard my story and decided that they would stand by my side, no matter what!

The women's room was fully covered but they moved a piece of the wall whenever they wanted to talk to the men. It was odd enough that, instead of men hitting on women outside the walls, in the cells it was the women who flirted with the men. To make it worse, we all would hear everything they said. They knew each other outside, when going out for shared toilets, for fresh air, to talk to visitors or for stretching legs.

"Yes, I love you too," said one of the ladies, Simret, in the next room. This was how they communicated.

Then one of my cellmates, Fisseha, said, *"Konjo,* I knew it."

"So you miss me?" she responded.

He said, "A lot, baby, a lot."

He actually had a crush on the other girl, Meski, and Simret was poking them both, trying to instigate a love-war as they called it, which was about to happen.

Then Meski took it from her and said, *"Deche bela,"* meaning 'may you eat the soil' in a literal translation.

He said, "I would kill a lion for a kiss and bring you its cub."

Meski replied, "Your lips are ugly."

He smirked. "More beautiful than your friend's."

Simret rolled her eyes. "You idiot, you are so ugly."

"Come one, don't get hurt this easy."

"I know how your girlfriend looks like," she said.

"What girlfriend?"

"Oh so you have a girlfriend and you play around!" said Meski.

"No, *konjo*, she is messing with your head," he insisted.

All we had to do was laugh in between the flirts, subtle provocations, also exchange of cigarettes, money, phones and almost everything important and they would just pass from room to room and to each other. I then said to myself, if I make it out safely, this is not going to be a boring place in my stories. For the good part of it, people knew me; even better, they had humour and literally tore each other apart with no mercy. The women were worse; they would tone down the men and would point fingers when they talked and squeeze before all men — nine of us here and forty over there. The people in the other room were said to be neighbouring farmers disputed over land or cattle, driver's assistants hurting someone who approached their car, falsely accused poor souls, thieves, drunkards and a few more with stories of other petty crimes. My cellmates introduced who they were and where they came from. On the part of the crimes committed or accused, they would say it with the transparency very rare outside the walls; there was a different culture inside the jails that was unusual to my awareness.

While he was wrapping up his talks, a policeman came, opened the door and pointed fingers at one of the detainees. The guy rushed out and came back in no time. He then started to check all our mattresses. Broken glasses, a knife and a lighter were taken out.

He then continued saying, "They said you could try to do something, or someone may get recruited to harm you while you are inside. They are very anxious that you are here; all of them are afraid that something will happen because of you."

My parents and siblings were notified of my situation, people circulated towns talk, social media campaigns were set ablaze the authorities did not know what to do with me. First, they tried to block people from coming to the police station and said I was not allowed to talk to anyone for a day. But as the pressure mounted, they gave in. My mother brought me food, drinks bottled water and all that I needed. We all shared the food, drank what we got, and it was time for bed-time story, almost. The teethers would know the women's wall, and we would hear "She does not love you now," some would sing traditional songs, and all would clap, a few would be singing church songs, others would play cards and the rest some sort of games. People were trying to make the best out of the situations they were in.

In the pitch-dark outside, the little flickers of light could be seen from afar. The cold temperature took over the night and utter silence gripped the area, for except when the detainees would cough or sneeze. I tried to look through one of the holes towards the front wall. The policemen were swinging torch lights and moving here and there.

My cellmates said, "Andualem, the cell has never got this much attention and checked out from outside. They keep coming here, would stand for a brief moment and would go back. And then another one would come and another one. It was police, then regional security and at some point, the army. You made our cell recognised."

Late at that night, around just after midnight, a man was hoarded into the room, sighing and gasping his pain out. He said he had swelling all over his body because of the beatings. He told us that the security officers would stop anyone on the street and start hitting them with the backside of their guns or the heavy sticks they were carrying. They were patrolling the city and seemed very agitated, he said.

"They destroyed my body!" he wailed and started to cry *"Wano! Wano!"* — meaning, 'What shall I do, what shall I do!'

"Ne suntay one?" — 'What is your name?' asked one of my cellmates, Ayele.

The man faintly responded, saying, *"Ta suntay Bibisa."*

Then Ayele said, *"Mantta Bibiso hayiza"* — meaning, 'Mr Bibiso, shut up!'

A young man, Fuad, who came from Jima and was based in Arbaminch, said he was jailed in my cell because of a false allegation of rape and that he was innocent. I did not know what to believe and not, but he seemed a good guy. I just wanted to hear more about him. I realised Fuad was not buying Bibiso's story. And he called everyone to get up, for by then we all started sleeping. He suspected Bibiso thinking that he might have been sent by security forces that put me in jail at the first place, and that he may have been sent to infiltrate our cell for evil plans.

We all sat, and he said, "This is a very dangerous time in Wolaita, and Andualem is in an even more serious situation. At this time, I cannot trust and take people's stories for granted."

Then Ayele asked, *"Tadiya min enadirg?"* — saying, 'What shall we do then?'

Fuad responded, "We need to take shifts and guard Andualem. He needs to be protected in this cell. They were divided into three, with two groups of three men and one group with two. Each group would stay awake for two hours and the last ones with two people to watch until we would be called out for breakfast. In about eight hours, I became from a freely roaming man to being guarded all the time, now being watched even in shifts — it could not get any odd at all.

The next day, as it was December 20, the deadline, people in the whole city wanted to go out to demonstrate. Around nine a.m., the youth went out and many were already arrested and brought to the police station. Several academicians, civil servants and students were brought by the patrolling police and were dropped inside the temporary detention centre. The youth were heard chanting and would then keep quiet. We heard that the police and the army are dispersing the youth and were standing almost door-to-door to prevent people from coming out to demonstrate. One of the university lecturers was astonished that he never saw this number of police, regional security forces and the military take over a city like this.

Demonstrations were happening regardless, and the youth changed routes whenever they saw patrolling cars approaching. It was a constant battle between the people and the security forces that were excessively flooded in all corners.

Around eleven a.m. local time, a second man was brought to our room arguing with one of the policemen and bashing him out in between. After he said, *"Ta nena erays"* in Wolaitic meaning, 'I know you'. He then said, "The whole city is talking about you." He introduced himself as Mesele.

Mesele was pointing his fingers towards three of the cellmates and said, "These guys, especially these three, don't trust them. They are murderers!"

One of them, Sewunet, said, "How about you? Don't we know about you?"

Mesele said, "You kill for a living."

Sewunet countered, "You kill for what?"

"I will cut your throat, you maggot," said Mesele in anger.

Sewunet replied, "I will lay and wait for you."

"You know me, you idiot, I will kill your sister first," Mesele then said.

"Man take it easy, you are taking it far," said Sewunet in an attempt to calm Mesel down.

"Then shut up," said Mesele.

Fuad and I looked at each other. May be this was why he gathered any sharp lighter and anything that could cause harm and passed it on to the police. We had four murderers and one of them seemed to be their alpha character. Everyone was silent and sat still without any movements or even coughing; it felt a big boss was around.

Mesele continued and pointed his finger at Fuad. 'You, what brought you here?"

Fuad started fidgeting and mumbled, "I did not do it," he said.

"What did you not do?" Mesele asked.

Meski said, "He did not rape that girl."

Everyone laughed, even many in the bigger room giggled.

Simret asked, "You mean he did not rape the girl?"

Mesele spoke, "You idiot; of all idle women on the earth, why did you do it?"

Meski said, "He actually did not do it."

"So why is he here?" Mesele asked.

"Her husband forced her," Meski explained.

"How?"

Meski replied, "He told her to choose between this man and himself."

Mesele chuckled. "He must be a chicken head. What was your name again, young man?"

He answered, "It is Fuad."

"Tell us how it happened," he almost ordered him.

Fuad, a young man moved from Jimma city to Arbaminch a few years ago. He got accustomed to the city, the people around and later on he opened a broker office where he facilitated buying and selling. He was a man who lived by making deals happen and guiding them to his advantage once both sides were happy about it.

On a weekend, he wanted to have some fun in Sodo city and boarded a bus. The travel hours may take between four and five hours depending on the driver and the car. It is faster on the way back as Arbaminch is a low land. He met this pretty girl in the car and the got close to each other in no time. They talked about their childhood favourite songs and movie choices to pretty much everything. The trip went as if they flew, not went through land transportation as they both did not know when they arrived.

As soon as they got off the bus, they went straight to Birzua Pension and booked a room and locked themselves for two long weeks without noticing it. It was romantic talks, evening sidewalks, a lot of hugging, so much kissing and sex, then sex and then sex and one more after that. They were like wild pigeons mating every time they land on a tree, grass, on the ground or electric poles. They both lost control of what was happening and none of them had the energy to stop it.

To make it worse, they both shut off their phones and were so irresponsible to their loved ones and family members. At the end of the second week, the girl said she needed to go out and be back. Fuad agreed with her and went to a café for a cup of macchiato.

When he returned to his room, he found the girl crying and disoriented. She told him that she was a recently married woman and that her husband returned from his work place and was looking for her all over the city, in Sodo, even far away where she had relatives. Her brother told her to return to Arbaminch immediately and that things were not good. That was when they both were caught when they arrived at Arbaminch and were surrounded by an angry mob of her family, her husband's friends and all that were there at the bus station at the time.

"Poor man. What do we make of this now?" said Mesele.

Ayele said, "a man caught between love and responsibility."

Simret spoke, "no, it is a naughty man caught red-handed."

Meski opined, "no, rather he is here because of a hot affair and madness that went rogue."

"Sorry, man. Does she love you?" asked Mesele.

Fuad replied, "she still says like that."

"Her husband is stupid. He did not tend her enough and now when she runs away, he takes hostage of the situation," said Mesele.

Simret spoke, "yes, you men suck!"

"Shut up!" said Faud.

"You are still naughty, you know that," said Meski.

Simret asked, "is he hitting on you?"

"No, I saw how he was when my sister visited the other day."

"No, she said she liked me," said Faud.

"Fuad, I told you love would destroy your life," Simred turned and spoke to Faud.

"No, you mean rape would do that," interrupted Meski.

"Wild sex habits will surely do," smirked Simret.

Fuad shook his head. "you two are not fair, you know it."

Meski said, "OK, I'll correct it; untamed sex will ruin your life, handsome man," with some pitch in her voice.

Everyone laughed again. Even Fuad also giggled and cursed at her. And Meski said, "come on."

Simret added, "maybe someone should write a song."

"This artist who is with them, why isn't he composing a song?" said Meski. Among prisoners, there was an artist from Arbaminch who happened to know Fuad.

Mesele asked, "do you think people will like it?"

Meski replied, "everyone likes strange love stories."

"Then her husband will kill both of them," said Simret.

Fuad spoke, "the police said one of the reasons is for my safety."

"Poor man. Are you going to marry her?" asked Meski.

"You two ladies will get this man killed." Mesele shook his head.

On the third day of my arrest, many people came to see me. A few travelled from Addis, some from Wolkite and others from several districts. Elders and religious leaders, the youth and activists demanded that I must be moved to a cleaner and safer place.

A policeman came and said, "We are moving you to another place. Your people are not giving us a space to breathe, some even call us during midnight at our personal hours. Take your things and follow me, Mr Andualem."

I gathered my things and waved a goodbye to everyone and followed him. I jumped on the back of the field pickup car with two other policemen and we drove while people were cheering loudly. I was then taken to the zonal police headquarters and was given a much cleaner room to stay by myself.

Now that visits were permitted, I was kept busy greeting people, talking to them, listening and waving when they were leaving. Towards late afternoon that day, I started hearing a chanting that felt like football fans chanting on their way to the stadium. But this one was different; they were chanting for me. And singing. They were singing Mahmoud Ahmed's popular song that is sung for the love of the country.

The youth gathered in several groups and put a heavy strain on the police and the military and demanded that whatever the police were accusing me of, it is all of the youth that did it and they all wanted to be jailed with me. They were so many that the police were afraid that people would raid the headquarters and disrupt everything.

A high-ranking officer, and old-time friend of my father, came and started begging me to talk to the youth and send them back home. I asked him why they were worried this much, and he told me that the police force was not enough to handle if they all decided to be jailed.

"We will be overrun, and this is going to cause trouble," he said. "My son," he continued, "please explain to them that we are trying to keep you safe and that your case is being followed by the federal government bodies, embassies and journalists. Tell them you are safe, or else it is going to be a problem for all of us."

I was never as proud of the people. Because growing up in this city, a lower-ranking police officer would beat people, do almost anything they wanted and get away with it like nothing happened. Now that they feared the people, this showed that the youth were doing a great job of awakening among the masses. I came out and the crowd was cheering! After I spoke briefly, they all agreed to go home. And see me the next day.

On the fourth day, a health officer came to visit me with what appeared like a timely message and said, "Listen to the elders, they are always right, and you are wrong. And they take your wrongs and own them." I asked him what he meant by it. And he went on to say, *"Agree to whatever they demand. Whether you did it or not, that is not what the elders want. You know the culture. They want to see that you honour and obey them. If you obey, they will own any accusations against you. Disobeying is not an option. If you excuse me, I have to leave as many people are coming. And by the way, good luck. If all goes as our attempts, you should be released and sleep in your bed tonight."*

After dialogue and mediation by elders, religious leaders and influencers, ambassadors, with constant voicing of the activists and the youth, I was acquitted and was told to sign on a paper and walk out free.

Walking out free from Ethiopian jail does not come free of cost, as I was doing some auditing work awhile back. Most of these were in search for answers to the questions: 'What did I trade for my freedom?' and 'What did they gain to ensure they too have a better deal out of the situation?' among many others.

To the surprise of many people, I had no clear discussions that took place both at the local and country levels. I was aware that open and genuine conversations were needed. At times, I was reserved, and on the others, I saw the need for talks of shaping matters before wide circles would be involved. As I saw that all that was desired was personal level of talks, but informal, this was not to my taste. Therefore, all they wanted out of this was to seek personal gains and leaving what was public and common to them. All they obtained was that I was not willing to do any of it and that collective questions would have to be kept alive by the people.

But I was soon to realise what I was to let go if I wanted to see the eyes of my son again. A man, Maleda, came to my parent's place in what appeared like a friendly visit, while from the look of it he had something to say to me in private. There were so many people coming in and going out, he had to sit there patiently for almost two hours. We were only the three of us, an old man who always tells jokes, warms the house and cheers up everyone who is visiting me. At some point, I was noticing that this was his way of gracing my presence at my parents' house. He comes, and laughter comes in with him. He would make people laugh their challenges away and see issues in a much calmer and composed manner.

"A joke and wine would never hurt anyone," he would say, and would smile before adding, "but my children, don't tell this to my church's men for none of you would save me from the hell," and laugh.

Sometimes, we just laughed because his laughter was so inviting to just join in and crack it up with him.

Stabbing and Exile

Maleda tilted his head, hinting for me to follow him to the veranda. He then excused the old man, who just said, "Don't take him far from here, my son."

Then Maleda responded, "No, our father, we will be here at the veranda," and we both got up.

Maleda, seemed seriously stressed during the two hours he sat with us. He surely did not come to tell me one of those gossips so that I would try to bend and sway their direction, follow and control what is circulated to avoid plans of hurting our activists and the youth. This time, it was a third round of attempt against me. As I looked deep into his eyes, he was seriously worried about a potential injury that may even amount to death, or maybe I was just overly scaling up what I read on his face. I was really trying to grasp the eventualities and compose myself to hear the news he had come to break.

He said, "You were arrested first."

I responded, "Sure, everyone knows this."

He continued, "Then they stabbed you and tried all their best to make it appear as if it was something else."

I agreed. "Sure."

"You know some of theirs were given a mission from the zonal president and the regional guy to set you up, attack you and make it disappear?"

I nodded. "Yes."

"You also know few people closely working with you left the town that day."

"Yes."

"And you know this is what everyone does when there is a planned attack and they want to look innocent and uninformed, even after orchestrating this all," he spoke.

"I have heard so."

"You tried to inform some people that night saying you were in danger?" he asked.

"Yes," I told him.

He continued, "And no one responded in due time?"

I replied, "Sure. I was surprised."

"You said on a radio interview that what happened to you was an appetizer before the main dish, as in a pilot before a movie series. And Ethiopia would be going through a hell."

"Yes."

"If I am right, the police visited you here at your parent's place?" he asked.

I answered, "Yes, they did."

"And they asked you to say it is a robbery and not a political situation?"

"Yes," I confirmed.

"But the guys did not take all your money, left your second phone and your wallet."

I nodded. "Yes."

"That day, you met with someone who said, 'We will make the country governable for Abiy'."

"He said so," I affirmed.

"You kept quiet."

"Yes."

"Well, for the most part of it, you have all the picture, my friend. You now know who is doing what, why and that they hate anyone like you who is here to offer solutions in authenticity of people's capabilities than faking it for manipulations. They see you as a serious threat. But they lie to you to hide their fears. They are afraid of your soul. You are their nightmare and we love this. Because we had no one that would stand all their arrogance, wrap it up, trash it, lick the wounds and walk tall again. We envy you. Many of us do."

"But it came with a cost," I said.

"We know you never cared about materials. We have seen for as much material you gained, you gave it away to people and those around you," he said.

"I am not a saint."

"We know this too."

"So at the wider country level, the wounding, inflicting psychological pain and injury will still persist for some time to come," I noted.

"Yes."

"How about the uninformed mass?"

He then cried, sobbed a lot with his shoulders narrowed and his face looking down at the cement lines of the floor. A few thin tears dropped on the floor.

The old man was asking if there was a problem, saying, "*Ta nato metoyi di?*" in Wolaitic.

I answered, "Ayibika bawa," — meaning, 'There is no problem'.

"*Yake esuwan wursite.*"

Almost giving us an order, he said, "Wrap it up quickly."

Maleda wiped his tears, cleared his throat and said, "As you know, the country is going to enter into the darkest phase which you know about. And that some individuals will be the target. And the intent is to get rid of any sensible person with social posture they do not afford to own.

"A few of these will be jailed as what may appear like wielding total power and standing as the only face of the state authority, but deep down they will actually be protecting their own from potential security threats and retaliations to what has been committed."

"What is your worry concerning me, then?" I asked.

He said, if you do not leave Ethiopia before the moment, you may be neutralised either with significant physical injury that can leave you at the hospital for at least a few months, or even get assassinated. My advice is that you fly out of the country in less than three months. Save yourself first. You will know what to do once you are overseas and the people know this."

I asked him, "What else is possible?"

"If you mean by staying here, not so much. You may have to work for them and serve their interests or at least let them get away with what they committed and the hell they are about to bring. It will be up to you to decide. Work for them or leave the country, be in exile once again in your life. Maybe you are better off there, I don't know. We need you here, but what can I say, the people can not interfere with your personal convictions."

"Well, my personal conviction is what made me stretch my hands to the people," I said.

"Yes, that is why it is hard for anyone to even expect anything more than what you have already done on your own. And it seems many are very sad about this situation, but they will understand and accept any path you take. The people have a very deep trust and attachment to your thoughts. Don't take this lightly. They see your judgments as accurate. For the sanity of all of us, we want to know that you are with us once this all mess is cleared up."

At an evening after I was called on a party duty, I was invited for a dinner and to an evening chit chat with friends. I had a bad feeling, but these are individuals the people use to convey collective calls to me. I had to obey as in responding to the people's call.

This was the darkest of evenings in my hometown I have ever spent in my entire life. After we ate dinner, meeting five members of a family at a restaurant, and a jam and rushing of security officials, intelligentsia and unknown faces communicating with each other in super-fast speed in a compressed timespan, I knew something was to go down this evening. I had to pretend to make a phone call, go out in the dark and check if the fall was for me, or if I was about to witness something terrible against an important figure.

Over five people came to watch me in less than five minutes forcing me to make unnecessary phone call. Once I was sure that I am targeted, I was to either call for my security back-ups or using myself and exposing the depth and extent to which this was planned. From the looks of it though, the security chain meant that this issue must be sanctioned at the federal level than local capacity.

I chose to take the hit and fight back against all the individuals in the food chain that agreed to my attack. Because, if they miss me they may come after my family members and significant others. And I was convinced that I must be the one they will have to target. To begin, I sent a short message to a colleague, with an intent to use it as a reference, indicating that something terrible was to happen to me. A few people including him went out of the town, which was the game any time something is to go down. I took note of all individuals that posted on their social media of their absence that evening.

It was also critically important to note that I was not in my home town in a personal capacity, and the individual to whom I sent the message notifying about an imminent attack on my personal security was responsible for calling me to come all way from Addis Ababa, and partake in the party responsibility, also at a collective public level role. I was making sure that if anything happens to me, it would not be a hit on an individual, it was to be understood for what it was. As an attack against a people's cause. This was my way of saying 'you cannot have the cake and eat it' to the people who staged the attack that is to unfold any time.

After two and a half hours I was asked to move to another recreational place which is not the first choice of my taste. But hey, people called you and minority among these are setting you up, just go by it put an end to their drama. Because at this point, it became super clear to me that this is not sanctioned by the public, rather it was select individuals with vested interests of theocratic and political upheavals covered up with lies.

To paint the security context of my city that day, zonal police and militia forces, the regional special forces, and the military were heavily present in every corner of the streets that nothing would go unnoticed by the agents. Besides, if something heavy goes down, the security must have agreed or spearheaded the process to bypass all layers of stringent government eyes and ears in place. I was beyond sure that it was a targeted move on me.

I was with a human rights activist, also one of the five family members at the dining hall, who was younger than me and did not have much experiences in the game. I was watching his back to make sure that he would not become a sacrificial lamb in the process.

On our way home, two men approached us and brought out knives. I told the activist to run a way as fast as he can, and I just saw him vanish in a microsecond.

I asked them what they wanted and looked at the face of the specific individual I remembered seeing him in the city before. As soon as I recognized him, he run fast towards the dark and I was left with the bigger body building type who took out one more knife.

At this point, I was telling myself, if what I saw was two knives in the hands of a body builder that my bare hands would not be a good match to survive this at all.

He demanded me to give him my phone, I gave him my iPhone. He then asked me for money, I gave him from my pocket. He started stabbing me immediately after he took these. He sent his knife to my left wrist, and so much blood was rushing over my clothes. I still had my wallet and my second phone. He did not care, even if I did tell him I had more money and one more phone if he wanted.

He said it was these hands that disrupted their work. And he stabbed my right hand between my metacarpals and the digit of my right index finger. He cut me in the middle of my joint almost separating the two bones of my index finger and my right palm. My hands were soaked with blood, and I was not sure being close to him or running away was the right move as he still held two knives. His chest was pushed forward, the left knife in the front and he was ready to charge towards me.

His third attempt came directly at my neck! Oh my God! He does not mean to rob me. He means to kill me for God's sake. What should I do?! Questions raced through my head and I was in a position of defence. But I was not sure if what I did was anything helpful at all. I raised my left shoulder and leaned towards my right side, hiding my neck. He stabbed me on my back on the side of my left scapular bone area.

I told him that I did not see him and that he did not need to finish me. We are not enemies and that whoever had sent him was wrong. He was adamantly determined to end me right there.

As soon as he missed my neck on the left side, he was attempting to stab the right side of my neck. I used my right hand pushing the knife away from my chest area. He stabbed me on my right wrist as a response. On his last attempt he went for my leg and stabbed me on the side of my right calf muscles.

When he reached for my leg, I was sure that he wanted to drop me and kill me on the ground. I could see it on his face that he was thinking of his next move. In a blink of an eye, I run away as fast as I could.

When I looked back he was chasing me, but I was not going to be caught. I was not just running. I was literally flying!

It was almost after five minutes of running that I heard a 'chuap-chaup' sound of my blood in my shoes. My blue jeans had been torn apart right by my right leg and was soaked with blood, my jacket had holes in the back and around my wrists. I literally looked like a movie-make-up artist's mistake.

In about twenty minutes I was taken to the hospital after a brief stay at the Soddo City Health Centre, in front of which I was stabbed. Since the main gate was closed, I had to run away to the entertainment place we were at. The guards refused to help me out and said that they were told to stay away from me. This also made it obvious that this was not the political mass, but rather a few individuals who sanctioned this because they were threatened by my performance in leading social movements.

I was stitched up, and the news had already come out. My shock was that they had already written five speculations of why it may have occurred.

Social media was on fire, with several lines of stories that just kept flooding in. This was when I realized that people were ready to post things, that sounded like they were already written and were saved in advance to be 'leaked' after the attack. It was all a well-orchestrated drama the actors of which became very obvious by mistakes of their own making.

I realised that I had maximum of five or six weeks to leave Ethiopia before things would go bad both at home but even overseas. As I was in discussion with a friend, who gave me accurate account of the Covid-19, its level of aggression and the speed of its transmissibility, I learned that the virus had a potential to spread in millions per day. He was based in China and closely monitoring a nearby city to the incidents unfolding.

This sufficed my judgement that we were about to enter into a crippling situation where the whole world would have almost forgotten its own history.

I whispered to a few Ethiopian public health experts of what is to tarnish the whole world and that the virus must be categorised as a health security threat at the country level, I realised the people were picking my message three months after I told them. I even re-posted it with a wrong note to get their attention. What was very strange was that they paid attention to the wrong note, rather a stimulation, than the previous actual post to notify of an imminent threat to the public. A high-profile individual reacted to it publicly later on. This shown me that people among high profile individuals are slow to learn and much slower to respond.

It was at this time that I realised that borders would be closed, societies would be shut and that international travels would be blocked any day.

I called my brother, his buddy and my friend and told them that I was flying the same night and that all was set. It was a close shot, and time for me to pack and leave Ethiopia once again. Not like one of those moments knowing that I could return but with uncertainty if I would be able to see my parents and loved ones again.

Chapter Three

Going Global

Smelling like Berbere

I grew up hearing that Scandinavia is close to heaven on earth where milk comes through water pipes and juice is cheaper than water. A friend who visited Scandinavia awed all of us saying that even idle donkeys of Ethiopia would have secluded treatment, as he saw one on a show at a park.

It must be said that quite several people have a sense of moral superiority hidden in key words in their subtle expressions. Literature seems to paint Sweden as the land of emotional detachment, slow closeness, conformity, while I would rather take this country of the Vikings with rationality, selectivity and expectation to a functioning social harmony. Surely though, I have not seen heaven yet.

Yet when it comes to Sweden, personally I have a hard time to be in the harmony everyone seems to play safe. At least my parents who visited Sweden had almost the same impression as what they envisioned before coming here. Yes, juice is very cheap, milk can be poured down through a tube from somewhat a large container placed on the table, busses are on time, trains work quite efficiently and apart from recent developments, relatively crimes are low. In the eyes of my parents, Sweden is close to heaven on Earth. I would say it is not only a nearly perfect place of the Planet Earth, though it may hurt feelings of some friends, it is one of the cleanest and well-tended countries. This said, I am not discounting its recent worrying attitudes towards immigrants, tendencies of self-pity-induced negativity towards none Swedes and overall decline in social space and the palpable deterioration of the usual open mindedness.

While these are worrying changes, the social consistency and public harmony remain as the treasures of Sweden.

If Sweden is to be considered as the leader of Scandinavia, while a few of Scandinavians may disagree, it is not as far from how it presents itself to be as compared to many countries that claim to be leaders of a thing or two. Sweden is what it says it is, for the most part of it, if I cannot say totally. Because wealth may not go beyond showing measure of economic output, mostly just to belittle low-income communities also as a show off known spoilers, learning about the similarities and differences of the organised rhythm of life may be a better thing to do. The Swedish collective beats sound a lot like unimaginably fit social performance as passioned stroke dribbling as Malian drummers.

OK, in the era of Google, Wikipedia and WikiLeaks, what can we learn from each other, right? Several Swedes would say they smell like milk or cheese while many Ethiopians may not even realise that they smell like berbere, a commonly used spice made of red pepper, ginger, garlic, onion and several other ingredients.

My dining experience with a Siri Lankan-Swedish friend made me realize the smell of his cloth. Which meant, I had to do laundry of my cloth and smell it with good inhaling to learn that my cloth also had a smell baggage I brought with myself. To this day I do not prefer eating food with berbere because of its after-laundry smell regardless of how much perfume is sprayed.

The aspect of whether I am doing fair to a low-income country by comparing it with an advanced economy should not hold us back from noticing a few relevant points though. Experiencing policies of a society mostly built through the ideals of social democracy, the collective is very important in Sweden as it is in Ethiopia. With varying degrees, both countries have a certain level of similarity both in the collective society they have and while the individualism dominates the Swedish way of life, Ethiopians also have it expressed differently and to varying levels.

Swedes are individualistic at personal levels but that has never come to a conflict with the wellbeing of the collective unless we want to be picky and mention the outliers and exceptional. Social space is heavier in Ethiopian rural life, while it is a bit looser in urban areas but still strong as compared to Sweden.

Swedes have their version of Moses from the Bible or his rival prophets across other religions. The Swedish 'law of Jante' or 'Jante lagen', which imposes the will of the mass on an individual, is present in Ethiopian society, with its version, that does more than it thinks and thinks more than what it says and says more than what it writes. Because one of the rules of bearable social life in Ethiopia is the art of doing away pretty much everything by secrecy and 'inexpression' of feelings, thoughts, decisions and actions. In present day Ethiopia, empirical thoughts come last as fables, tales, legends and myths have already been entertained. Emotionality is also what ravages people's lives as rational thinking is a set up for weakness, and altruism is taken as foolish.

Except the 'ruling class', or today's governing body, individuals may fall through a crack if they are not part of, or born from, 'the specific tribe'.

The rules of the play towards individuals or groups not part of the 'specific tribe' are rather changing in Ethiopia and some of the Ethiopian 'commandments' are not written and are not clear to all either. One of the 'commandments' is that rules do not have to be followed. In a way, this promotes inconsequentiality of choices and bearing no responsibility for the decisions made or actions taken.

Some sins would cause plagues and curse in the eye of several superstitious people while a few people seem to be immune from heavenly calamities, even if that means they commit atrocities, kill, rape or massacre in mass. In a way, that sounds like disasters are clandestine works of people than wraths of the heavens.

Speaking of ethical standards, I am not quite sure if I can say Ethiopians are what they say they are. Most Swedes I know are either self-confessed atheists or vaguely somewhere exploring, and while I know many Christians too, most Ethiopians that I know are self-confessed Christians, Muslims, Catholics, Waqe Fetas, Bahai and Atheists. Atheism is a silently growing urban reality these days. I presume that this is because faith has not been delivering its promises.

Spirituality has been central to Ethiopians to the point that sometimes science finds itself cornered. While there are hospitals clinics and specialized centres, people seem to prefer low educated and ill-informed superstitious figures and witchcrafts for complicated issues. In a setting I grew up, one can be surprised that spirituality was almost everything, literally everything. This is just changing very fast, for good or worse.

If there are almost no clear lines drawn to differentiate right and wrong and the line is left for the imagination of the beholder, this is where reason is not there any more rather non-static, non-definitive views of reality become predominant. At times, reality is staged to the point that pretence becomes sort of fact and impressions take the place of what can be close to what we can call truth. Where reasoning is shoved off, wanting to smell the scent of rules or to observe its influence on behaviours and routines of people is a vain attempt in today's Ethiopia.

Consequentiality of creating and maintaining social harmony, without going all out ideal to the level of the Swedes, but just good enough to make things work, and avoid undue suffering of the people is something of a far planet to our social engineers, scientists and influencers alike. I don't even want to line up political 'leaders' in this, as just the thought of it can be nauseating.

Saving Birgitta From Suicide

I fled to Sweden a month prior to my registration date, as I understood that they already had encircled me, were recruiting my friends and choir members. It had been a very planned and long-acted move much beyond what I could bear alone. Sweden was my country of silence. A country of sanctuary. Here, I was to heal, regenerate and stand back on my feet. Here, I was to understand where all of it went wrong, why and who was responsible. About all these, I needed answers.

My encounters in Sweden made me grow to like the path I chose in focusing more on the humanitarian efforts, while I was struggling to set my feet on the ground for myself, let alone making it to reach out for others. Within the first three months of my arrival, my mates and I were invited to a party. On our way back, we all jumped into the bus and took our seats. Then I saw some encounter happening between a girl and the bus driver. He was raising his tone and she was trying to make an appeal, but how would I know what they were saying — as it was in Swedish. The buss stood still. I then went straight to the driver and asked what the situation was. The girl said she did not have money for one trip and he was refusing her to get on board. I paid it and went back to my seat.

The girl came and sat on the first seat on facing towards me. For some reason, she thought it meant a lot and she said she would be glad to pay back the favour. A few of my classmates thought that I was not giving her a chance because I didn't like girls. Very typical misunderstanding. I just did not think that it was big enough as a favour, and even if it were, I did not expect anything back. For otherwise it would mean taking an advantage. She on the other hand would not take it lightly.

I had to show a stiff neck to make her see it as something she would probably have done to someone else too. This situation made me realise that while there is so much wealth in Sweden, it is such small moments that may affect some people at the personal level than what societies plan at larger scales, which may also turn out to be of no help for such people. Some issues can slip away even in advanced societies.

The Lund University Clinical Research Center is where I conducted my master's studies. It is located in the beautiful city of Malmö. The library we study at is a two-storey building, the back of which faces the greatly calm lake in a large park with walkways and bike lines. The slowly walking elders, bikers, joggers, lovely couples and groups hanging out make the atmosphere lively. The straight-lined trees with perfect cues, the greenery of the vegetations and the grass sooth my heart that needed a healing of unresolved pain I carried with myself. The coloured pigeons and ducks and several other types of birds and rabbits make the most of beauty and the harmless company of nature. I love the park as it is pleasant to study and stare at it or take a half an hour break between studies.

One weekday during the mid-spring of 2010, I decided to take a longer route and spend more time meditating and taking my slow walk in the park. I was watching people feeding the birds, and couples caressing and kissing, others glued to each other and walking slowly all reminded me of my high school years where lovers walked on sidewalks holding hands or hugging. Past most of these, I was making my way back to the library.

I was rushing a bit to catch up with the time and saw someone sitting on a bench and sobbing deeply. I tried to ignore and focus on my way as I had studies. While walking, I saw that it was a woman in her mid-age and just crying without even making a sound. At first, I said to myself, man what if she reports to the police and say that I am harassing her? They warned that such incidents happen in Sweden sometimes. The other side of me just said, *Man up, go back and talk to her*. I returned and went to the bench she was sitting on.

I asked, "may I sit on the bench please?"

She answered, "it is not mine. It belongs to all."

I thanked her and sat down. Then I asked if she could talk to me.

She replied, "I do not want to talk to anyone right now."

"I saw you and returned to talk to you, if it is OK," I said.

She insisted, "You made the choice, now leave me alone."

I sat there for a few minutes.

She then turned to me, gave me a look and pulled her eyes away.

"If I were you, I would talk to someone who is paying me attention and is interested to talk to me," I said gently.

"Maybe I am not in the mood," she countered.

I said, "maybe you are."

She replied, "whatever," then went quiet again.

I said, "I would like to tell you something."

She asked, "like what?"

"A story of two people that I knew in Ethiopia," I explained.

She remarked, "if it is interesting, may be."

"You will tell me your impression later."

She responded, "ok, tell me then."

I said to her, "my name is Andualem, by the way."

She replied, "mine is Birgitta."

I began, "The other day, I saw on a CNN show that an Ethiopian American mother was selected as the best mother of the year. Her story goes like this. Her husband was killed by the government Red Terror operation by the military junta, and she fled to Sudan with her six children. They lived in a refugee camp for several years and made their way to the USA.

"As you know, raising six children all by yourself in a country where you don't know the culture, lifestyle and have no one to help you is not just unthinkable, it is also unbearable for an average Ethiopian mother. What is amazing is that the woman made it and managed to raise all her children, sending them to school and tending to their needs. She had to switch between jobs and be their mother and father for everything. Her colleagues nominated her for the year's best mother award and she was selected. This is the first story."

By this time, Birgitta was crying again. I thought, *OK, instead of showing a strength of another woman to lift up her spirit, I have done quite the opposite. What a waste of time!* I was just feeling it was not working.

She then said, "Andualem, sorry for crying, but the woman's story shows how little things can break people into pieces here in Sweden. I am trying to see myself in her shoes and I don't know if I would make it for a day. So, what is the second story?"

"There was a young man who grew up in a middle-sized city around the Southern Ethiopia. When he was younger, his parents used to struggle to put food on the plate for the children, buy their school supplies and clothes. He was a gifted young boy who lived in a spiritual context, wrote over four hundred songs and acted in dramas, wrote poems and read them for as many as twenty thousand people. When he was close to finishing his high school, he dreamt of building organisations, a humanitarian organisation to help children and assist his people in their needs. After he finished his first-year studies, he travelled back to his hometown on a vacation to see his parents and friends. While having an evening walk with his friends, he saw a boy, about five years, coming towards them. Not one of his friends noticed the boy as they were joking and having fun. The guy stayed behind and asked what the boy wanted.

"The boy said if he wanted something, he could help.

"He asked, 'like what?'

"The boy answered, 'calling the girls from there.'

"He questioned, 'from where?'

"The boy motioned, 'the hotel over there.'

"'Do they sit there and send you to call for men?' he asked.
"The boy replied, 'yes.'
"'Do you do this all the time?'
"The boy again said, 'yes.'
"He asked, 'where are your parents?'
"'We live near Mercato.'
"'Do you have parents?' he asked the boy.
"'My father died. And my mother lives.'
"'If I give you money, what would you do?' he asked.
"The boy answered, 'I will take it to my mother.'
"He gave the boy ten birr (equal to almost eight Swedish Kroners).

"The boy thanked him and rushed towards Mercato, the direction of his house. But the guy knew in his heart that the boy would have to do it again sooner or later. And he thought maybe this was the time to resume the humanitarian organisation establishment work he had begun while he was in high school. One of his friends called him and asked him what he was talking with the boy about.

"He responded, saying, 'It was nothing.' And they carried on with their walks.

"As soon as he graduated from the university, he was employed as a health care staff at a great hospital in his hometown. And he also opened the humanitarian organisation office and started its operations to fulfil his dream of helping others. It was not long before bad people and some at the government offices started to chase him and try to shut down the organisation. They shut it once and it took him a whole year to build things again and make it operational.

After half a year, they started giving him troubles and threatened to shut it again. They threatened the American donors working with him and chased them out of the country. They wanted to put him in jail or cause harm to him. They bribed the police to hurt him and find a reason to arrest him.

To save his life and his organisation, he left what he had sacrificed his everything for and fled his country. They claimed the organisation and took its control through some of his staff members. He is now working student jobs struggling to pay his rent and bus tickets, talking of nutritious food is something else. He is living here in Sweden."

She said, "Andualem, it is you right?"

I replied, "Yes."

She took her tissue paper, wiped her tears and said, "Do you know why I was crying earlier?"

I replied, "no, but I would like to know."

She said, "you would not want to know."

I asked, "why?"

She said, "hear me out and you will understand."

I responded, "I am listening."

After a lengthy silence, she started to struggle with her tears. "You see, Andualem, as you had challenging life because of poverty, bad people and unfair government, I also had challenging time not because of similar things but mostly because of my own choices. When I was a teenager, we started smoking cigarette and got into alcohol and stuff, you know. Later on, we all started smoking weed. But the fun did not stay long, we wanted to have something stronger. We got into the stuff you know, like crack and stuff. I also took heroine many times, mostly after drinking a lot. We did not know but it feels to me now as if we were in a life-ruining contest. My friends, me and all of us. I damaged my own body and soul, you know what I mean.

"Later on, jumping from a boyfriend to another, I met this cool guy who really took care of me. I just celebrated my 38th birthday, I have a loving boyfriend and we have been living in his apartment for a very long time. We love each other so much; he means a lot to me. I just failed to deliver to him, you know."

I asked her what it was that she did not deliver.

She said, "I went through an operation to remove my uterus or I would die soon. I agreed with the doctor and removal was done. Now, my boyfriend is happy with me and always says that I am enough for him. But I feel guilty whenever I think of not giving him a child, and this eats me inside out. I get into depression and would not wake up even after days. But this time around, he had just had enough and could not take it. I don't judge him. I was depressed for almost two weeks was not waking up or being there for him. He is very kind, caring and loving for me. But I cannot help it. Then we fought, and he said I should leave his apartment and we must break up if I cannot let go of issue of a child or anything I cannot change. I left his apartment and have been sleeping on benches for four days now.

"When you came I was contemplating when I should kill myself or if I have any reason that is enough to hold me back. I could not control my feeling as I saw no reason and it all felt like I have no reason to stay alive. Andualem, it is a very deep wound inside, you know. I was even making up my mind on how I can take my life. Then you showed up.

"I was thinking that while scarcity was giving people a hard time in poor countries, many in richer countries also suffer from mismanaged abundance and few go through the pain of not accepting what is not possible to change."

I asked her when the last time she ate.

She told me that it was before she left her boyfriend's apartment.

I said, "You must be starving."

She replied, "I have started feeling hungry now."

"Maybe it is because we are talking about food. Would you like to follow me, please?" I said.

She asked, "Where?"

"Somewhere to buy you food," I replied.

She said, "Andualem, you don't have to do this."

"Sure, I do. I cannot forgive myself if I don't."

"I don't know what to say, Andualem."

"Let's walk and decide on our way," I suggested.

She smiled. "Sure."

We started walking slowly and passed smaller streets and made it close to where there were restaurants and fast-food outlets. She wanted to go to Subway or Seven Eleven. I wanted her to have a proper meal. She insisted and entered a close-by Seven Eleven shop. She ordered a sandwich with chicken and a few more items in it. She also ordered bottled water and a cup of coffee. I just got my usual black coffee and we started to sip and walk to a public place to sit.

Once she was done eating, she said, "Andualem, I will not die. I will live, and you are my guardian angel. You saved me from committing suicide and perishing for a reason another woman would manage to hold on to. I will remember this day for as long as I live."

We kept in touch for a few years before my usual travel life took over and my communications started to lessen with people.

First the boy challenged me to change the path of my life, from the previous wish of working as a professional and coordinating the humanitarian organisation in spare time. I have not just put my full time, I put my life on the line for it. This chased me out of my country and made me a fugitive without any political cause. I was just thinking, *was it not good enough as a reason if I were here only to save Birgitta's life?* As if someone were there to give me answers. Birgitta, on the other hand, may be a lucky person for now who regretted from suicidal thoughts and decided to lead a normal life, would mental health issue be something I should on focus after my master's studies are done was what I started to contemplate. Talking to Birgitta made me realise that mental health is something that needs adequate attention and I would try to give it a close look. She had no idea that I was to be deployed in Iraq and would spend the next decade dealing with issues of overall vulnerabilities. A little Ethiopian boy at the first year of my undergraduate and a Swedish woman at the beginning of my master's held a grip of my life for two decades much more than how much my studies themselves influenced. I stared at her for my last brief moment and thought, *If you only knew where you are pushing me to step into, lady, you would pray to all Gods, deities and angels while you probably may go for additional atonement to Satan not to harm me for an exchange of the lion calves of the world.* These two people rocked my world.

After deployment in Iraq, where I was working with mental health and psychosocial support, also as a development advisor, I learned one thing pivotal about myself. I love Ethiopia to the level that at some point, I flew four times a year as I miss the people every time I leave the airport. Having some dollars enough for a start-up, I went back in 2013 to see if I could open a clinic and start it from low. I was aware that I could aim for something big and roll it like crazy. Since I have big enemies it would not be wise to call for their attention. But you see, this was the problem. They were following all my Facebook images and status updates of flying to Uganda, Brazil, France, Denmark or the Netherlands. This was a period where most Facebookers were so naïve to post almost everything without putting a serious thought over unintended consequences.

In my attempt to open the clinic, Ethiopia became more of a hating stepmother. The government of the time turned the country into a jungle of their own where they rule and do as they wish. It was during this time that I was trying to import machines. Permit process is so subjective; different officers would tell two different criteria to force you quit. In one attempt; I went through all the processes of obtaining licenses and all the required documents. A day later, I was told that there was a new directive that was to make me start everything from day one. I tried this for seven months and decided that I must leave the country once again.

But before this, a friend of mine from our postgraduate studies proposed that I work for the Dr Tedros Adhanom at the Ministry of Health at advisor capacity. Dr Tedros is now leading the World Health Organization, based in Geneva. My friend is from Oromia, one of the coolest friends I have. You know those kinds of friends you can discern their heart and that any conversation would mean you are literally enriched. I was secretly wishing that he were a minister and I wouldn't second guess to work as his advisor. I wanted to serve the country, but my issue was that the government was so brutal to its people that I would not forgive myself for enhancing their cruelty. I informed him that I would not accept it and left for Uganda instead for I had an offer for a post.

Kampala

Back in the day when I was in Kampala and even in Nairobi, I would rent the motor bicycles, 'Bodabodas' that are known as very handy and faster to get around. The accidents, and designated hospital beds for motorbike accidents would make me think twice if it were now, yet I must admit it was not just fun, but also motorbikes made it possible for me to look around in both cities in a short time period than how much my friends did in a several years. Going around the city corners, sharing experiences, making friends, eating at unexpected local places and exchanging genuine social encounters remain priceless in Kampala as also in Nairobi.

The country has a tenderly special place in my heart for a reason I cannot explain. Perhaps, it is because I was treated very kindly and that I found Ugandans more elegant and open-minded than most of my fellow Ethiopians. The first time I travelled to Uganda was on an internship/scholarship.

Eating matoke, G-nuts and spinach for dinner and drinking some soda with a group of university students, grinding our presidents, sullying out celebrities or impersonating professors was fun sitting under an open sky filled with evening stars.

Ugandans have one thing so special; the ability to move to almost any music and their way of dance. From little children to adults. they break it down so cool I am just amazed how people are close to having fun any time they get the chance. You see knees bending, legs widen, hips moving, a smile and a snapping sound. Laughter and joy are so close to daily life that anything seems bearable here.

Not that everything is accessible nor that all people have wealth to show for, it is this richness that they make the best out of what they have that is amazing about the people. But at some point, a condemn would be thrown, and I would pick it up even if they were speaking any of the local languages in Uganda. They would even add HIV/AIDS and that it was a way of fighting the disease together by reminding each other. It is like let's have fun, but they had to be careful about HIV/AIDS.

What I recall was that the dean of the university booked a meeting at the reception hall at Lund University before I travelled there. He asked me super serious question that sounded easy just because he was polite and super diplomatic.

He said, "So Mr Andualem, how do you see we talk about a scenario in my country?

"You see, Andualem, there is a woman in rural Uganda who is married and has three children. One night, her husband comes, you know for sex, and she refuses. The man angry at her behaviour asks her with a demanding tone. She then says, 'I am in love with our neighbour's wife' and turns to the other side and tries to sleep. Now I must warn you that our police do not operate like the Swedish or our society is not supportive of a woman's free will in the usual straight sexuality and her taste of expressions." Then he laughs, offloading it all.

His question was what the fate of this woman would be. I was figuring out why he would want to discuss this instead of inviting me to his country and telling me a thing or two to entice an interest to my visit. It was high time that debates on issues of sexuality and abortion t at some point became Uganda's most debated topic that created a traction that even President Museveni would say a word or two about. For obvious reasons, this woman would be kicked, violated and probably left on the streets for more abuse. Her family would be torn apart, and the neighbours would also end up divorcing with similar situations. This is to see in a contrast where you have the Swedish 'no-taboo on feelings and well-functioning welfare system' that can rescue these women almost in no time.

His soft-spoken approach meant that I just needed to think it through if I were to talk about scientific approaches to sexuality in a way that would not expose people for harming themselves, their families and their way of life. It made sense in such a way that things are supposed to make life better and that a comfort of one shall not come at the cost of another. Probably the word balancing may work here better.

I realised it was an informal interview session without saying so; had it been that I said terrible things, my trip would be cancelled.

"Mr Andualem, if you make friends in Uganda, condoms shall also be your close one," he said. He then laughed at my reactions to his statement that dropped out of the blue with long *hei-hei-hei-hei*.

"How do you think I come from a country ravaged by HIV/AIDS and I still find myself healthy and alive? Don't take HIV so easy in Uganda. We lost a generation to it. Many of my close relatives, friends and acquaintances perished before our eyes just like that. You would meet a new friend and after a while, you hear they are gone. HIV is a horrible thing, man. It has destroyed our generation so much that only elders and the youth are left. So, buy as many condoms as possible since you have quality ones here, I assume." Speaking of this though, it appeared that President Museveni had managed to open this page to a new chapter where oil, mineral and the service based Ugandan economy is the main storyline today.

I came to Mbarara, a beautiful city, located on the southwest of Uganda with one of THE most awesome people on the earth and a very warm and pleasant weather. I like Uganda as a country, and then I love it for its amazing people. As a master's student doing my internship, I was to adapt to the guys and ladies, see how things go and get along with pretty much everyone. This would mean making new friends, that stayed in my life to this day. Somewhere in the conversations though, I would be asked for my opinions, or how it is in Sweden, or Ethiopia and so on. As it was contentious issue, raised at the presidential level and official statements being made on the media, and stories of arrests, talk of sexuality was at its peak around 2010, and long afterwards. It is even discussed a few times now too.

I shared a villa compound with four people from Sweden, two girls, a guy (girl, I guess) and my professor. Kjell, was a student and a Swedish parliamentarian and was a strong advocate for sexuality rights under a banner of research student. We used to hang out at the school compound, eat together and just chit chat with the Swedish students, and with my professor occasionally.

What I realised was that some students that normally hangout with me would distance themselves whenever Kjell was around. And some of them started getting pissed off at me and showing me the face. I knew I had no negative encounters with them and was left puzzled as to know what went wrong. To make it worse, I was more interested in the Ugandan social life, the culture, turns and twists of their daily lives and something was blocking the way.

One sunny day, I was sitting at the shade sipping my coffee all by myself and five students, three guys and two girls, came to greet me. Talks were started and after a while one of the guys went saying, "Andualem, some students are not comfortable now."

I asked, "Why is that?"

He replied, "Because you are hanging around with the sexuality preacher."

"You mean Kjell?"

"Yes."

"But he is not doing that."

"What is he doing then, when he goes around and tells everyone that he is into men and that Uganda needs to be like Sweden in this matter?" he said.

I replied, "I did not hear him say that."

"He frustrates everyone around here by talking to us on how we should think in this country," he went on to say.

"I did not know this either."

One of the girls said, "Do you like girls, Andualem?"

I responded, "Yes. I actually have a girlfriend."

She then said, "I am prettier, no?"

I said, "Eh…?"

"I know, I know you still love her," she said.

"Yes, I do," I said.

"But she is not here," she insisted.

"We keep in touch."

"Someone here has a crush on you, Andualem. What are you going to do about it?"

I was still confused. "Eh…"

She turned away before smiling at me, kept giggling while walking and left.

My professor from Sweden who was also with us in Mbarara city has a hobby of looking at birds with his binoculars, or even just adjusting his eyeglasses. He would stand there watching the birds, stare at them and spend an hour or two just doing that. I never saw someone do this before, and when I grew up, birds were for either chasing, catching and bringing them home to keep them in a small box where we would feed them. I was stunned! It actually took me time to learn a few things about their nature, colours, what differentiates on from the other from his explanations.

On one of the Saturday evenings, the two girls, Kjell and myself sat by the sofa and were just hanging out. What we saw during the week, a few jokes and dashing out at some things kept the evening great. At some point, the boyfriend of Kjell called on Skype and excused himself to talk to him.

After returning from the talks, Kjell became a bit off the pitch and started to poke me around. In a complete honesty, what happened triggered me to actually mind what was happening more than I would want to.

Kjell literally said, "Andualem, you are not really much attractive to me," and I just lost it.

"For one," I said, "I am not hitting on you, if that is what you feel."

They then said, "But still."

My response was, "You are not straight."

They asked, "So my opinion does not count?"

"Not about what is attractive in the world of straight people," I said.

They then said, "Well, I am entitled to it."

I replied, "For me, it does not count."

They asked, "Why?"

"Because I am straight, and it is a straight woman who can tell me if she thinks I am handsome or not."

They then asked, "What if a straight man said so?"

"Straight men don't put too much time on gazing each other when there are plenty of girls around. Who would waste their sight?"

And 'they' was just laughing.

After policing *her* talks, and telling that beauty was in the eye of the beholder, I said, "As for me, it would only work if you were straight and a girl. I don't really care about your opinions."

Then something else came up and people started talking about what was published on one of the Ugandan red papers that had some women leaving their number after expressing their sexual fantasies to the bravest first man who would call them and see. I was on the roof thinking over Kjell's attitude of having such strong opinion over me; it made me think whether the students were not as biased as I thought and if he personally were just doing it wrong.

Few days later, I was passing by a narrow alley towards my room and saw Kjell standing by the shade and arguing with more than ten students about issues of sexuality and stood for a brief moment to hear what they were discussing about. The more They talked, the louder they get and at some point, two or more students would shout at *her*. Some were using slur words, others were spitting on the ground and They were making everyone angry at *her*self. I was just shaking my head and slowly started walking. Kjell was actually turning everyone against *herself* instead of being respectful to the culture and that if They knew anything better, there is a Ugandan way of doing it so that they could share thoughts. No, they had an assumption to have had superior knowledge and they were just to accept what they had to *teach* them.

For fair contrast with Kjell, and to try to avoid attitudes of straight perceptions, I would want to say about a local star who left Thailand with her boyfriend and stayed in Sweden for quite some time. She broke up with her boyfriend and later on decided that she is not a girl any more. After a few visitations to surgeons' appointments and psychological follow ups, she managed to get a male private part. At the time we met, they were now a *he* and got a male name, Richard. Richard met with the ex-boyfriend and explained the situation and life is to be accepted as it is and they both should move on.

I rented a room at a large two-storey villa in Stockholm. That is where I met *him*. We had a shared kitchen and would stumble on each other, and talks would begin almost about anything. The transgender man would explain to me how it works with hormonal issues, psychological shift, noticing the gaps between his perceptions and what happens, and the all-round issues related. In all of this, *he* appreciated the rights and respect Sweden offered which is incomparable with what one would experience back in Thailand. It is already hard for a star, and harder for regular people. Richard is grateful about Sweden and its tolerant culture while Kjell would not put an effort to learn, see things as they are and trust Ugandans to take charge of their own matters.

The same day Kjell was arguing with students by the tree shade, they came to the veranda where I sat to watch the sun set and listen to the birds and just read a small book I brought with myself. Obama was the President of the United States back then. I was already contemplating what to say if he opened up on these issues and use Obama against the Prime Minister of Sweden for my case.

They asked, "How was your day?"

I replied, "It was good. Yours?"

They said, "Mine was good too."

"Good to know."

"Yes. I saw you today when I was talking to a group," said Kjell.

I nodded. "Yes, I saw you too."

"How do you find it?"

I said, "it was aggressive."

They nodded. "Yes. They all were on my neck."

"No, I mean the way you handled the situation," I told Kjell.

"I did what was right," they said.

"You mean attacking people's cultures?" I raised my eyebrow.

"No, I did not."

"Do you see that you keep poking them?" I said.

"That makes them engage in discussions."

I said, "Then you lost your case."

"Why?" they asked.

"Was the point to get them engaged in a discussion only?"

"Of course not."

"What are your motives then?" I asked.

They replied, "So that they learn."

"About?"

"Sexuality and rights."

"How do you know that they don't know?"

"Well, you heard what they were saying."

"Well, they were deflecting you not because of the topic, but because of how you approached them."

"What are you trying to say?"

I spoke, "Respect comes first."

"Fu*k respect!" they cursed.

"Well, I heard them swearing with anger towards you."

I said to Kjell to assume that all of a sudden, President Obama flies to Sweden and orders all the pharmacies shall get shut down, and that all practices need to be duplicates of how it is done in the USA. He says this to the face of the Swedish Prime Minister. How would people react?

They responded by saying, "Well, the president must be crazy."

"But what you are doing here in Uganda is crazier than this," I said.

They said, "Andualem, you are stretching it too far."

"No, too far is when you say culturally disrespectful expressions to several students in one spot in other people's country."

I told Kjell that I did not have to say I was straight, and that they were to feel comfortable to the point of no need to introduce this where there was no need to express private orientation while people are about to be introduced to each other, at least not in Africa!

I have a Congolese friend, Luis, with whom we have more than twelve years of good friendship. My parents met him in their visit to Europe and he still is one of my closest friends for thin and thick in life. He is a genuine, thoughtful, intelligent and kind man. We usually hangout occasionally, eat some good cultural food, or just any favourite picks and trash and praise each other's leaders based on their performance of the time and have elaborate talks about how things could get better in Africa, and how it can improve its ties with Europe, the USA and others. A while ago, I got a phone call from him urging that we talk on some important matter that was so acute, and it bothered him, and he did not know what to do. He briefed me over the telephone and that it was about his brother in Paris. Luis's brother is a good guy, at least this is what I know from my experiences.

After eating our lunch, we changed the place for my favourite latte, and his preferred tea and sat at Espresso House, perhaps the most popular coffee shop in Sweden. They have great snacks and bites too. I like it.

Luis said, "Man, my brother's situation is bothering me."

I asked him, "Why is that?"

He replied, "You know this guy just altered my thinking."

I asked, "How?"

"Man, he just said he is not into girls any more."

"No, you are kidding."

"No, I am serious."

"How was he before?"

"As long as I remember, he was straight, into girls and had girlfriends and so on. But now he tells me something else," he said.

"Since when? When did he tell you?"

He replied, "He said a few years have passed."

"What do you want to do about it?" I asked.

"I really don't know. My mother is expecting us to get married, have children and make her happy one day. And this... what can I make of this?"

We paused for a brief moment and then talked about how he could re-orient himself about his brother and remain as close brothers as they had been. And that nothing should change on the part of expressing love, having the familial commitments and all that. I was not sure if I made sense or not, but out of honest desperation I mumbled a few words.

A few years passed, and Luis and I were at a bar sipping some drinks and trying to catch up. We briefed each other on our updates; and he did about his long-time girlfriend. Before her, Tania was his girlfriend who used to come with Lena when we met.

Somewhere down the talk, he just picked at the table and said, "You know, Andualem, Tania kissed our friend Lena right here."

I was extremely shocked. Because Luis loved Tania from all his heart. She was studying to become a chef at one of the known schools in France, and he had to fly to her almost every time before she moved here. He sacrificed a lot, brought her to his family in Congo and did all it took to keep her with himself. But Tania somehow thought it would be fun to hurt Luis's feelings while she was gradually distancing herself from him. And loving another guy, I can take it. Or just saying she does not want him is still OK. Coming and kissing a girl in front of him was more like a knife in the chest than a girlfriend telling him to break up. Seeing this though, Luis seemed to have told his mind that anything could happen and that he was not to take it personal or seriously, rather just let it go.

On my second stay in Uganda, I was volunteering based in Kampala with frequent field trips around Pader, Agago, Kitgum, Karamajong, and my favourite in the area — Gulu city. Gulu is a regional city, modest and vibrant in its way. The Kidepo National Park is a well-kept and less-frequented great place where lions, cheetahs, elephants, African buffalos, zebras, antelopes, impalas and birds on acacia trees would not need to be seen through binoculars, as they may just pop up on the side roads in numbers. The open field valley and savannah with fresh breath would be one of the greatest feelings to remember. As it is close to Congo and other countries, one would see different people partly on business and partly on leisure. Chances are that you would meet American soldiers, humanitarian organisation workers, businesspeople, professors and university students. In the partying department, the Americans and the Ugandans seem to rock it better than when a British or Irish would be there. I just don't know why but they click better with each other.

I became rich in the wisdom I was absorbing from the ex-child soldiers, Kadagos in the local term, from how one can survive in the darkest moments of life, learns skills used for a brief part of life, preparing for a new world, adapting to the unknown future normal, knowing how to celebrate life with all its shortcomings, how to forgive accept and embrace enemies, and most importantly how to love again, even those that knew they deserve the harshest of your punishment. A significant number of Kadagos have now managed to become medical doctors, engineers, photographers, artists, teachers and community workers while most of them are poor farmers.

As the Lord's Resistance Army Leader Kony was said to be roaming around the area, together with his Kadagos in the local term, the stories we hear in Gulu were not always cosy. It gets intensely worse when you hear them in Pader. It is in this district that the LRA burned and destroyed villages, raped women and brutalised the whole area.

One day, the LRA soldiers were said to come to the village shooting and burning crops; they were terrorising the whole community of the area. It was a young woman who was telling me this story, and started by saying:

"…they forced us to drag the bodies of twenty-eight people they killed and called our remaining relatives to gather outside. They shouted at us and ordered us to chop the bodies and prepare them for boiling them in large pots. Their intention was to make us eat the flesh of our own relatives after letting us cook on the outside so that everyone could see. We were cooking in many pots and people from far thought we were inviting the soldiers to eat regular food. We were boiling bodies of our own siblings like potatoes or, you know, fish. It was on an open field with bushes and trees and could be seen from very far. Outside the cottage houses, many soldiers were making sounds and shooting at the sky every now and then. They would be ululating or start beating family members of the dead ones. One could hear the burning sound of houses, crops, bushes and wailing women silenced after a number of yelling and a cry for help. Most people had run to the mountain top, while we were the only ones left. And they got us. You will hate to know about us. We all are not like that," she said.

In about time to force them to start eating, the government security forces were said to have arrived, started a fight and intervened. The stories were so horrendous and mind jolting that it is difficult to tell or hear without tears, sweating added with the hot weather and one would just wake up to moments of gasping, soaked with wet cloth and remain shaking the head. It vibrates my nerves even now when I think of it.

As I was working with Mental Health and psychosocial support and development, such stories are not new to me, but this one remains a thing of its own. *"Andualem, you need to be careful to know who is telling you the story, it can be Kony's recruits or government soldiers in civil for your information, my friend. If people feel you are on the other side across the table, terrible things can happen to you as well. People have deep scars, never to mention that it can be any of us, ey! But they like you hiya* (meaning 'here')."

I was getting a warning. A friend of mine saw that I was so consumed by their stories indiscriminately that I would sit with almost everyone who would share their experiences. This meant a risk that I may get attacked for knowing what I am not supposed to know about. To this day, the LRA issue has this dark side of it, that is very sensitive and dangerously intriguing. It was a close call to say that I needed to draw the line. What may start as an issue with LRA may turn out to be linked with the death and remnant loyalists of Idi Amin Dada or President Obote's death. One thing I normally hate in this is when a story starts a circle and the trails lead towards Kampala. I could see the story tellers marking the dots one after the other that somehow link countries and leaders or organisations. It is always dangerous to know the first account in raw and uncensored stories of atrocities.

The generous sociability, music, dances, food and easy conversations among people mean a collective way of coping mechanism. It was a kind of inherited and deep-rooted practice of self-healing and restoring dignity, the sense of togetherness and creating a shared safe space. This is possibly how such communities prevailed post-war situations and previous traumatic incidents. None of this is without a lot of alcoholics, few cases of psychosocial crisis and mild to severe mental health conditions more prevalent than the figures among the general population. This being so, I must say that such mental endurance, collective strength and emotional ability to restore a way of calm in the entire community is a whole lot of unexplainable process in its own.

Gods of Africa

Dhugasa used to come to my dormitory and discuss very elaborate matters from faith to ethnicity and culture, from ideologies to civilizations, modernity to modesty or even personal matters like the girl he was in love with whom my other friend loved and that I was trying to keep both of them away from getting in trouble with each other or pressuring the girl from making a reasonable decision as to whom she really loved and wanted to call her boyfriend. My other friend, Galaso, would say, he stands no chance as Dhugasa spoke her language, Afan Oromo, and would snatch her away from him. In the end, she let both of them go but was closer to my other friend.

Dhugasa was not that every other medical student that thinks they are on their path to a good social and economic status by the time they graduate. In every conversation I had with him, I could tell something deep was bothering him to the point that he was failing to fall asleep for many days every now and then.

He would come into my dorm, one day and passed by me, went out to the balcony and sat there watching the girls passing by, hitting on some, laughing and greeting some of the guys passing by.

Then he called me and said, "I will be here until you are done with your reading. I would like us to talk about a few things today."

I knew he came with some intrigue that would keep the rest of my afternoon engaged before it would be dinner time and all the 'gangsters' would flood the room and shooting jokes and eating together would replace the peace. The noise was equally fun, but when I want to have serious talks, I prefer quietness, especially when friends like Dhugasa have something to say.

I went out to the balcony, dragged a chair and sat down. He was sitting on the edge of the thin support of the back of his chair, while putting one shoe on the chair and another on the upper protection of the balcony. I gazed at him and saw that he had this ease psychologically. But surely something deeply troubled him.

He looked at me, calling me Andrew, and said, "Why don't you stop going to church? Why even are you a Christian? Why shall I stay as a Christian? I am just wondering if you thought of this," he said.

Galaso gave me a nick name, Andrew. A classmate from Diredawa gave me a nick name Jack. My parents and relatives gave me seven nick names. I was rich in this. Sometimes Galaso would call me Andrew Jack, borrowing Jack from my Diredawa friend. Because Dhugasa is Galaso's class mate, he got it from him and used to call me Andrew once in a while.

We debated over several issues for very long time. A few of these issues are deep topics that touch religion, philosophy, politics and real-life social matters.

Dhugasa came back to my room and started a conversation, saying, "Christianity is not Oromo faith. I assume it is not the Wolaita faith too. Our religion is Waqe Fata and you guys worship Xosa (God — in Wolaitic). It is better I preach you about Waqe Feta and you teach me about Xosa. Maybe they are similar or can complement each other." He had some examples, practical scenarios and lengthy analysis about basic concepts of Waqe Fata. But I was somehow lost, as his statement that Christianity is not Oromo nor is it Wolaita just shook my skull around.

I was halfway thinking he was sinning, halfway it felt he saw faith from ethnic ownership angle and this made me wonder, *what can make a man think something like this? And if it is under a normal circumstance, where is this coming from?*

To complicate it further, he said, "Andrew, Christianity belongs to the Amhara; not you, not me," and he sighed, took out a tissue paper from his pocket, brushed the chair and sat on the chair properly. He said, "The Amhara own Orthodox, they dominate Islam and have influence in protestant religions, you and I don't matter in these. Especially Orthodox, Protestant and Catholic are in their pocket, I am sure you would agree to this."

This goes against all my thought balance, emotional equilibrium, faith reliance, moral compass and ethical conscience. It is against me as a person to question faith this way, but he threw me off the cliff, I would say, and made me think, could this actually mean something?

We talked for a good two hours and a half time, before everyone else returned for dinner and evening library hours. What Dhugasa started as exercise of questioning ownership of faith ended up in me being troubled by the fact that he stayed in the university for almost twelve years without graduating. He developed psychiatric disorder that hindered his studies even further and that it was quite an unbearably huge burden for him and his parents.

I knew that some Oromo students have very deep dedication to Oromo political parties, and the Oromo cause, that some would delay their studies by a year or two to do political mobilisations and recruitment and coaching university community. And that he also was part of the leadership, beyond all of this. I just felt that this young man must have been hurt to get to this level. A sane individual would not stretch all the strings, go all the distance, question everything and be as bitter and scary to many people without being provoked to the core.

His grievances and other situations all made me take bad occurrences with grain of salt. The worst is that people don't question or explore links and leaders instead pray to God and go through hardships without noticing it.

Some people do know, but significant majority is unaware that pain does not fall on its own, and there are responsible individuals for incidents. Further to this, there is a purpose these altered conditions serve. They literally condition an individual's and a group's future reality. This is not just an act of interrupting with their fate, it is also meaning we actually have a country that somehow edits and decides what kind of life your children can have.

In a truest sense possible, beyond any doubt, these acts of evil hands alter generational truth. Once you have the upper hand to alter truth, you are a 'god'. When you are a 'god' you own faith, cultures, society, the state and all there is. Perhaps this is what Dhugasa was trying to picture and determine its depth, colours, contents and weight.

I guess that is what he meant when the Amhara nationalist party's former executive committee member openly said, "As God created heavens and Earth, Amhara created Ethiopia." Assuming many of the readers believe in God, or the rest in the highest power, or greater good, we all understand one thing in common about this. It makes more sense as what he wanted this mass to believe in comparing itself with God, making them a deity of some sort.

If all agreed to him, the perfect expression of everyone would have been 'we are God'. Almost the same expressions as my friend who said, "God is Amhara." Yes, you are reading it right! So, we have some people who not only believe in being god, but if they succeeded in rallying everyone behind them, they would want the mass to say that they are god. If God is Amhara, and if Amhara created Ethiopia, these individuals mean that they are creators of Ethiopian heaven and Earth. What is important is that many of my Amhara friends actually believed, at least back when we discussed, that they created the African Union. This would mean, at African continent, we have a people's group that probably perceives itself to be the god of Africa.

If you are god, you own everything. You decide whether it will be the good or the bad to happen to people. The people you want become wealthy, healthy, well-to-do in life and have the assurance of improvements for the future generation. You are the alpha and the omega. You are THE GOD who was, who is and who is to come. You are the supreme to concert everything that has to do with culture and the way of expressions are to look like. You are the embodiment of how the people's life looks like. And most importantly, you are the truth that walks on the earth. As God is believed to be the source of perfection, and that Ethiopia is not a perfect country (not yet, at least), and if God is not responsible for what is wrong, not the Amhara elites either; it must be the fault of all other ethnic groups!

What was happening at the university was the business of the people in the city as much as the staffers from the area took the university matters into their possessions. I am not saying that everything in the university is this way, but if you look close enough, you should be able to sense it. But there are moments when the sensing is not needed to the point that the incidents around manifest themselves in their own even without any of your efforts. It was time for exams and we all were really squeezed.

Me being the man roaming around Internet centres, sitting to read on leadership and organisational management, proposal writing and searching for potential donors, I am twice squeezed than every student who spends most hours at the library and never goes to church or any other social functions.

A collegemate came to me and asked me at a break between lecture sessions. He was so nervous, in what appeared like the stress a psychology student would have as if their assignment is assembling the total equations for nuclear plant turn key. To his advantage, he is from Amhara region and some of the information trickles to him in some way.

He rushed to me and started asking me questions that later made me feel like left out in my university. Since the university is a federal institute, this would technically mean I am cast out from the Ethiopian institutional and academic sphere.

It also made me feel like I cannot expect fair chance of competition and that whatever I see at the university, for as much as there is genuine process of measuring student competence, there was a lot of shady work going on depending on who you are, whom you know and what you do. Coming from Amhara region, being Amhara, even among the Amhara the Gonderians had a better chance.

He started to ask me questions:

"For as long as I see, you are not a hundred per cent on the studies," he said.

I replied, "I have other goals too, and you know it."

"Don't you also want to have good grades?"

"I do. But I will do the exams, and all should just be fine," I told him.

He said, "Why are you acting like you don't care?"

"I care," I replied, "but I also feel it is not really something I should worry about."

"No, no, you have the answers."

I said no.

He asked, "Then why do you ignore it?"

"Because I don't believe the teacher would know how smart or dumb I am just because I can or cannot answer questions," I replied.

We both paused, and I just started feeling uneasy since this was a common question that some of my mates asked me every now and then. At the same time, I was sure he was just scratching the surface to see if I would ask him back.

"You seem to be uncomfortable with something," I noted.

"Yes, I worry sometimes. I am sure you too feel this sometimes."

I nodded. "Yes."

"*H'ooo.*"

"What is bothering you?" I asked again.

"We are in trouble," he said.

"What happened?"

"*Tewegn bakih,*" — meaning, 'Leave me alone on this'. This is usually the Ethiopian way of saying, ask me for more in a subtle way.

"*Ende mindinew esu. Bakih nigeregn,*" — meaning, 'What is it that concerns you? Please tell me.'

He replied, "*Fetena eko wetual,*" — meaning, 'The exams are leaked.'

"*Besmam!*" — meaning, 'Oh my God!'

He continued, "*Bakih min waga alew, motenal,*" — meaning, "We are dead."

While the burden of study would mean one thing for some and another for others, some students such as Dhugasa were left to suffer at the school for over eleven years. It is not just fair, but even slightly different from normal, to say that if the school were a hot bed for everyone, it surely was a hell for people like Dhugasa.

Having his typical Oromo name, and him being not that much reserved to say out loud what he thinks, nor being a person short of expressions; his experiences are not the occurrences of a usual medical student. Whether he questioned who God is, if God is for Oromo, or if he asked me if I ever felt as a real Ethiopian, and if I never felt, 'excluded in a thing or two', I would not dare having any judging tone, for doing so would actually send a signal of justifying actions of the perpetrators that ripped him off his dignity and walked on his fate.

Many Oromo and other students, among many others, were ambushed from dormitories and murdered only to have a mass burial in secret locations, some going to Kenya, Sudan, Djubouti and elsewhere, to stay at refugee camps to make it to the UK, Europe, Canada, the USA or Australia.

For many among the Wolaita, or the Oromo like Dhugasa, that went through indescribably painful and oddly heinous experiences in present-day Ethiopia, propelling one of their own to the Arat Killo Palace must mean for what it is! This is a victory at the global scale which history will remember inscribing on golden bar as a generational achievement. Dr Abiy Ahmed Ali, the incumbent Prime Minister of Ethiopia, the chief of Ethiopian National Defense Forces, is an Oromo through his father and as he confessed publicly and Amhara on his mother's side. This must mean something!

It surely is not a story of every other average power grabbing, or some political plot that eventually yielded state capture, this is a global history in the making. Africa's political landscape will surely change. No one can be sure if it will not rearrange the global map or we shall learn if it won't alter the course of Ethiopian history, if not that of the entire world.

No Quero

I flew from Addis Ababa to Stockholm, and from there to Costa Rica with my then fiancée. We were invited to attend a wedding of our common friends. Dr Miguel and his fiancée Carola. My fiancée was photographer at the wedding. I must also say that it was my persuasion that converted her photography talent into a profitable company that helped her to travel to Miami, Costa Rica, Brazil, Peru, Bolivia, Italy, Portugal, South Africa, Zambia, Zanzibar, Victoria Falls and to several places in Sweden. Many of these trips I also participated in on different occasions.

Costa Rica remains among special countries that I am blessed to have visited, twice surprisingly. Travelling to Costa Rica taught me of my value in this world in two dimensions. The first was that I do not have the basic human rights in the eye of immigration agencies of several countries in one hand, and special treatment for coming from Ethiopia on the other.

The most exciting and unexpected encounters were also parts of the same trip. The first time I went to Costa Rica, at the arrival, I was asked to present my passport. The officer at the counter was so excited that I was from Ethiopia and he went asking for coins, souvenirs or anything special about Ethiopia. It was not in a sesnse of a bride, it could have sufficed if I gave him a cent or a keyholder. I could not believe it! Being an Ethiopian is celebrated too.

To my surprise, he did not check my papers well or did not even ask me questions that had to do with my trip. He just said, "Sir, you are very welcome to my country," and I knew that I was going to have fun in this country. To be honest, I was not greeted and welcomed like this even in my own country. It is unforgettably and with truest honesty, a very special treatment. No one in their sane mind would un-love Costa Ricans or resist from not falling for this beautiful place on the earth, for real.

We stayed at a family place in San Vito, made great local company and had all the attention of the small town on us. The people seemed to have met black people before, but finding any black person on the local shops, restaurants or a café was rare. Once again, the generosity of love and care by all people meant that what we saw in San Jose and Cartago was not just a smile ritual for tourists or short-term visitors, people mean it when they love and respect each other here.

For many people would find synergies and shared views, practices or cultural reflections to connect with. The language, though, can be difficult for many to express themselves in English, and my '*ola*' and '*gracias*' did not help much either. For most part of it though, we would understand each other and get along much easier and without a lot of exhaustion one would anticipate.

Some of the amazing musical instruments that I saw were bamboo or wooden pipes that are blown to make amazing sounds. A guy, Lucas, brought an Elm Didgeridoo pipe, wind musical instrument and handed me over to try it out. Except breathing in, I was terrible in making anything musical at all.

He was laughing at me and said, "You are an African man, these things are popular there. You should know how to play them and make a woman fall in love with you. Come on, strong man." He was having his day teething me around. He then taught me how one can blow in a certain way and make this base sound very deep and graciously amazing.

In Wolaita and neighbouring ethnic-siblings, there are many shapes and type of musical instruments made of bamboo pipes which have closely similar functions and notes. The Elm Didgerido appeared relatively narrow by the mouth piece closely 4 cm and the edge 5—7 cm diameter and could be as long as close to two meters. Made of earthly brown colour and smoothly polished, the instrument is one of those items that sound awesome and look great too.

The Dinkiya and Chacha Zayiya are played during spiritual rituals, annual celebrations such as the Wolaita and it sibling's new year Gifata, weddings and funerals. Wind-based musical instruments are very central part of the people's and kingdom's events and celebrations in the area. Now that we have the likes of it resembling in Costa Rica, I realised that the culture of Wolaita and its siblings are just a part of the global music family and that with the correct connections and relations, these are global gifts to celebrate, not just market them for formal rigid purposes that were used in recent public life.

At a hill, that sits on a river bed on one side and a wide field on the other, the family of Lucas owns a farmland on which they grow many kinds of crops; such as coffee, bananas, maize, beans and cassava among many others. They would be heard complaining that the local laborers are not frequenting as much and that at times they fail to get enough help at the time of coffee harvest among other farming works. The indigenous people of the area would be seen roaming around going to and from farms, mostly in the mornings and evening after work hours, but also some do rush on the narrow alleys trying to eat lunch and make it back to work quickly. In their haste though, they would turn and have a gaze at me and turn to their road and continue rushing away.

I saw the indigenous girls that put on long and wide dresses, wearing a few handmade traditional jewelleries, with their hairs split in to two with braids tied back and letting the rest of hair float to the fresh breath of the wind going through and making them look like may be more authentic than what they think it looks. They are pretty, reserved and cognizant on being observant of my presence there.

Their silence and at times angry look towards the Lucas' family or anyone they saw on the road made me feel like there must be something awful in the past that is not dealt with but hey, I am on a wedding trip, and that I am to learn about anything that comes through my way without judging or getting in to people's business yeah. No, my mind was asking me why the indigenous people are not seen happy, comfortable and affectionate to the likes of the Luca's family and passers-by. I just couldn't help it from asking myself.

Lucas's family owns almost the whole hill all the way down to the river, must be several hectares of land. On the top of the hill, they built a large restaurant on what looks like a ranch, with fishery, swimming pool, eating area and coffee shop. The fishery has layers of fishing ponds dug every two meters on which the water runs from the source on the top and passes through each pond on which the fish are seen through the water barrier.

One day, Lucas, his brother and sister-in-law invited us to have a walk to the river to the see coffee farms, neighbouring people's work and go through the river and have a relaxed day. We were Izla my then girlfriend and me, Lucas, his brother Gabriel, Gabriel's wife Marta and two children. Marta carried the little baby and Samuel was walking with us.

Samuel was about four years old, but somehow a seven-year-old in a younger body. Very clever, at times angry and stubborn, yet a lot fun to be around with. You would never get bored with him or lose the idea of what to do with him. We passed through neighbour's farmland, cutting through bananas, sugar canes, sweet potatoes and cassava.

We were greeting people, with my faint '*ola*' and taller appearance was looked at and asked a few questions before we would more to the next. It was here we saw the indigenous girls and some men doing farming works, whether it was tilling the soil, harvesting, storing or placing different items in special places for crops. I saw some of them doing fence work, while some were fixing broken ones, others building them from scratch.

The ladies are quiet for most part of it unless someone talked to them. After a while, we made it to the river; very clean, calm and slowly flowing down the valley. One could see small fish, frogs and insects running over or close to it.

While we were chitchatting about big and small issues from the USA news to what was happening in San Jose, the weather and malaria getting worse, eating fruits in between and Samuel splashing the water over us, we were like a little family that were on a short-distance excursion than just going down on a visit of adjacent river. When we were about to return though, Samuel was just having the peak of his fun and did not think that he should just leave it for our sake and go back to the boring walking up the hill, which was also tiring for his age. The boy knew what he wanted and what he did not. And he did not take it well when the adults wanted to cut his fun-time short and tell him to stop and climb up the hill.

Samuel was very furious at his father. He rushed to the river, held a tree branch and took a bunch of little stones. He would take one by one and throw them at us and reject our plans of returning home. The boy did not say it, but it felt like he was thinking, *'Who the hell are you to tell me when to stop playing and to go back home? Am I not a person enough to decide when the fun is over, and it is time to go back? Wouldn't I feel hungry if that is what you all are worried about, and if it is more for my sake than yours, for that matter!'*

What he did say was *'No quero!"* — meaning, 'I do not want'. He said this literally over a hundred times very fast and not even catching his breath properly. *"No quero, no quero, no quero!"*

Lucas said, "You hear the little man, Gabriel? He is saying he does not want. He would be crying the whole way back and keep nagging his mother until the night of this mishap. He is super angry. Maybe we should not force him, I would suggest." We all realised that unless someone dared to force him, no one of us would persuade him and walk him his way back. All nice talks, prepping up and inviting mango and fresh banana did not do the trick. He was determined to stay for as long as he wanted to and that nobody else was to decide for him, assuming they would know the best to speak on his behalf. No, he did not think so. While the mother was angry and intimidating, probably because she would be the one who had to prepare lunch soon, the father said, "We should stay a little bit longer and return when he feels comfortable." He said to him this in Spanish and Samuel got happy.

I just said to myself, "You cannot force a will out of a child in this country!" Adults in San Jose pinning the government to the wall when approached to snatch their land and offering them compensations they felt would be enough for them; a child refusing to walk back home and stay there until he felt it was time. The 'People's Will' is not easy to crush, nor is it impossible to make an unfair deal. People are respected in this land regardless of any possible gaps in Costa Rica.

What Works in Turkey?

A while back, I sat with a much older man here in Sweden who presented himself with Assyrian, Syriac background that he draws from Iraq, Syria and Turkey. While he grew up in a deep village of Turkey, his wife grew up in Istanbul back in the day. His family from the entire village escaped the atrocities of the Turkish government and scattered all across the world. He has a sister in France and others in Belgium while his wife's relatives are in Australia, Europe and the USA. He lived in Belgium and Norway and finally brought his American wife to Sweden where they live to this day.

In soul searching, his wife turned him and his entire family from Syriac Orthodox into Evangelical Christianity she brought with herself from the USA. Later on, she read the Catholic Catechism and found out that the Vatican was responsible for the change of the Sabbath from Saturday to its present status of globally observing on Sunday instead.

This was her compelling reason to convert the whole family with her to Seventh Day Adventist. When he was telling me this, I was looking at the bookshelf he filled in with world and European history, Oriental history, Turkish history, philosophy, communism and a few books that touch capitalism. While we were talking about converting his faith from one another, he sounded more like a political and philosophical man than faith-centred person in his speeches. I asked him a few questions.

"Why would you as a believer choose communism and abandon it later?" I asked.

He replied, "I would say as a former communist that Jesus was the first communist. Even a communist Muslim would say Mohammad was a communist too."

"What makes Jesus a communist?" I wondered.

"He will teach people to share one if they have two, and care for others," he answered.

"The acts of solidarity then," I said.

He replied, "yes."

"Do you think Jesus and Mohammed would have been friends if they lived on earth at the same time?"

"I would not be so sure about that," he replied.

I asked, "why?"

He said, "Because Christians and Muslims would have lived side by side and peacefully in Turkey, Syria and Iraq, among others."

"What went wrong between Christianity and Islam in Turkey?" I asked.

He answered, "I know several Muslims who are really awesome people. I still keep my Muslim connections back in the village, also here in Europe."

I asked, "what is the issue then?"

He replied, "I would say followers of both faiths who are aware of politics share the blame."

"Tell me more about what Christians are responsible for," I said.

"We grew up seeing Islamisation of Turkey just like Christianisation. You know everyone with a belief would want theirs to grow and expand. One problem with this was that Islamisation wanted political support and mixed a bit of what can be equivalent to cultural Arabisation. The more politicised Islamisation became, the more the political people started to be hostile to Christians. All our land, public space, faith centres, shops and livelihood were being taken away one by one. In the end, killings and atrocities took over. The only chance we had was to stay and watch our women raped and our lives destroyed or flee to other countries," he explained.

"Does this have to do with your conversion to Communism?" I asked him.

He replied, "yes."

"Did you see a problem with your prior beliefs?"

He replied, "yes."

"What did you believe in first?" I asked.

"Faith would guide all aspects of life," he replied.

"Wouldn't that mean theocracy?" I wondered.

"You could say that," he said.

"You also had secularism to a great degree as compared to many societies."

He answered, "Yes. But the faith had been dominant over our public space.

"What went wrong with it?" I inquired.

"We were told to turn our right if the left cheek were hit. This time, it was not with the hand they hit us. We were trained to be sheep while they were the worst of wolves. They had machine guns and we have no time to turn our cheeks before they killed our people. They found us defenceless to their easier success of eradicating us from our lands," he explained.

"So, you felt faith itself betrayed your people," I asked.

He replied, "yes."

"When did you decide to say now it is time for communism?"

"After I came to Europe, mostly in my experiences in Belgium and Norway, I was done with theocracy and thought that communism would be better."

"Would communism have built a functioning and self-sustaining society?"

He replied, "no."

"Why is that?" I asked.

"When individual greed is high, the collective wellbeing becomes a sacrifice. Then the very sense of communism falls apart," he replied.

"I heard you don't like capitalism," I said.

"I never did," he admitted.

"That was why you refused to visit the relatives in USA and see the country," I said.

"Back in the day when I was staunch communist, I believed the USA was a filthy country."

I asked, "what changed your views then?"

He responded, "relatively, the USA has a well-functioning society."

I said, "more of the impact of democratic values and capitalism and the people who believed in themselves, I guess."

He said, "yes."

I asked, "how do you compare it with communism?"

He answered, "Capitalism is more rewarding than communism. It seems it can self-govern, restrain anomalies that would have killed it and manages to control the present and slightly even the future."

While he was telling me this, I was pondering where I could categorise most of the western-educated Ethiopians that are out in the media or whose publications are swarming much of the digital space. While many views that I mention here are around, I was trying to sniff if there is any sign of capitalism, perhaps in the very Dutch-styled or Scandinavian sense of Social Capital or just raw form of capitalism in the USA. I just settled with my mind, saying, "But Ethiopian elites are restoration disciples of feudalism and are trying to bring it back and station it in cities this time around. They can be considered as Modern Urban feudalists except that it is a mix of urban land ownership and a drop of capital." This is because the notion of several present-day Ethiopian elites, parroting out liberal terminologies and free market, are replicas of the Roman empire traders whose wealth depended much on labour exploitation than the capital itself. You would not see any capitalism and wealth expansion in practice. What you see would be deprivation of the mass and benefiting few without any productivity. The idea of expanding wealth through stimulating and prospering the mass is not in their logic, I would say. It is a fall back to the past in a modern package.

He also sounded like the American theorists who claim that the 9/11 attack was to show the concentrated impact of radical cultural Arabisation video with time lapse of centuries and that the only way to make a compelling case to convince the mass and march it against present and imminent radicalism was to visualise the impact of protracted cultural take-over and demographic alterations. The only difference between his claims and the theorist's is that while they sound presumptuous, he sounds very real. I must say though, at times, the separation between presumptions and fact can be thin line.

Then the man was staring at me and said, "You went away. Where have you been?"

I replied, "Thinking about where I can locate Ethiopians."

He asked, "is it good?

I answered, "no."

He then asked, "how does it look like?"

"Terrible," I said.

"So sad," he commented.

"Yes. I am also thinking of the spiritual part in this. As most are self-proclaimed believers."

He agreed, "sure, it has a role it plays."

"Wouldn't Jesus be a capitalist in a sense that he needed to have two to be able to share one?"

"You can say that, but accumulating wealth was not his motive," he said.

"How about Mohammed?" I then asked.

"He would also be the same in this regard," he replied.

"Would Jesus have a problem to live in a capitalist society?" I wondered.

"He would not have a problem except he would teach people not to destroy everything around themselves and assume it would not catch up?"

"Are you talking about the climate now?" I asked.

"The climate as in the environmental aspect, but the social, political and wealth dimensions too," he explained.

We had a very honest conversation about issues I wanted to learn at the first-hand than what books or other sources of information would offer.

People are persecuted because of their faith, what they stand for and not. In all of this, nothing is more striking than being denied of the right for existence and the ability to live in an area once people called home.

Wolaita is the New Jerusalem

A mountainous and topographically rich Sodo town has about the same temperature (+27°C) during the sunny weather and may get colder during the rainy season as compared to the capital city Addis Ababa. For what it is worth, the city is architectural failure than the breath-taking beauty that was naturally bestowed to manage. Sodo is a somewhat geopolitically important city in Ethiopia. It intersects seven townships and two regions in its present-day stand.

Sodo is close to the lake Abaya, Mount Damota, Hawassa, Arbaminch, and most national parks and national reserves in the Southern Ethiopia. What I consider to be one of the richest things in Sodo is its fresh breath and a really suitable weather. Daily temperatures are somewhat moderate thanks to the mountain that keeps feeding it appropriate rain and spreads clouds over the town to make the daily life bearable.

It is here that the first American missionaries arrived at the southern part of Ethiopia and stationed there to spread protestant Christianity. The SIM and Sodo town have a very long history of few farmers converting to Evangelical Christianity and later be the reform force taking gospel across pretty much all over the South and even up to north Ethiopia. You would hear that this expanded and has its foothold in China, Pakistan, India, South Sudan and Sudan among international destinations.

The social movement was accompanied by expansion of schools, abolition of harmful cultural practices and paving way for a much-modernised Southern Ethiopia to take the leap much ahead of the rest of the country. The only city that may contend, but may not necessarily outperform in social progress, might be Addis Ababa. This just amazes me when I think of it as it is mostly farmers and poor men of villages that sponsor the expansion. I would not want anyone to take for granted that the people have excess in life.

The bittersweet truth is that Wolaita has become one of the seriously impoverished areas of Ethiopia due to political incongruency. The mindset of the people and the political ecosystem of Ethiopia do not always fall on the same foot. It is from this insufficiency and poverty that a pastor would fly to China or Pakistan and that their salaries are paid in dollars. It is from these farmers that the story of being God-chosen people in Ethiopia has gained a collective belief, not just conversion to Christianity.

The Wolaita call their land the Second Jerusalem. 'Wolaiyiti Yerusalame' is a song that magnifies and visualises what is kept inside as a deep belief in being God-chosen people.

Tana siqidi goday Xosay kitini bolasa Saluwa kantidi duge

Sa'a yiis nu ashuwa mayidi Yeletidi pilxosa awa Mentidi suta gusidi Masqaliyan hayiqidi Hayiquwa xonidi

Hezanto galasi Paxisi!

Wolayiti Yerusalame

Loosely translated this old song can be understood as the following.

> Because he loved me,
> he obeyed his father's will and
> came down to the earth,
> he was in a flesh,
> born to a mother,
> judged by Pilate,
> spilt his own blood for me,
> died on the cross,
> and risen on the third day,
> with victory over death,
> he did this for me here in Wolaita, my Jerusalem.

My parents were extremely happy to have a baby boy — my elder brother — and deeply sobbed when they lost their second child because of miscarriage. When my mother was pregnant for the third time, my father really wished to have a girl as his second child also to see my mother pleased as she also desired like him. But no, an adamant boy was born and yes, just as you guessed, that was me. I came to this world by saying no to my parents, a rebellion. They wished for a girl and in some way, I just meant, 'You are going to wait for it.'

I was born a resistant, for sure, but was also one among rebels too. The people of Wolaita were in struggle to bring about a shift in a belief instead of taking Axum as a holly site, composing a song 'Wolayiti Yerusalame' — meaning Wolaita is Jerusalem. This can be seen in a steepest contrast to the widespread narrative that stated as if the Amhara region is where the heartbeat of God stops every time God thinks of Ethiopia.

This is rather a defiance to say Wolaita is Jerusalem. Listening to some other Christian songs, narrations and debates that Jesus walked through Ethiopia with St Mary as little boy and that some would even say that God is Amhara, and that if there was any country God loves more than Israel, it is said to be Ethiopia; it is a cult, a heresy to believe that the heavens would choose Wolaita of all places of the country. I for one believe in either getting people laid back to say exactly what they believe in such matters or would confront as a breaker of discussions.

Once, a long-time friend of mine said *"Endemitawukew Egziabher Amara new"* — meaning, as you know God is Amhara. I joked off not to show any seriousness of this claim and that I would want that God cannot exist if deity is sized and is fit into an ethnic identity at the first place, and of all ethnicities God would have chosen, I could not see anything so special for the Holy Trinity to have bonded with only Ethiopian ethnicity. But what could I do other than offering some boneless smile and shrug it off for that moment.

This felt so much like what a friend of mine from California used to tell me, that he loves Jesus and has a question of whether deity would want to be associated with a tribe in Israel instead of all of us in the world. We would sit with a common Jewish friend for fresh fish grills, tilapia for most part but any type whenever they run out of it. He would tell me that we needed a new religion for Ethiopia if we feel God is too much Jewish than being the deity of the Wolaita. But this man just jokes away anything and would just say I love you, and you guys love me, and this is my religion.

You see the people of Wolaita are going against such a notion by claiming if there was any place in Ethiopia God would chose especially, it must be Wolaita for otherwise gospel would not have come through Sodo. In short, people are saying, no quero, 'we do not want' without saying anything about what they do not want; they are talking about what they want instead. For as long as it sounds arrogance or any other similar, if you have already believed that St Mary, Jesus' mother, walked through Gojam of Ethiopia back in the day, as the legends claim, it is also a belief of a group of people on its own. You can't help it; your only option is to respect people's belief. This is not just disagreeing to what the majority of urbanist Ethiopians are told almost every day, it is much deeper than just that.

Almost every single Wolaita clan has their own deity and are tolerant towards the gods of their neighbours, to the king's, the merchants, farmers, metalsmiths or ceramic potters alike. All of these believe in one creator whom they all call Xossa. Among their gods, there is no distinct space and comparison at all. You have your God, I have mine, and all is well. Tolerance can never get better than this.

That is also why Christianity and other similar forms of faiths did not penetrate until lately, the cultural fence for as long as they existed. Islam stayed with families with royal ties that came from Jima and Arsi. While this is true, as a principle, monotheism is not a friendly philosophy for the Wolaita. As they know that if deity is to be only one, all others and their followers are to be targeted, one way or another. Beyond this, though, it also carries the attitude of 'who are you to choose deity for me' in its unspoken form.

This then means that the Wolaita prefer the freedom to choose their gods, their way of life, moral principles and ethical standards that agreeing to a prescribed and imposed words on a paper. This means that it is easier to develop democratic, tolerant and a free society in Wolaita. If you can be open to tolerate many Gods within a family, which bring all sorts of diversity and at times contending understandings, you will probably tolerate other ethnicities, cultures, ways of life and people's preferences.

In this sense, Wolaita is a sacred place for its people and they can never accept the idea that a geographically different far place is Godlier than theirs. It did not matter if it were Jerusalem, and the land is Israel, even after they accepted Christianity.

They do not buy it! Instead, they said 'Wolaita is the New Jerusalem' on one hand showing they accept Christianity among their people, and on the other if it is about the issue of God's favourite place on the Earth, it can never be anywhere other than Wolaita. This means, they are telling their 'converters' into Christianity that 'yes, we love your God, but we also love our land which your God would probably call as the new favourite place, would you tell him that please?' with the tone that they were not buying it of being tourists to a foreign land and buying their stuff to feel closer to God.

Our New Holy Planet

When the Wolaita are saying Wolaita is the New Jerusalem, they are doing two things without even saying it. Here is how I understand it. In a nutshell, against the fact that all three Abrahamic religions claim Jerusalem as their holy place, the Wolaita are saying that Wolaita is their

Jerusalem. One specific location, of all the places on the planet cannot be supper holy place while the rest of places are unimportant to be scared place.

For the Wolaita, as a country, Israel is not any holier than Ethiopia also Jerusalem is not any better than Sodo. By stating this they are confessing their belief that Wolaita is the new Holy Place. They prophesy that Wolaita is The New Jerusalem! This is a new revelation, of its whole new Bible written for itself. A birth of a new religion if you may, not just a new denomination or a sect departing from an existing one.

To me they must have discerned the truth behind all world's dominant religions claiming the same spot as their special location and what this means politically, socially and economically and decided that Woliata is by no means any less than this. Technically they are saying Ethiopia is not less worthy of a country than Israel. In effect they are saying that Ethiopia is the new holy land. Probably people like the Ras Tafarrians can deeply relate to what the Wolaita mean by this even if their perspectives and references can be different.

To begin with, the world is assumed to have had been run by either holy scriptures or some other guiding notes which all have one thing in common across all types of faith practices globally.

That is, you have God's promise, His favourite place on the earth and chosen people who live in it. That if you are from there, then you own the truth. Owning truth means that your opinion and choices of pretty much everything takes precedence to anyone else's 'clumpy views' that don't hold water. This positions people at the height of privileges and special treatments that must be defended by history, government and religious institutions.

Looking at it from this perspective, when you hear someone claiming that God is Amhara, you ask if there is evidence to back this up — if it matters in the first place. If God is Amhara, what should the Tegaru say? Also what should the Wolaita say? You see that the Wolaita believe that their country is a holy land. Because, when you ask real questions, people would want to claim that Orthodox Christianity has been championed by the Amhara people and that God has entrusted them for this. Personally, I would not dispute this apart from just listening and asking questions.

To begin with the Arc of Covenant, that is said to have been brought from Jerusalem by son of Solomon and Queen of Sheba, if this is accurate and morally fit to be told as a story, is found in Axum Tsion in Tigray. This has nothing to do with ethnic Amharas. By being so, if God were to express himself in any ethnicity other than Jews, it must be that God is Tegaru, not Amhara.

Second, the Wolaita are saying that for as much Old Testament-based view of seeing Axum as the sacred place of God in Ethiopia, and that this is snatched by the Amhara elite, not even used by the Tegaru, the New Testament-based scared place of Ethiopia is Sodo city, Wolaita in general including the wider Southern Ethiopia.

This is because the American missionaries, led by Dr Lambe, went to Wolaita while the Scandinavians went to Wollega and that the Wolaita see the entire south tied up in a belt of God's grace and his choice of bringing gospel through the Wolaita and the Oromo who later were joined by the Kambata, Hadiya, Sidama and many others. In this sense, the Wolaita believe that Wolaita is Jerusalem that is a sister place to Wollega and the rest of the wider South. Then God must be Ethiopian than being just Wolaita, Oromo, Amhara, Tegaru, Kambata or any other.

This is not only a view of smashing everything the common urbane is supposed to uphold, but also replacing it with a much acceptable, tolerant and very relatable presentation of what God can be and where He would have a sacred place if it were important at all. This is a clear act of defiance and saying NO to what everyone else is told to say yes to. It is a protest.

It is a disbelief of ancient norm and a belief of modern norm that is yet to be installed in the society. It is a no to the past and a yes to the present, being a tool to craft the future with something that makes no specific group blessed, rather gathers everyone else as equally sanctified people of God.

It is a belief of saying no to human imposition and saying yes to what is a probable will of God; that God is a friend of everyone, not just select few, to the point that He can only be free of self-jailing Himself into some ethnic cage. It is a dismissal of human assumption that God must relate to human identity to be complete. In Abyssinian sense, God has to be Amhara to be holy enough, which the Wolaita are not buying for a penny.

In this sense, the Wolaita are rebellious as a group of people; rebelling not against God but against human manipulation and a set up for a faith-protected exploitation and ethnic dominance. If you see a Wolaita going against the state, this is at the core of their philosophy simply put. Many may not articulate it this way, but this is a shared feeling among the people. It is a dominant worldview of the Wolaita, that God is for all, or for no one. Which means, if God exists, God-ness is for all, and if God-ness is not for all, then God may not exist. Let alone God being Amhara, if Christian deity is not for all, it is farce according to the Wolaita.

This demands universality of not only God, but also anything that must be accepted by the mass, be it social, economical, political, behavioural or personal matters, it must be universal, or it is not acceptable. It is a very explosive thought of nuclear proportion.

A group that can take the risk of joining the fallen angel by assuming there must be a higher throne than what is being prescribed by the God-is-Amhara line of thinking. The Wolaita would want to join the anti-Christ than accepting fables and trickeries for political, economic and social manipulation. In this sense, the Wolaita would win the heart of God and Satan would presumably say, I would probably do like them.

The governance for Ethiopia has never been clearly studied or observed with a great detail in an objective and empirical manner, I would say. If it is studied, I am very sure that an honest study result would tell us that Ethiopian state is ethno-theocracy.

While being so, it is more of an ethnic cue where people are waiting for new leaders to from their ethnic group, instead of wishing the best one emerges from anywhere in the country. This also means some people wish that leaders are come frequently from their ethnicities. Ethnic dilemma has no ending even in issues of Ethiopian spirituality. The idea of seeing a foreigner growing up in Ethiopia and rising to the power is like a turtle having a chance to outpace a horse. It is impossible in our time, while we don't know about the future. Those who tell about unity and pose as anti-ethnic sentiments, are the worst among deeply ethnocentric people. Those are the true faces of Ethiopian racism.

Like any other ethnocratic segment of a society that also relentlessly believes in the romanticised theocracy, the present-day Ethiopia is owned by whoever that has a control over the intersection of faith and the state, and the state itself. In this regard, the Menilik's expansion war can be understood as a campaign to cement this upper hand over other ethnicities.

When the Wolaita were engaged in a very bloody war with the then Abyssinian army, which later became Ethiopia, they were resisting to be incorporated to a state controlled by a single ethnic group that also owns the God and its truth. Because for the Wolaita, what they would later call as their God, which the protestant faith brought later and the truth it teaches have not been theirs yet.

For a young man who grew up defying much of what was around myself and seeing the God-is-American or Jesus-looks-European way of presenting views and sanctifying self-image close to God's deity and telling me that I am here to accept it without questioning, I have just been a true Wolaita in Ethiopia and overseas. I carried this with me almost everywhere I go, and I feel I have it around me here in Sweden where I am at right now.

When the Wolaita say Wolaita is Jerusalem, and openly say so and confess the city as the New Jerusalem, they are saying '*No quero*' to the mainstream narrative and are refusing anything that comes along with it. They are saying no to the notion that someone would assume to know better, and incline themselves to the throne and say what, why, when where and how to do.

Technically by saying Wolaita is the New Jerusalem, they are also stating that Ethiopia is the holy land. And if Ethiopia, an African country is holy, not only its mother continent, the whole planet must be a sacred place. Therefore, planet Earth is Our Holy Planet in the eye of God, according to the Wolaitans. To call the Earth Our Holly Planet is the Ethiopian prophecy.

If the society cannot force the will out of children in Costa Rica, trying to squeeze the will out of the people should not be done by the Ethiopian governing bodies too. In this, the Wolaita are not just saying *No Quero* to the beliefs, and confess their own, which they started as soon as the Americans arrived at the area. It is then the sense of autonomy, cultural preservation and the feeling of already having global touch of expressions.

Bonfire Master

Dr Miguel is a Costa Rican engineer who lectures at the university in San Jose and has been serving as an advisor to the president. Before I dive much into this, I would like to say that he has decided to spend more time on research and coaching students, or perhaps groom them to deliver for his country, and slowed down the advisory role recently. This is to my advantage and liberty of sharing his true-life testimony, given his roles and issues tied to it. For me, Dr Miguel, and now his wife, Carola, and so many great people come on top of my mind any time I think of this blessed country.

One thing peculiarly great about Costa Ricans is that they never fall short of showing love, respect, curiosity and above all the true value to friendship and family. I am not saying that Cosa Rica is the only and best country that shall be taken as heaven on earth; no, no, that is not what I mean. I am not saying that all the infrastructure is the greatest and that the service is beyond measures, it is the people I am talking about.

In the end, what we remember is not the smooth flow of services or the high-rise buildings that nothing more than concrete, some wires in it with glasses coating to make it appear to be grand. It is about the moments and how the people make you feel and seeing how they value your presence with them. It is any little thing they do or have to commit only to see you pleased.

Costa Ricans beat any country on the earth, I would argue. Comparison fairness aside, unlike Ethiopia, Cosa Rica is one of the greatest countries with the most open-minded people on this planet as of now. Let's settle on this. And Ethiopia has millions of miles to go.

Once the ladies, my fiancée and his wife, indulged in their talks of beauty or things that I have a hard time to figure out, I sat with Dr Miguel who told me how hard it was to pass a lot to acquire land for construction of new apartments or complexes to accommodate the growing demand of housing or his wife coming in and telling us how congested the roads are during rush hours that she can finish a movie series standing on the roads for quite a long time.

You come to Ethiopia for experience as to clearing an entire city for development purposes where you rise several hundreds of buildings all at once. Of course, not without a problem as huge corruption means farmers are displaced, livelihoods are affected and so on. I am sure it will cost the government to the point that it would collapse, but this is more of political than the fact that development policies are not accepted by farmers or other politicians. If we discount that, there can be something to learn from each other.

Deep down in my heart, I knew what I meant was to see if Ethiopians could learn how to do business with Americans (USA) and be of good force in the global partnership, without negating the west or the east unduly. In my heart I was asking myself, what my take away is from my trip to San Jose, that took enormous amount of money and over sixty hours of combined flights. Still, the talk remains about our countries, the global big economies and their best practices.

Because Chinese loans have made their way into the treasuries of Costa Rica in no time, it is obvious that one can partner with anyone in the economy. Perhaps some people from both countries may do cross-Atlantic business as well. It would not hurt, I would say.

While we were diving into the talks, his wife said something regarding what Pope Francis said — after saying a few things back and forth, he would say no the pope does not believe so, he says this instead. When I recall, he would say that occasionally and I said to myself all in my mind, *why care about what the pope says, what do you say? What is your wife saying? And what would any Costa Rican say?*

To cut the hypocrisy out, isn't this what an Ethiopian Orthodox, Protestant, Muslim or Catholic follower would say? Wouldn't they have a reference to their bishops or so when a question comes to that point where all other perspectives are dashed out and that the ultimate closure is needed? We all are the same on this and no one is different, even none believers have something else in its place.

My shock with Miguel's statement implying he would accept what the pope says than thinking through as a PhD holder, and man of high intellect. Well even with this, you see education is not a measure of intelligence as we have doctors in Ethiopia who would hire tutors and do almost nothing other than appearing during presentations, read what was prepared for them, mumbling a word and two during opponent pressures and leverage the professors to give them pass grades and graduate in the end. Even those who study in a proper manner fail to see that their degree is not definitive of how much they can think, do and change.

For people who don't figure this out, they will be caged in the box their degree offers and they realise they did nothing meaningful other than what all other graduates like them did, especially if they never asked those key questions that define why they are here on Earth in addition to having a degree. Plus, education itself is participating in seminars, presenting borrowed knowledges, theories and practices while they all may mean nothing other than reference for intellectual rituals to give you access to some offices.

But once you make it there, all that you know means close to nothing, that you are just an educated *kulli*. Oh, *kulli* is a labourer loading or offloading from trucks in Ethiopia. As opposed to several Ethiopian intellectual kulli's, Miguel has done amazing things for his government, knew how to balance faith, culture, maintaining international friendships and personal life balance.

Miguel's mother invited us to celebrate the Christmas Eve at her place at San Jose. We arrived there in time. Seeing Miguel's mother, her coolest designed villa and having panoramic view to the entire city made me appreciate that this man and his brother could design such crispy clean and well-imagined villa made me appreciate that it is possible to be creative to country, but even so to self too. Why not!

We were invited to Lebanese meals, and any and everything best that you would find in major cities. Meze, olives, some snacks, fruits and laughter in between made the eve so special; perhaps one of the unforgettable nights in my life. Miguel's mother is a Lebanese woman, his father a Hispanic Costa Rican. I don't think it can get any better than that, at least to my personal taste.

One thing you can tell is great about the Lebanese is that when they land on the right foot, in any city I have been to, they make something great out of pretty much everything. You see they know how to befriend the Americans, the French, the Chinese, the Indians and many in Africa. They own shops, clubs, bars, restaurants, casinos and entertainment points in many cities in the Middle East, Africa, Europe, Latin America and some part of Asia.

They don't just work hard; they work super hard when they find something they love and see a way of making life in it. I recall that in many restaurants, especially bars and clubs in the Middle East, the managers are usually Lebanese. If it is not the manager, it is the vice, or the owner or shareholder or they consult them. If all fails, you at least eat their food, listen to their music or are invited to some specialty.

Fireworks would crack now and then to give some coloured lights lighting the sky lines and make the city smile before fading away. We were talking about almost everything from grandiosely praising President Obama, Oprah Winfrey to Tyra Banks, or how Jay Z and Beyonce were at some event. You see, this is also one thing you notice that when you talk to a non-African, especially non-Ethiopian, you have a wide range of issues other than ending up either cursing or praising politics back home.

One special thing about Costa Rica is that it has no military, or if it is there it is only some police and a bit upgraded forces trying to guard Nicaragua and other close by nations would not cause harm. Apart from that, it appears that Costa Rica is a country with no enemy, literally no hostile nation or group at all. To me, the Costa Rica's abolition of the instituted military is the greatest human accomplishment I would ever imagine.

You see, one of the things that make Ethiopians bitter towards each other is not just the countless and meaningless wars and fables of superiority in regional wars, it is rather the active choices made by people to dwell on the myths, legends and tales that promote hate. People in Ethiopia are taught to believe that there is an enemy somewhere that needs to be fought against, making them fail to see that this turns people against each other. What is worse is that almost every sympathizer of this sentiment wants to freeze people in time and hold them prisoners in the past. To understand this one may want to sense the time references in discussions with these types of people.

Much of the time perspective is about the past than anything to do with today or the future. This is a very simple diagnostic tool. They simply indulge in history so deeply than the quality of life today or the aspirations of how the future should look like. And if the present is not the exact copy of the past, their content of speech is more towards agitation and gravitating violence to bring it back. It is very important to note that if Ethiopians do not change this mentality, periodic wars and the use of violence as a means to advance a cause will remain inseparable from future realities.

Before I dive into this, any war concluded without yielding social progress, economic advancement or political enhancement is meaningless to me no matter who has won, which hero it produced or what history has to say about it. Especially so, if lives are lost and social order is disrupted, many are left with amputated limbs or lose their sight, and all that we get is some ear-deafening music, rigid presentation of history and a few people sticking their noses up in the sky.

I believe the war was already lost even if the trophies and spoils were shred within the boundaries of Ethiopia. Worse is if it does not mean widening of the global market and revenue expansion for the country.

Then, only people of today that are deeply brainwashed with ancient thoughts wage wars to satisfy the intellectual urge of our days to looking just like the past. Turns out that I want to live for today and dream and work hard for tomorrow. I do not miss the past with all its glories and miseries. That is why I think; at least in Ethiopia, war is meaningless.

No matter how I feel about it, war is inevitable if people's thoughts and actions are not guided towards war aversion, violence avoidance and suppressing aggression that arises to defend the sense of entitlement, to imposing one's own perceptions of superiority (or the counter thoughts of levelling this up) on others through a means other than dialogue and an intellectual exchange of ideas.

On the day Dr Mehret was to speak to over twenty-five thousand youth at the Millennium Hall, and the PM was expected to surprise the youth with a few motivational speeches and swinging his eyes all over them, I was sitting with two ladies.

We sat on the guest sofa and one of them was well-connected with all prime minister's networks of Mele's, Hailemariam's and Dr Abiy's circle. Helina, a tenacious doer and a dissecting thinker, wanted to know what I thought of the event at the Millennium Hall. The second woman, a physician, was among highly accomplished individuals to whom key people would turn to when it comes to countrywide tense situations.

We were served with snacks, some Kolo (mix of roasted barely and peanut), fresh coffee and the talks began. It was high time and that optimists were on their hypes, they would just hear and say how Ethiopia has changed and that the future is brightest, and they are happier than ever.

While the initial speeches, music and show-offs were taking place at Millennium Hall, the three of us started some crazy but realistic talks. It was a question partly of Dr Mirheret's psychotherapeutic and social moulding of the mass from professional perspective, but in its truest sense, more of from the western approach. Or if the approach is Ethiopian, the technical orientation sounded to be of western sort.

But when questions are asked in Addis, it means you need to understand the element of questioning with bias towards faith, and somehow spicing it with concrete and vital questions to ask. For me, I had to try to distance myself from the perspective of faith at that point as anyone can get hurt and all the talk goes down to the dust. But the conversation was very critical and anything we say may or may not be listened by pilots on the power seats. It was a very close call.

Helina asked, "so how do you see the event at the Millennium Hall, and do you see this will change people's perception towards progress?" This was one of the buttons I was trying to avoid.

It is important to remember that much of Ethiopia's mental grasp of what is acceptable and intolerable, is set as a consequence of previous wars, than openly accepted intellectual debates, books, shows and cinematographic moulding. People accept a winner of a war and justify its atrocity that is used as a means to get there, and the victory justifies this. It is an unfortunate collective state that demands violence for a paradigm shift towards accepting the new and intended understanding. This is a precondition that everyone agrees on, communicated with this unspoken language, while fragments of indifferent voices can be noticed here and there. I paused to reflect on this before opening up to these ladies.

Truth be told, even if I do not believe in it, I said, you see, war seems the only option left to make people accept that there is no other way, or at least no U-turn to the Old Guard which are the past now. And this may mean that the highly localised crisis will have to progress towards a clear war where forces of the right and left need to confront each other and one must come out with a clear win to determine who to follow. I am not saying this is what I want to happen. But feels that there will be armed conflict.

As you know, currently there are many bosses in the city. If we have one country, there must be one government led by a boss. One direction and an idea we all follow. If this is slighted by anyone, then they need to prove it with conflict. Because, for as much as people want to talk it away, as if we have intellectual class that believes in and adjusts based on merits of better ideas at a debate table, the Millennium Hall is just a good drama that won't make a change we want.

This shall continue, but it will not be good enough for mass behavioural adjustment suited for a situation in which political leadership is afforded. In such cases, even if we hate to accept it, we must have a war. And the war must be with the level of precision that a clear win will be forecast beyond hundred per cent at the planning phase. This will make it possible to do politics, not without challenges but with practicalities manageable in Ethiopian standards. Well, the South must know how it will be spared and that no one would be caught in a crossfire.

When I was done, the two ladies were shocked; the physician had already got a pale face. I sensed it somewhere in the middle of my speech, but I thought she would agree after she heard my justifications. She did not buy the justification either. 'What happened with you?', 'You are wrong!' and many other objections were forwarded.

At some point, I felt like it had to be said regardless since they asked me why I would not be at the Millennium Hall, clap our wishes out and do away with my worries. Often, truth is uncomfortable to hear and difficult to swallow when a younger and supposedly a guy distant to powers would say such a thing. Happy for her that I was not one of those who had close ties to power, but hang on, could she be sure? I mean, seriously.

What pissed me off was that almost a year and some months later, a war broke out and the start button was at my hometown. Yeah, it is one of those things you fight to be implemented knowing it may affect your own people. But a lot later, the government was provided more than adequate and accurate information openly and at intelligence levels that there were false flags sent to it from Sodo by some dubious people who wanted a conflict to happen there too.

I made this clear to some key people in an open manner, but all was ignored, and innocent youth were attacked. This to me was something I may forgive as a moral act, but from a political perspective, it needs proper investigation sooner or later and that serious political stand has to be taken to ensure such stupid things would not be repeated.

One thing has become clear, the war in Tigray made the government much stronger, at least for now, and more legitimate and to a greater degree more acceptable though the leaders seem not yet sure of having the competence and the human capital they need. I mean the people who would need to tell them that a war is needed when it is a must. Now, I am not implying a need for another round of war, I am just saying that some people as hard as a rock and as soft as a sponge are still needed. The competent league of the best and brightest is also there, this I am sure about.

The challenge I see is that in a medium and long run, this group will have fatigue and lose the push and urge driving their motivation and commitment to deliver. What is also lacking is the perspective of the southern Ethiopia, economic issues are going to hurt everyone, social trust will grow to be lower (though it may seem better on the surface) and minorities will be suffering as the governing body is predominantly hired to tend to the demand of the two majority groups (Oromo and Amhara).

This is not because attempts to handle these are not in place, it is because some lack the insight, the capacity and higher eagle eye to see through false narratives, PR stunt, regular government house drama and some biased questions that create an impression that real questions are being answered while in contrary these would be overshadowed by rather senseless issues being raised by groups that want to silence the minorities and intellectuals that are well-wishers for all.

Everyone knew that I refused to serve the Meles' regime, rather my mindset did not fit the old guard's discriminatory tone towards people. A key issue I had was not just that they hurt the Wolaita and people around, but the very idea that the 'right political mindset' in their eyes was hating the Oromo and the Amhara. Worse, you cannot show sympathy to your ethnicity for which name calling of 'narrow minded' is tagged.

I was in serious conflict with this idea of hating the Oromo and the Amhara, though I knew in my heart that some Amhara were exposing themselves to this notion displaying exaggerated self-image, show-offs to satisfy emptiness, lacking the understanding of listening to what non-Amhara had to say, and being open enough to see non-Amhara as sincere contributors towards a common good.

I still do believe that in a world where we are known for poverty, underdeveloped infrastructure, not so much advanced society, cities that are not liveable and low-life standard, assuming oneself as better than the Americans and saying all Ethiopians need to listen to their order (not advise) is just stupidity at best and an idea borrowed from ice age, if any better.

I once sat with a friend from Afar and a second one from Amhara to discuss about issues of various themes. We sat and had debates for quite a long time to see if there were learnings to be drawn, ideas to be shaped or issues to deal with. One day, though, the Afar guy seemed highly irritated by what was going on in Ethiopia and started cursing the Amhara elites.

He then started saying, "My friends, I must say this to both of you, but you especially must listen" — pointing at the Amhara friend of ours — "I am going to be very frank about this. Some of your Amhara elites and the graveyard do not know enough about when to stop taking and start giving. Your elites are very demanding and investing in them is not a profitable business, I would say."

The challenge with few of Amhara elites is not this simple, and I wish the list were this short. They never fall short of fuelling the Ethiopian political flame that runs with the deep sense of hate towards the Amhara.

Amharic is another problem for the Amhara unlike English is probably a 'blessing' for the British. If it is not a curse to all of them, it surely is a nightmare at least to most of the people as much as I understand. You see, a language is a blessing as it can open the heart of your crush, or the gates of business possibilities, international partnerships or just a simple social door to a great and playful ambience.

As several people would agree, Amharic is a language of soldiers, being so it is a language of aggression and conflict at worst, competition and hostile contest at the best, and anything can come in between. English was not the language of handing flowers and roses throughout history.

Yet, it developed itself to be a handy tool to anyone who has interest and access to learn its basics. But to make Amharic a true language of cooperation, beyond superficial gestures, the language and its use needs a serious re-engineering if it is to be a tool for good, continuing to stay alive and pleasant to use.

It can borrow practices from English, French, Spanish or Chinese as to how to make it industrious, desirable and part of social and economic progress having competence and fair competition and its rewards to its global peers. As it was once imposed, for good or worse, sweetened forceful thinking will only yield more repellent reaction and loss of appetite, if met with well-meaning people, while it would surely breed hate and the horrors it hatches once again.

Back to Dr Miguel; he is a true doctor who has built his mother's house in a fashion that looks like the house is constructed with a layer of carved large stones in squares and is put one on top of the other. What makes it look so gracious is that on the glasses they put the colour they chose, the site it is standing at and the whole San Jose being clearly visible in an astonishing style.

The interior is on another level, I wish I were a good expert to explain about the choice of the light system, the size and colour of lamps, the sofa and tables, all household items, the open kitchen, the doors and the toilet, the bedroom and guest rooms that makes the house just so that you just want to throw some dollars and beg them build an exact copy for you for any price they ask.

Well, I am not sure how many Ethiopian architects with PhD would be confident enough to design their parents' house, or lawyers to win a case for their siblings and so on. Imagine these being political architects who tell leaders what, when where and how to do a particular task on decisions that affect the fate of over a hundred and ten million Ethiopians for the coming decades for good or worse. I am sure there are countless great people, and I am sure they do to the best of their capacities. I am not doubting this.

At the same time, a country that has more than millions of graduates, and more millions to be added soon, having a number of PhDs, post docs and specialties would still have a population that has as large as thirty-five per cent living a life in shackles and fifteen per cent more added to this not being sure about planning for their lives for even three months, and the rest of the fifty per cent of the population worrying about the continuity of the country, security of their children at school without mentioning the level of poverty, spoken and suffered in silence.

It hurts to be aware of this, especially seeing that the political economy is designed by graduates of Harvard, Princeton, Oxford and a few more world-known top universities in the world.

In fact, it is my fellow Ethiopian doctors that shock me in a truest sense than Dr Miguel, by referring to the pope as a dedicated Catholic, who actually delivered greatly to his country, community, parents and his own family of two kids and a wife. He is honest to his religion, his career, family, country and president. Well, Miguel is a real presidential advisor if I must say. Tested and delivered.

Well, I would not rob the pride of Ethiopian advisors who have astonishing track records and omitting without mentioning at least one of them would not do justice to my conscience. For his elegance of coming from Dawuro area, Mr Gessamo may actually be more phenomenal having proven world class competence, for shaping the governance, through advancing the capability of the Ethiopian Prime Minister's Office, that is best known as having limited resource and a struggling premiership of the world. A simple example would be that running a country of over 125 million people with a budget less than medium sized company resources of advanced countries is not an easy job on its own.

The greatest things about his service years is that he delivered in Prime Minister Meles' government, one of the top-notch advisors of Prime Minister Hailemariam and has been serving the whole transition period for the incumbent Prime Minster Dr Abiy Ahmed.

He worked on areas of legal matters, whose touch any one with good scent of legal affairs can smell; he is said to have wanted to retire and take personal time, or perhaps write a book or two.

I am sure his book would have offered us an insight into the real reflection of us, at the place all the power of a hundred and ten million people is converged and concentrated at a single spot of the country. It would have shown us openly of our true characters, images and intents of clandestine nature.

I heard recently that he submitted a resignation letter and was waiting the prime minister's office to approve his request. He comes from the Southern Ethiopia; expectedly, surviving and thriving in Ethiopia comes with the price tag of outperforming and top delivering among colleagues and being healthy enough to keep cool when stupid assumptions are made about your people or those you sympathise with.

We drove from San Jose, made it through Cartago to visit the mother- and father-in-law of Miguel. We met with biomedical scientist mother of Carola and her dad, an artist and famous sculptor in San Jose. The mother conducts research at the bio-medical institute and is a senior member of the staff.

This is where Carola has got her biomedical genius and is also working with researches like her mother. She went after the mother. Her father is a man of charisma and the style of playmaking. Speaking eloquently and relaxed, he appeals to the relaxed mood of anyone who sits with him. His career is also a greatly impressive success story of a sculptor. One of the famous sculptures he made is built at a square at Cartago and stands magnificently.

The sculpture depicts the old-time Costa Rica whereby farming was done using a pair of oxen during the era of subsistence farming, which is sadly the status of every eight out of ten Ethiopians today. It spoke volumes to me in the way of seeing how far Costa Ricans and the rest of the global north has come, and where my people are left at.

It is a reflecting mirror but a lot more powerful than just a mirror. For a mirror would show you what is before it. This sculpture is a depiction of the past and the present and in Ethiopia's case no sight of change in the foreseeable future in a single image.

Maybe it is me who is overthinking and is taking this matter too seriously that just appreciating the quality of the sculpture, what it meant to the city and why Carola's father was selected to do it for the municipality. There I would be on the side of positive feelings, appreciation and good mood instead of having and dragging the baggage of feelings that I am bringing from my country. To be fair to myself, this is not something I should worry about as much any more than people who are making daily decisions that could turn things around and make the practice better.

Dr Miguel took a pause from his work to drive and show us around, where we travelled to many parts of San Jose and several destinations across the cities. The rest of the way, we had our maps with us and a list of cities for our experience, parks to see, wildlife and beaches to touch, the white sand and splash on the clean turquoise waters on the shores.

As we came here for the wedding of Dr Miguel and Carola, and as my girlfriend was their photographer, I was a running man to assist the photography or just left with guests from the USA and many areas of Costa Rica to interact with them or stare at the thrilling nature and get carried away.

The wedding was to be performed at the Hotel del Sol Bahia, by Playa Potrero at Guana Caste province of Costa Rica. As we were on the north-west of the country, we were not that far from the neighbouring Nicaragua. Looking down by the palm trees, around us, the open restaurant cottage behind us and the beach to throw our eyes at, it was one of the very magnificent and happy weddings I have ever been to.

What makes the event extra-ordinary was the varieties of food to eat, drinks of all sort to your taste the warmth of the weather and the blue-sky roofing over us, the world-class hospitality and the tranquillity people had. All was done, the groom kissed the bride and they were pronounced husband and wife.

As the night was taking over, the scenery of the setting sun, the fresh breath of the beach, the dark reddish sky and the carnival hats and wearables made the evening uniquely colourful.

The music was not just on, it was literally lit. It felt the people were there for a birthday party than a wedding which is usually surrounded by competing family members of both sides showing off their stiffness and dry smiles and if they loosen a bit just dancing for the show. No, these were not taking their moments for granted. They all danced like crazy, from my favourite bachata to the common merengue, salsa to reggae, then time came for some African dance.

They turned on Shakira's "This Time for Africa" song from the South Africa's World Cup opener. The one thing I am a disaster to is dance, and to dance to expectants that want to see some wild and deep South Ethiopian moves, Jesus, help me!

It would be an insult to the world to say I am bad at a dance and refusing on the very song selected for my sake, what a shame! Except that they all got up and danced the hell out of the music, and at times clapping and smiling at me, which for a while made me feel like, are they for real or just prepping me to keep my mood up? It was hard to tell on my end, but they were rocking it. Ladies would break and shake it like crazy!

"These people know how to live a life, man," I said to myself.

We then returned to the Miguel and Carola's villa in San Jose. Their villa is a spacious one-storey beautiful place to live in. We stayed here over the night at a guest room, and it was time for some adventure.

Leaving the two love birds and their guests behind, we headed towards the Panama's bordering towns, and in-between we would make stops in cities and beaches. We took the buses by coastal line and travelled Uvita — San Vito — Sabalito — and finally stationed at Rio Sereno. It was here my girlfriend came as an exchange student and shared so much memory.

The parents and family of Lucas, Marta and Gabriel were going to host us. From here, we headed towards Palmar Norte and made our way to Corcovado National Park. In this park, we only wished to see a jaguar, tamandua, tapir, margay, poisonous frogs, several types of monkeys, crocodiles and dolphins among so many wildlife. We had stops in places for spending time going on canopies, bathe in natural hot springs, horse rides guided by indigenous people towards deep into their villages and showing us around their way of life. This is among the best encounters worth my memory for as long as I have spent time with indigenous people of any country.

One thing I may not appreciate enough about Costa Rica is how the society preserved the ecosystem and invested a lot in protecting the parks, wild life and put positive print on the climate. While nature has gifted the people with beautiful greeneries, rivers and ocean water bodies, wild animals and so on, they too are taking good care of it. And that it pays off as compared to several countries that say a lot and do little.

From here, we headed towards Playa Uvita we passed on our way and stayed at a resort there to spend some time on the beach and visit the Marino Ballena National Park. At the Punta Uvita, the beach is shaped like a whale once the water subsides and the shore is shallow. We spent the whole day wandering around, sun-bathing and taking tons of pictures as my girlfriend took it to herself that almost everything was worth photographing. For me, a few pictures would suffice; for the rest, I just wanted to lay there and try my best so that the sun would not hit my skin directly. My skin gets burned like no other and even peels off if I am not careful enough.

I don't joke around when it comes to the sun-bathing. This is also one thing that I learned after I came to Sweden as to why my parents would warn me not to stay by the sun for a very long time. Apart from its continued take-in; it would give me headaches. I still wonder if they knew that my skills come off and burns exactly like I am burned by fire. Strange thing for me as someone from Africa! Or this is how I feel any time it happens.

As it was a New Year's Eve, the day went with holiday vibes, so much music on the beach, the resorts rushing to prepare for the night and the anticipating tourists and locals alike. We stayed on the beach much of the day.

During early evening, we returned to the resort we stayed at, took a quick shower and changed our shorts and put on some good cloth. We still had simple shoes as we knew that we would be back to the beach sometime later. For much of the early evening, we were at a nearby restaurant where we ate some fresh fish and had some cocktails of the local sort.

Around nine in the evening, we walked towards the beach and found us a good space where we did not have too many people around. And at this point, I knew what I was about to do. I went and gathered dry wood as if I was back home doing it for my mother from a small forest close to my hometown. As back then, my parents could not afford firewood, let alone use ovens and microwaves they have today. Most of such activities came on my shoulders as my younger siblings we too small and my older brother did not care about anything, and issues of our home were the least of his worries as a student.

Gathering wood on the beach to just cheer up my girlfriend and make a company of people to soon surround us was more of an act of luxury than the burden it used to be when I was a boy. She was laughing at this African man, just doing his job as he used to, but instead of the African woman doing it for her man, it was an African man doing it for his girl; it kind of enticed her.

Once I had enough to start the fire and put extra on the side for later, I went to a small local shop to buy matches and gas to get the fire start quickly as by then the time was approaching 10:00 in the night and the craze was about to begin soon. I rushed back, passing by couples, families and gangs of young men, and made my way back to the firewood waiting for my hands. I started the fire, and it slowly gained more light, catching a wood by wood. We stretched what seemed like a bedsheet over one of the big wood trunks and sat over it. I opened some soft drinks, and we had some salted nuts, dried fruits and snacks to chew on.

When the fire was fully burning, we had to drag the wood trunk and sit a bit further from it. By this time, people slowly walked to us, brought wood for themselves and sat around the bonfire. They would greet us, greet each other and sit in a row circling the fire. One additional line also was made on the side facing the water surface.

Then people started sharing beers, snacks, sodas and anything they brought with themselves; it just felt like we knew each other and came for a bonfire night at the beach. But we did not know each other, we were just people attracted by the fireside and the beautiful beach. All of us were there for one thing though, we came to celebrate the New Year's Eve.

People were telling all sorts of jokes and personal stories, encounters they had in Costa Rica and others about their travel experiences. Some local people were also there speaking Spanish and mumbling some

English words. It did not matter as much, because there was an unspoken sense of equanimity of being together and the vibe of celebration visible to all. As the master of the bonfire, I would move the woods, check the fire was OK and that the wood was added adequately.

This was the moment when I realised that when people mean it, all can gather for the things that make our moments meaningful, create the aura of happiness and attract the positive energy that connects us all. For most part of my global experiences, I saw people having more or less the same reactions towards openness, the will for togetherness, the gravitation to the good and the longing to just have that one person to start the cheaply found bonfire, make it available for everyone alike and let them bring themselves and surround the heat and the light generated.

I saw humanity, collective trust and the feeling of belonging among people that just met on the beach. The power of positivity does more impact with lesser cost than any force used; the cost of which is not just immense, it also claims lives in most instances.

While I was contemplating, firework broke out near us and almost everywhere. People were cheering, friends and families hugging and kissing each other, wishing a happy new year and dancing to the music being played. I was in my heaven. All I had to do was bring wood, stoke fire and sit, and now you get a bunch of hippies, happies and jumpers. It could never get any better than this.

The next day, still having fresh memory of the bonfire effect of last night, on the very first day of the year we drove up the hill going deep into the forest of Marino Ballena National Park. We arrived at Oxygen, sat on the side of the mountain and looked towards the ocean underneath that makes it the extension of the edge of the swimming pool. Here we spent the whole day, eating, drinking and swimming occasionally for as long as we had the energy. After enjoying our sunset, we drove back to our resort to prepare for the journey to San Jose and then back home to Sweden through Mexico.

Chapter Four

Club of the Conditioned

Menelik's Success or Tewodros' Failure?

One thing that I really want to be blunt about is that looking at the history of Abyssinia (former name of Ethiopia), faith, laws and principles had already made their way to this land before big superpowers were even conceived. We are talking about three thousand years, the former prime minister of Ethiopia, Hailemariam Desalegn, awed me and two guests in a state visit while he was hosting us by saying that it extends up to five thousand years. I then recall hearing from Prime Minister Abiy that Ethiopian history can stretch as far back as five to seven thousand years, yes seven good thousand years, that looking what has happened and has not happened in this old-aged country is very important.

As for me, in-advancement today means lazy, chaotic and unorganised past which then is a window to look through the glass ceilings the history jibe is hiding from us. See our past for it would be the first step to know 'what not to do', if we want to see progress, that is. Yes, history has those rosy victories of this and war spoils of that, but how about what they have not actually done and perhaps failed to do if they ever attempted? Honesty would mean that present-day Ethiopia itself is a failure of King Tewodros than success of Emperor Menelik, right?

Except the impatient British that did not spend enough time to study the idea of Ethiopia that Tewodros conceived, they rush into getting in deadlock with him, that prompted him to force them to create him a war arsenal, which then eventually led to his death.

For me, the time period between Tewodros and Haile Selassie is a momentary pause of progress towards democracy. Haile Selassie's time may have been an unacceptable feudalist empire, at the same time, many ministers and officers that run the state machinery were trained overseas and that the process of betterment was visibly initiated.

Fast forward, from the time of Tewodros to Prime Minister Abiy, and perhaps the time of my son's generation, one thing will be time-cross-cutting reality. What Tewodros struggled with, the excessive intimacy of the state and the church, and present-day role and contributions of the predominant faiths to what Ethiopia looks like, cannot be any different except that their levels of closeness or views of own contribution differs, which then makes it very hard to pin-point at their roles.

In a sense, faith used to be the hiding sanctuary of Ethiopians from what goes around every day, this public position of beliefs will soon be replaced by something we all are not sure of, presumably adapted to realities of this generation rather, or even remain untouched. Across the years, between Tewodros and Dr Abiy, one faith centre stands firm against all tests of time, generations, governances and global changes: the Ethiopian Orthodox Church.

The pro-secularist Tewodros-ians known for starting the difficult work of design and architect as well as digging down for the foundations of the modern Ethiopia, it cost his ruling class for going against the Orthodox church, state faith by then, and his vision was laid for a rest together with him. Menelik was the most dubiously smart of them all, bold as his eye but a deeply secretive as his skin colour and skilful in manoeuvring different groups to his end and to the advantage of his empire.

Saying one thing to the white allies of the west, posing as a Christianise, and even a moderniser, said quite the opposite to the priests telling them to defend their faith and more importantly the 'Ethiopian culture of the forefathers,' by which he squeezed the culture to the Shoa expressions — loosely taken. Menelik painted himself as a mother of the nation, the provider, protector and affectionate darling, hence Emiye Menelik! He had always done one for himself (the republic) and the rest for the mass.

In all of this, though, he would say one thing to the white western allies, its complete opposite to fellow countrymen, and another to the priests of the church and made sure that he would compartmentalise all of these so that honest and intimate conversations would not happen among all of them in a horizontal fashion.

If this is not being smart, for the time he lived, I don't know what intelligence is to be honest. His demand to the church was clear — strengthen my empire — and he literally earned it at the expense of people's suffering and unresolved trauma.

To my understanding, the faith suffered a setback of not expanding across the rural areas, remained closely attached to the state presence, which was in and around townships and cities than deep villages in the southern Ethiopia, with several exceptional cases. This is without mentioning the international spread, perhaps its chances of expanding in the rest of Africa, or at least paving ways for the generations of Haile Selassie's empire and later, missed out.

What I am saying is that there is this side of trading out spread over consolidation. Yes, expansion within the country followed Menilik's soldiers and later rulers, that widened the religion from before Menilik's era. At least, this is what any ecumenically conscious and expansion-aware Orthodox faith followers would most likely say — I presume.

As compared to Menilik, the 'all are fine' Haile Selassie is rather interesting figure to me in his special way. Since he lived in England and travelled to many countries and was very popular across the world, he was more laid back in some faith issues as compared to Menilik.

His Majesty Emperor Haile Selassie had more joints than the all-muscled Menilik, and he was flexible enough to attempt accommodating different views. This is a statesman in a country you have a state faith, he is the one who even accepted himself being worshiped as a deity and allowed Ras Tafarians start to make their ways to Shashemene of Ethiopia.

He surely did not instruct anyone to invent a new religion, have temples and preach about him, but if it comes on its own, hey, why not! Let's see where this would lead us. To be frank on this, there is no confirmed state outlet that implied it this way. But let's say there is a meaning to a statesman allowing something strange and foreign, even as if it is from another world, that you are a God and your worshipers want you to give them permits and land in your country.

His strategic decision, which the American missionaries stated as God's guidance to allow them to build their station in Wolaita, which may plausibly be him sending away what he probably thought as a burden to the northern people to the least or using them as pacifying force against the resistive Wolaita people. It is a known practice by African leaders to inject religion as social tranquilizer, by inviting Catholic and Protestant missionaries against repressed and angry people of Africa.

With this though, of acting with the role of nursing and cultivating a young faith at risk, the Ethiopia of Haile Selassie's time was not new as history is my witness. When it was at its worst times, and at the moments it could have just perished only to be remembered by history, the religion made its way to Ethiopia and stayed until its bones were strong, muscles could carry and make it walk or run for that matter, Islam stayed and found itself a home (though question of religious justice remains unanswered to this day) in Ethiopia. Judaism also sought a sanctuary in Ethiopia in its worst times.

Contrary to Ras Tafarianism, Islam did not call the Ethiopian king of the time you are our Allah-God. Rast Tafarians did to Haile Selassie. He let them in regardless. This only increased his popularity to the point of immortality in history, thanks to the Bob Marley beats and Reggae music that carries his image, the flag of his time and quotes his speeches.

A Government in Auction

So how much did it actually cost team Jawar to dismantle the government dominated by veteran old guards of Tigray and undo its wheels? I had to do research and cross check this fact before making up my mind and ask my subsequent question to understand it all and have a picture of what the security system of Ethiopia looks like, where it was, where it might possibly be and where it may get, if it gets there at all.

What is seriously concerning is that Addis Ababa is a host of the African Union, as a globally known fact the security of leaders of more than fifty-four states and international delegates falls on the hands of Ethiopian security forces. Also, that being so, the Ethiopian security is supposed to be much stronger than most AU countries at least, and by assumed competence it projects and comes short to be crushed for as little money and coordination as the system of ruling through tyranny, then in short, the security in Africa is so porous. It is already yesterday that they must have revamped and revitalised their systems.

Now, when I talk of this, don't get me as someone who is educated at top security schools in South Africa, Israel, Russia, the UK, the USA, Germany and China where many Ethiopians boast to have been trained among many countries I did not mention here. I don't have any certificate or any legal training except a one-time basic awareness training for NGO preparedness due to missions and deployments in war zones.

I have no bad intention except that part of the story means that I had to show uncooperating face with some people whose ulterior motive is to hurt people and use their powers for their greedy end. This is where I draw the line, you can be greedy and as a human I understand such souls but using security as instrument of repression and causing imposed poverty on others remain intolerable to me. Very simple.

Speaking of not cooperating, since I hated the previous government from the deepest core of my heart, and my father hating it even for longer, most of my family members paying the cost for all our 'sins' because of this, any good towards some individuals in the power circle I did out of concern for the Wolaita and all Ethiopians; most importantly, it was because some of the grave mistakes the Old Guards did were about to cost the country to come to its knees.

Some of these points were not more than a moment where I tried to wake Daniel Berhane and a few other Tegarus, especially Daniel as he was closely linked to Getachew Asefa — security chief of Ethiopia and a former college mate of mine who was closely attached and hired to follow former Prime Minister Hailemariam's circles including Masqale Lera and his team. It was from notifying that the grievances must be told by Ethiopian journalists first than BBC and other foreign media or clarifying that the land issue of Addis Ababa is a serious security matter. And that any grievances are to be paid attention to.

To make it clear, once again, I tried to avoid direct contact with PM Hailemariam until I was sure he was quitting his premiership and vacates his post for a really, really and honestly good reason, but I stop this here.

My former college mate, Angesom for our easier flow, himself was not aware except that we had an encounter at an airport in Vienna; me en route somewhere for field work and him and Masqale Lera within Hailemariam's close circle landed on a state-level visit to Europe. I was sure Angesom thought, *is this guy is still roaming around? Look at him.* I assume he had a quick thought in his mind, *Ah, this guy is doing much better for himself than what I thought at college.* Because they never believed that graduates would be better off on their own without party blessing.

But I was evaluating how tightly Masqale and all PM Hailemariam's close circle are monitored by Tegaru security apparatus. I was unduly provoked and made to wake up by force, and now I cannot unsee what I see.

I also would want to remind my readers that Angesom is that college mate who reported bad about me after he expected flattery and I wanted to check who was following, why and to what end. Now, you see how closely they knew me even from high school and followed me at the college and fail to understand that for as much as they were following me, I was counter learning about them. Partly because all they did was delay, destroy or dwarf my success and they hated me so dearly. Partly because, I wanted to know who was protecting my country and if we are safe at all, and surely their motives, rationale and their mindset.

This is because understanding how the security operates tells more than what they say in rosy TV speeches, what they pay to be released on music, or printed outlets or social media for that matter. The pain of my family and myself meant that I tracked the security of the Old Guards to understand why and how they hurt the Oromo and the Amhara that they hated deeply.

This then would help to reflect to similar circumstances of my loved ones and the general public. I remember what my father used to tell me. The most efficient war is the war of the mind, not of the metal or any object to be used. I knew I was in a war even if I took it with faith, a sense of ease and intent of not burning out.

When my assistant in Addis Ababa was recruited under the table to try and undermine me at a bar, and my attempts of opening a clinic, medical tourism firm, closure of my NGO and even denying the big investment projects I suggested, some of which I had source of finance, were all tied to the fact that I am in a categorically hated group in the eye of the Old Guards, my mother's clan in my ethnic categorisation, if it meant anything at all.

This actually opened my eyes as it made it easier to follow the path of the powerful circle and find trails of grievances across other ethnicities and individuals without even saying a word. I am not saying clan arrangement is the only path to follow, but it rather made me see the tyrant circle for what it is. So, as a combatant, rather a born fighter, I was in a war with the darkest hands, and I was sure my fight would not end even after the Amhara and Oromo feel they are done with their bit of the war.

I am also not linking my struggle, by any account, with what is going on in Ethiopia that is spearheaded by the Oromo and enhanced by the Amhara, the Wolaita and others. The tyrants made me feel it is personal to me and that if they made my life a living hell for thirty-eight good years (well, I lived and live better than their top paid or owning people, but it is not just the material but the fight at the spirit level makes you know that it is not over because you can pay your bills in Europe).

When I wanted to know how much it cost the Jawar team, to crush the previous powerful circle, I was confirming to myself that I started paying for this way back without it being noticed. The Airport scenario at Vienna, conversation on my father's sofa, constant denial of my deserved personal progress, were just quick good examples to mention. This is discounting minor but equally annoying situations.

The previous players had more porous security than it made people believe and that is also a reflection of not the gaps in the tyrant circle rather the listener being fooled and not knowing this is happening to them. OK, for honesty purposes, I am not dismissive of what the tyrants did, nor am I ignoring any questions that may arise of having anything positive at least to some Tegaru artists, intellectuals, politicians and businessmen.

Well, this is a known fact by the circle of the Old Guards themselves and something they learnt later that some people were not to be pushed and that they were wrong that I am hard pressed. Now that this is settled, as an architect who moulded the previous security apparatus in recent years, how come Getachew Asefa failed to understand this that I was not to go against of all people in my hometown, that, if no positive relation was sought, how about leaving me and my family in peace? Like, forgetting that we even existed. Not that it did not go that way.

The loopholes in the previous government's security were not just that they were choosing wrong battles and that they were missing the bigger picture for once at country level, AU, and how this would play out with the USA, Russia, EU, China, India, Japan and other key global players. They are bad haters and poor in judgement of when and who to recruit. And that they really underestimate the individual's ability to see through deception and the intent to hurt someone at the core.

Rigidity over inflated self-image, the hierarchy born through false sense of prestige, unperceptive of the subject tricked control, the idea of ignoring performance, slashing merit, upholding clan ties, and assumption of quenching the thirst of perfection means that stagnation has been their reality much longer than when the world came to learn about them. I would sum it up as a lack of imagination.

Imagination is a great tool if you realise how much you have it and hurts a lot if you do not notice you have it yourself or surround yourself with the gifted ones. Worse would be you have good people like Gessamo, Meles's advisor, and fail to see that based on how you treat him and his likes, many others with the skills, commanding competencies and the quality of seeing through challenges of significant value to the national interest would just withdraw helping you out.

Lack of imagination is intellectual impairment, not just lack of having a gift. The gifted ones may have the gift of seeing the future events as if they are watching a clear, well-directed and well-acted movie, but we all have the gift of imagination if we start noticing it, paying attention to it, learn about and from it, and cultivate it like a plant until we see a fully ripe fruit. It is very natural to say that in this some of us are more gifted than others.

When I read about Addis Ababa masterplan, which was more like urban and semi-urban land policy, it was clear that the days of the old guards were coming to an end.

I was sitting on a meeting, as an attempt to mend connections between the Oromo and the Wolaita, both politically and at the area I wanted to focus 'people-to-people' relations. We all were notified that the meeting was sanctioned by the prime minister and that he had given his blessings to our discussions.

I was briefed that most Oromo major power sailors such as Lemma Megersa, Jawar Mohammed, Dima Negewo, President Shimelis Abdisa of the Oromia region and key individuals set an agenda and came to a consensus that this is important both as a state-level meeting but also as Wolaita-Oromo agenda.

Therefore, chasing me because of my mother's side meant that this group wanted to work with the Old Guards, or only the Amhara than with the Oromo, just because they are old royal blood. This was not big enough as a reason to dismiss building relations of two people groups that have lived side by side and intermarried and have blood ties.

I was opposed, pressured and fought against, but as soon as relations started to resume, the security improved significantly, and this also added to the stability of the country and triggered a feeling of trust between the two ethnicities, their politicians, businessmen, intellectuals and opposition figures. I heard even a music album was released, sponsored by someone inspired by this meeting. So, it was a very crucial meeting, the impact of which will remain as significant to both people.

The incumbent minister of mines and petroleum, as of when I am writing book, and former city mayor, Engineer Takele Uma, presided over the meeting at his office in Piazza (Arada) with state delegates from his side and several of us from Wolaita. After orienting that Addis Ababa used to be land of different clans, he declared that Addis Ababa is a city that is sitting on the land of Oromo clans and has a need for urban justice, making it suitable for Oromia as it is a chartered city, and the capital city of Oromia regional government, Ethiopia and the African Union. He then elaborated his vision of improving services, safety and infrastructure. We all delved into picking our notes and talking on what brought all of us on the table.

Before the meeting was called off, there was this one guy who was not listed as a visitor but was hastened to participate, and I was asking myself, why the hell are you here as you are also a messenger of the previous system? To shorten it, this guy later ruined the very intent of this meeting, disrupted all efforts and got a promotion as a reward. This is purely internal Wolaita rift, for the sake of clan and personal incentives at the expense of the people's fate. It is important to recall that this was a very crucial time in building alliances and agreeing on terms of partnerships.

It was because of this man's intrusion to this meeting I ended professional contact between myself and party chairman, as he defended this person and set me up. Clearly there was a breach that must have been sanctioned by Mr Dagato and someone at the governing party central committee.

While I knew that this will be one of major issues for the fall of Dagato, I was also sure that my personal security is compromised to a life-threatening level, except it was a matter of when than if something was to happen to me. For this I had a plan to professionally determine if my safety is in danger through consulting security advisors.

The recently ended war began at my hometown and a few people, including him, plotted to betray us and our people for personal gain as they underestimated us and thought that we would fall in traps they had arranged for us. Except a few points, we managed to recover most of the agreed points of the meeting, relations remained intact and we just left him alone as he would eventually touch the buttons from his previous ties to his own demise, since we knew that there would be a moment every politician would have to pull strings in search of leverage or some benefits.

We saw many like him crumble, so trash him and move on was my agenda for setting scores. And to make it clear, the table was not personal to me more than it is public and has to endure such incidents anyway. But the previous system managed to book a seat for an unregistered guy at a table sanctioned by the prime minister, give me a break! I cannot fight such things at a personal capacity, except that I set some political triggers here and there for proper reactions and left it from following it up.

The mayor mentioned about the Addis Ababa masterplan issues and what challenges it posed on the farmers and how much intense work they were doing. The masterplan was a political plot designed with a good package cover and poison inside.

On a chat with Angesom and Daniel Berhane, I tried to show them this that whoever proposed the Addis Ababa masterplan wanted the (former) government to fail as a government and this would define its existence soon. Except trying to deflect, arguing against, referring to legal terms and claiming about land acquisition, jargon terminologies, they both failed to see the picture I was building for them clearly. Anyone could see what the policy advisors intended in the proposed practice and staged a crisis to unfold for the collapse of the government but also the potential dismemberment of Ethiopia as a country.

Possibly, in my assumption, since I am not a policy maker, urban planning guru or a politician, why should they listen to me? This was a clear indicator to me that the Tegaru clique is systematically being detached from the reality on the ground and that, perhaps, there may be a greater good in the making. Besides, I am to be taken down and pressed down as their party operational doctrine instructs, I am not to be listened to. The City Mayor Engineer Takele did mention this policy in his talks that day.

Apart from the deteriorating security, which I hope may improve, I want to remain hopeful Addis Ababa has changed for good, and that people may try to make the best of it.

Was It Always?

I moved back to Addis Ababa and lived there for about three years. During this pre-Covid stay in Addis, I met this old woman, honestly devoted Ras Tafarian, from Trinidad, who lived most of her lifetime in the United States. We had shared an apartment at one of the residential areas of CMC.

We used to talk about a lot on a wide range of issues, really a lot, I mean. You see, she is this kind of an old woman who is literally stuffed with rich wisdom, tons and tons of knowledge, finding all exceptional angles to look at life and all that is around us.

She once came and said, "Andualem, you are among those type of people who are the thinkers, knowers and doers. There are not so many out there. This can be a blessing, but if you are not careful enough, it could also mean a curse in your life. Be careful about yourself, young man, be careful!"

It was less than a month that a serious incident happened to me, showing that I was fast enough to grasp what she said, but not ready enough to act up on it. She used to live in Shashemene, did a lot of leadership work, voluntary activities, fund raising and a lot of coaching and counselling.

The wisdom and knowledge, good enough to shape up Ethiopia to the level of South Africa at least, if not England, is present in Addis Ababa but hey, if I sleep by choice, who can wake me up, no? I mean this! I really do. It is truly sad to realize that enormous number of skills and expertise that roam around in Addis Ababa without getting the chance to contribute to the country's progress.

One thing that struck me hard was when I heard her refer to Ras Tafari's speech, just as people refer to religious verses, and made her point based on it. I am not saying she was the first Ras Tafarian I met. I was once almost over-lectured by a Ugandan Ras Tafarian about Ethiopia, how misunderstood Ras Tafarians are and so on and so forth. Not so usual for me to sit with an Ancholi Ras Tafarian.

For once though, when the woman referred to the emperor, I was mentally pinned to the unmoving stone. I became out of place. I was to switch from seeing a former emperor to sort of a living deity. She changed my understanding about the former Ethiopian leader to a very starkly different personality.

And when I started to gradually realize, her arguments made sense to me than my own reaction to her reference and using Emperor Haile Selassie as the source of her wisdom. Because all that she said was right and she was talking about the level of tolerance people need to develop to peacefully exist together for otherwise, countries could collapse and societies disperse, which would mean families can be torn apart and people can get hurt in the process.

This time, though, I was lost for the second time. What this woman was saying gave me a flashback memory of what happened in Syria and how a nation just crumbled in itself and inflicted wounds on its own citizens while the world either stood watching, or others added fuel to the fire to our global shame.

"This woman is right," I said to myself. She was telling me about what happened to the Ras Tafarian community in Shashemene due to recent political incidents, and that many were left insecure and alienated by the mob nature of violence happening around.

She did not go to a doctoral school, or did not even get a certificate, but she guided people to their ways to PhDs and what she was saying made more sense to me than many post-doctoral graduates that fail to see that the Ethiopian intrigue is waxed purposely to complicate things, make matters harder than they are, and darken any enlightenment around us.

Well, at least that is why Tewodros was left to die instead of getting proper help from his people as I believe, compared to at least some people who tolerated Haile Selassie who was somewhat friendly to people of other faiths, including Ras Tafarians and others.

Former President of Ethiopia, Colonel Mengistu Hailemariam, was a complete opposite of Haile Selassie though. At personal level, Mengistu would pay a visit to undisclosed churches, address his prayers and leave before the mass convened, but this was rarer than being often. His wife on the other hand used to go to church secretly and participate in the mass though she also went anonymously and had a walk of a cat wherever she went. She was also a member of 'mahber' Orthodox church tradition of celebrating saints' days.

I met a lady when I went through a minor surgery in 2018. I had a cyst formed around my inguinal area and had to be removed as it started to get bigger slowly. I remember showing it to a specialist from UK who told me to just leave it and that it was nothing. Only God knows how many people would believe doctors from overseas and get health complications later on.

To make it worse, he was supposed to warn me to get a check-up at least. He did not, so now I was lying on my bed after surgery was done. I was encouraged by my friend who is a physician not to get robbed off by the hefty price of private hospitals as they do really good work at government hospitals this time around. Another resident physician friend of ours was also there for my assurance, and me being me, I took the risk.

The surgery was great, and the theatre was as neat as it can get. Since I worked closely with a US citizen and orthopaedic surgeon in my first job, except complicated procedures, I was very familiar with attending operations, roles ranging from managing equipment to handling almost all surgical products since I oversaw the inventory to the warehouse and re-equipping work as added role; this is in case breakdowns happen or replacements or refilling.

Managing the risk of equipment theft meant that I was to handle the reserve equipment. Compared to the St Luke's Health Care Foundation sponsored hospital in my hometown and many expensive hospitals, I did not blush with the facility the Yekatit Hospital built in a country with limited resources.

I was given a room with another family as they said private rooms were all taken. But it paid me off to stay with this family whose father had serial surgeries that were complicated because the man was diabetic. His wife was nursing him; I was appreciative of mothers in Ethiopia whose love never withers through thin or thick.

Her kind words, manners of speech, respect, love and affection grabbed my attention. She also seemed to be interested to talk to me except that my headache from the spinal anaesthesia did not allow me to sit, sleep, eat or drink, let alone talk to anyone. Wounds were taken care of by nurses who paid a visit occasionally; the care was so good that I was not even left alone that much.

I could not wait to feel better so that I hear about someone I was always curious about as she is a friend of the former president of Ethiopia and mostly spent time with his wife! The toughest Ethiopian leader that yet lives. My repeated attempts to learn about this man were not fully satisfied by a few books written by allegedly his former aides and comrades; they offered me insights and left some trails at least.

Not the official man, occupying the seats of his presidency, but the man at his house, a husband, a father, a friend, his thoughts and the psychology of his normal life was what I really wanted to hear from her.

From Mengistu making fun of his comrades with his wife to his humour over home affairs, to all-serious public man being the friend of his wife type of husband, the *'kill-them-all man'* at his office to *'yene wud'* — my darling — to his wife, very loving to his children, Mengistu was a hell lot of a good father to his own children than how I pictured him from the stories of some confessions. His wife on the other hand was very wise, calm, quiet and articulate than even her husband as her friend told me. This fit exactly with the story of the former Prime Minister Hailemaram's wife.

At times when I sat with her, whether a short tea break or a lengthy discussion moment, I pictured her as the prime minister of Ethiopia, and said many times to myself, 'oh my God, if Hailemariam is a jazz, she can fit to either be a Deep House or a good Rap, but then the former first lady would never be a lamely performed opera though.

As compared, if the First Lady FL W/ro Zinash were Tizita, PM Dr Abiy would be remix of chikchika (Ethiopian rock beat) and hard rock. This is the thing about Ethiopia; we only know almost too much about the leaders (who have been men for most recent part) than their wives, what they did and did not, what they aspired to, agreed and disagreed with are not heard as much.

From the look of it, as I saw it, Hailemariam is more like a civil servant than a political beast that you want to see somehow appear in a leader at some point, his wife on the other hand, Former First Lady FFL W/ro Roman Tesfaye, is a lot more of a politician than HR tally at some payroll.

The moment Hailemariam turns to be a politician is when he sees a moment to convince you of something, and at least sway your decisions, leaning all the height he has over your shoulders, then you do know he has been employing this countless time to make his way through this ladder in a political path built with thorns, sharp nails and knife edges. She would ask and ask and say few words. Hailemariam also asks, but the former lady is more of a detective than he is. She would have made to be a more efficient and well-spoken leader, I would argue.

This is when, with some exceptions, of course, I wonder whether putting civil servants in the highest political posts is not poor judgement on its own. Whether it is in humanities, business and leadership, law, medicine, engineering and science or arts, most of Ethiopian graduates are more tuned into civil service, technical deliverables and ethical discharge of services than the leader types.

I do not recall universities that are cultivating the often risk-filled culture of creativity, the uncharted world of innovation, the unseen planet of questioning our truth and so on. If you are invited to a graduation ceremony, you would be so sure that majority, perhaps an overwhelming majority, is moulded into officer, physician or engineer technical cadres groomed for either four-by-four office or even worse glass-separated open space halls sitting with hundreds doing what every other graduate is doing.

If you mould a student to this end, the best of these is still not the best yet, how can you then leave the system so dysfunctional to the level of not being able to filter and either leading to other aspirations or equipping for leadership, I will say chances are that there is no capable system, or it is not there yet itself.

I am not even saying anything about those who hold the keys to offices that were supposed to be doing this. I will surely upset some people's feelings without wanting to. This would mean vacuum at the state level and its main arches. I do see the flaws of Meles and stop from asking myself, as he was already at the palace before people woke up to it.

At some point, one would pause and ask, knowing Ethiopian politicians and the dubious games played around leaders, mostly meant to trap into failure, how would the country look like if their wives were not loyalists and full of wisdom?

Well, this was what I was thinking about Mengistu's and Hailemariam's wives and pictured to myself the horror it was at his time. A lot more would have gone wrong if these men married short-tempered, sadistic and cannibalistic wives than the balanced, weighing, reserved and listening types they both were. A lot of mediation, atonement and at times threat-like appeals meant many lives were saved, much more jobs saw no firing and many businesses remained open.

It is just amazing to learn that for as much brutality and horror we learnt from Mengistu's leadership, the former lady's roles to have left a country to tell a story about is something that needs a closer look and hopefully some journalistic work before we lost the chance of learning about her struggles, dreams and hopes that were realised and failed; why, because of who, to what end and what would she do differently if she were to become the first lady again.

I am very sure W/ro Azeb Mesfin may also have some trails to lead us to the understanding of the things that matter more in the daily errands of the state house. As she is outspoken herself and appeared on the media a few times, I am much more interested to learn about her excellency the incumbent First Lady W/ro Zinash Tayachew and their excellencies former First Ladies W/ro Roman Tesfaye, W/ro Wubanchi Bishaw.

All these that are living have the chance to write us books, appear on media and even lecture at universities or create a platform for mass education and enlightenment via digital platforms. We have been losing out a lot of resource just because we have not looked for it or have not known its value yet. It is our lack of curiosity, flawed understanding of 'the Ethiopian Truth' that has been said by the men, and our ignorance to a notable degree to any thinking and probing intellectual representations of critical occurrences in our shared public life space.

Say someone would do an interview and some sort of FGD and composes a good book. What a picture of us, of our mothers and fathers, our daily lives, our shared struggles and successes, aspirations and hopes, fears and risks we would learn from the incumbent First Lady W/ro Zinash Tayachew and former First Ladies W/ro Roman Tesfaye, W/ro Azeb Mesfin, W/ro Wubanchi Bishaw.

I would also like to say that since we are more tuned into mostly faith-based streaming as a source of our information, source of knowledge and wisdom, that is, we are trapping ourselves into the world of men and have alienated ourselves from the women around us. If we look at it, this sounds like the opposite.

Omitted truth makes the half-truth false. A human is not just the same instead of being equal, a human is the truth of the world too. The absolute truth.

Truth that is spoken by men only omits the woman in the truth and makes the whole incomplete.

Such truth is not relative. As it is biological, and scientifically proven as well, it is absolute. And relativity has not helped any of this either. Because it robs itself of the fundamentality of truth; therefore, fails to make women equal without flaws of scale precision, that they both are humans and by being so are equal to the least and like the most normal there is.

Listening to my grandmother, on my mother's side, has taught me that few women do learn, process, save and remember wisdom more than millions of men. But they would not tell you unless they see you are curious enough, value what they have to say and that they see you are learning from the conversations. The incident that happened after the Ras Tafarian friend of mine advised me meant I never took her words for granted. A lot is missed out without learning from women and turn the tides to our collective advantages in this world of shared space where we breathe oxygen from the same surface of Planet Earth.

Her Shadows

The learning capital that has long been saved around women has to start getting tapped as the world seems out of inputs. Repetition of product designs, recycling of ancient concepts, repackaging long-forgotten ideas and rollbacks of discarded policies show us that the men's world has come to innovation fatigue and new force is needed almost yesterday.

If this is not the case in the west, I am more than sure it is the case in Ethiopia and the rest of Africa. If the intended 'equality' is to be achieved, then women must assume much greater social and economic roles than just political roles. Because it is those who control these two that also control the politics.

Let's say the next global agenda, call it Global Progress Goals — GPGs — the amount of total global capital and the proportion owned by women shall also be equal. The economic inclusiveness must be built in so that this would be the foundation for the global progress. What I am saying is that you make it inclusive, you do not call it. A gram of gold does not call itself a gold, it is gold, you know what I mean. The term inclusive is so detached from the reality that you must call your package with it shows that you need to integrate it in.

Development goal as in Sustainable Development goal shall be left to governments within their jurisdictions, as we progress globally as an act of chanting performed by seven billion people sharing the space in our planet. The world needs to narrow and concretise what it wants to achieve as arch impact while outcome levels must be left for states. This would then mean global progress goal is seen from the perspective of gauging performances of governances at highly concentrated form to what can amount as source of legitimacy and partaking in a shared will.

When we talk about 'the same' as in 'equality', it shall also mean like say by 2050, the global wealth appropriation must ensure that we have the total wealth of the world split and owned by women equally. If the overall global wealth is set at five hundred trillion dollars, for instance, Women must own two hundred and fifty trillion dollars as an aggregate of the global women's share of the wealth. To my astounding rough research as a reaction to Ethiopia's political intellectuals championing 'urban feudalism' in which instead of rural land, possession of urban land is the backbone of the economy, I tried to account how much of this land is owned by urban women.

What shocked me is that the land that has high commercial value is owned by men and that means women do not have a fair share of resources, especially if Addis Ababa is off the list, it even gets worse. I assume this is the fact in many countries, even rural lands are also not as much owned by women. Land acquisition must also be the agenda in terms of women's wealth and resources acquisition as a global effort. It seems, you don't have a say over what you don't own.

But then, what do I know other than such hard and objective measures of women's wealth, social space and political representation and leadership! I am a man! And I am not without flaws myself. Sometimes, I see my own flaws and learn a lot that what I perceived to be acceptable does anger women and that a lot is left to be learnt to do behavioural changes personally and collectively. But then some of them drive me nuts, as they do to many men of course, a few though take me to the roof!

My friend Helina, who would not call herself feminist, but in practice is, once sat with me for a lengthy talk. She said to me that she wanted to be above men so that she would not have to worry about being equal or not. In this, we had a very heated debate; we almost went on an all-out fight of pointing fingers and raising our tones; I thought we had both lost it. A few of her talks are for thought provocations, but the arguments carry a few threads of ideas that irritate me, not as hers but knowing this is what many would want to think in a self-deceptive or rather self-defeating manner. This bothers me in the Ethiopian context.

Helina said, "No, I literally believe we women need to be higher than you men. We are tired of this that you all have created and are fighting against us to keep it there."

I replied, "Helina! To me, you are risking pushing people to go against you rather than rallying them on your side."

Helina asked, "What are you saying?"

"Look, are you not talking to a man who is at least trying to understand to do his best?"

"But still."

"So?" I said.

"I am fed up, and I think this is what men deserve!" said Helina.

I said, "You know what I would do the moment you assume to be higher than me?"

"I don't care," said Helina.

"You will care when I do it," I said.

"What is that, that you can make me undo my decision of not caring at all and turn it around?" she asked.

"I will take you for lower than me," I replied.

Helina said, "Why, Andualem, at least you should take me as equal."

"No, you decided that I don't take you as equal," I replied.

"How?"

"By choosing to do what you say bad guys are doing against women," I answered.

Helina asked, "Andualem, you are not being fair."

"Are you fair to want to be higher than me then? You do know in effect that is making me lower than your equal, and this is even worse!" I said.

"Shut up!"

"No, seriously, this is a self-harming thought. It won't do you anything. It will give you false sense of security and that is all you get," I said.

"I hate you, you know that," she said.

"Yeah, yeah."

I cannot take this type of feminism at all. She asked me what kind of feminism I would accept or even convert to. You know, when people are baptised in an ideology and take it to the level they want to convert their friends, family members and significant others, I see myself in them often.

Such level of commitment is awesome on its own, just that it needs to be somewhat balanced with the view that sometimes to be cooperative to ideas, people don't necessarily need to be members; also, that a repellent approach would not just be a sure sign of a failing method, it also implies risking turning potential allies into bitter opponents for no tangible reason. Even if a person may not be a contributing member, they won't stand on your way at least. This is because, when many people think of feminism, they think of women's issues and consider that they are to be left for women. Here you have a bias from well-wishing people already.

Adding on top of this, there are millions of people, if not billions, that do not accept the idea of equality. On the face of this reality, making more allies or at least adding more neutrals is profitable than going head-on with already 'society-hardened' men and telling them that you want to be above anyone who has dominant testosterone. The moment you think of it this way, you have lost it there. Ideas that come in a uniting tone with building consensus than appearing as platforms of disenfranchisement would get a buy in from villages of low-income countries to affluent areas of the well-off nations.

One day, Helina invited me to her place located at the heart of Bole area, living in a great villa, parking few cars tended by security guards, garden staff, cleaners and a cook. For a single woman, she is well-off than the affluent men in suits. She prepared me a freshly pressed cup of coffee and we sat on her sofa for a talk. She just said something sounding more like a feminist.

At this point, I thought that Ethiopian feminism is coming out of the shadows. As this friend of mine is the real Ethiopian feminism in flesh, I saw that she was passing by me and sitting on the sofa. I saw her two shadows on the floor while she was walking with some tone of power on every gait section where her heels touched the ground. There were two strong lights on the roof. For some reason, as soon as I entered the room, they turned dim. One of the two lights became dimmer after a minute or so. I said to myself anyone who observes their lights getting dim, anywhere they are, any time of the day, that if this happens on its own in odd way, they must mind the darkness.

Knowing that Helina dined and toasted with a handful of powerful men of the city, sized them down to their skins, I know that she would skin me off if I were that loose brainless machos around.

I saw her rip off feared men of the Horn of Africa like a chicken wing. You don't want to joke around women who do it all only verbally and a real wrath follows. Truly said, my aura never denied me an impression around her and that I was more appreciative of her ability to stay herself while most of the powerful came and left, than restraining myself from projecting the true self in an open manner.

I am talking about a woman who is behind the political-economic backbone of the ideas of Zemen Bank, Mortage Bank, Real Estates, Malls, Transportation, Shipping Lines, Mineral Explorations among many others that saw Darios Gizaw as the man of the business and becoming the face of jail. She can empower and disempower equally that you may want to learn, that she was alone in not having more women on her side.

When the Imperial Hotel was purchased with some manoeuvres, to throw it on the hands of the para-military conglomerate Metek, Darios as an important piece in getting through playing the business catalyst. This would also mean the self-confessed pro- American group, at least to conceal its deep intent of siding with Russia behind the scenes, lost the political grip in Addis Ababa and capitulated to its retreat following the 2005 election crisis. It was her anger with Darios that put him in jail, which also begun the slow loss of information security upper hand the paramilitary conglomerate Metek.

This is not just a symbolic coincidence. It is truly real in showing that the entire system of Gabrovos, their financial firewall and the control tower of the public psychology would soon collapse. It is tied with the dismembering security dominance of the old guards and the demise of their grip in the Horn of Africa.

What thousands of elite security specialists could not solve started to be unlocked by a madly furious woman whom her boyfriend, Darios, tried to toy around like unsuspecting pretties of Addis Ababa. He poked the wrong woman and was about to learn of it in the harshest way anyone is taught. She had the money, the leverage and the intelligence and above all, she knew it.

In my attempt of tracking this storyline, I needed to reassemble bits of encounters in a friendship with a school mate of mine. She had studied in the Netherlands and was in close contact with me ever since. I would visit Liya's house whenever I missed homemade shiro or coffee as eating at restaurants and cafés can be tiresome in Addis Ababa.

From monotonous selection of food types to either question of cleanliness or etiquette, at times the service delivery or the quality of the food varies and makes it hard unless you keep changing where you eat. As usual looking at the menus in restaurants, one would see enjera this enjera that, not even any creativity added, one gets tired of eating this nearly every day.

A good challenge given my situations. Liya and I are close just because of familial ties; my father and hers as well and her uncle were in the same league of activists back in the day. Liya's father would become a friend of the late Prime Minister Meles Zenawi and the former Prime Minister Hailemariam and his wife the FFL Roman.

To make the story complicated, which I doubt she would ever be informed yet, her husband, Chisha, allegedly had a child with the sister of the FFL Azeb. Or, so tell the high-level military intelligence rumours to animate, beef his stories up and offer him that power only few could assume except the army chief and the prime minister.

He used it for the best interest of Ethiopia on two historically crucial accounts, that make me wonder if it is his trainings in Russia or his personal competence, a combination of the two makes me think something might be unclear to me. This is the security web of Old Guard style whereby you are lured to have sex with a lady right at the time she would get pregnant; confusingly, she would not know if it was her husband, or you the child belongs to. This would mean she would be the constant link to the two of you secretly or in open game. Now, who has a child with who must be checked through DNA test. I seriously mean it. Many children and adults would have different sir names if this wave of facing the truth starts. The Ethiopian Truth is buried in the wombs and hearts of our women than what is presented by men publicly or even secretly. I am very sure many falsely secured people will start to realise that they were being set up through such ties of trickeries and espionage drama than making them safe at any level.

To what may have sounded as inflated prepping up, I was challenging Liya to aim holding high government posts, and she managed to be holding a position of 'state minister' which is a rank lower than just the minister. This friend of mine was married to a Russian-trained military intelligence officer who used to assist the Horn of Africa operations.

While he has a superficially told story of working with peace and security, his actual performance came to the surface when I was searching for the few men responsible to foil the alleged threat of the CUD state capture that caused the 2005 uprising crisis.

It was during this time, I myself was suspected of plotting (based on false allegations, or anticipation that I would not accept the government of the time), that I hid myself in Gondar for about three weeks and managed to dodge an arrest and beating that many of the students suffered at the time.

At one of the nights, Chisha infiltrated former Minister of Foreign Affairs Siyoum Mesfin's security and had to spend his night at the shower room before getting spotted by his cleaner. It is at this point you know where the security of the country is porous, much more than what is known to the control.

This is when this man was either killed for recalibrating the security or was himself used to rebuild it. For his special character and performance, he was spotted by the late Meles who would personally assign him for special missions. One day, his colleague started what looked like a silly joke while they were sitting at Sheraton Hotel, monitoring the security for the late Meles. His colleague was from Tigray and had this sense of superiority over him and projected that he could get away with pretty much anything.

He would call him 'a name', some sort of ethnic derogative, and he just took out his gun, *pop, pop* on his legs. The security rushed in and dragged him and his colleague out; sending his colleague to the hospital, he was summoned to Meles right away. Meles asked him what happened, he told him exactly as it happened.

Meles said, "You should have shot him on his forehead," and he answered, "I was not ordered to kill him."

Meles said, "I know you were to be preventers together, but he breached by acting the way he did. He knows that he is living because you let him live. No one would blame you for it."

I guess Meles had this soft side for several individuals from Wolaita, and it is unclear to me why he would not be so to the collective.

Chisha was among five people that were recruited by Meles Zenawi himself to investigate, neutralise the threat and turn the tide to his favour. And this man was just the right person for it. His prize was the national flag of Ethiopia for the extraordinary performance of foiling a *c'ou de itat* that would have kicked Meles out of the palace.

In a very odd way, he also stands in the middle of the same building the Berhanu's party was plotting at, the Emperial Hotel, which was converted as a head quarter of the Metek conglomerate para-military industrial complex. At the time Darios Gizaw was followed while performing his business dealings that saw the military to overtake the building of Emperial Hotel, it was also this intelligence operative that tied his hands with the first serious blow to the political supremacy the Old Guards had across the Horn of Africa.

In what would later usher a way for Berhanu's return from Asmara, President Isaias Afewerki's frequenting to Addis Ababa and Bertukan Mideksa's appointment to lead the electoral board and so on, the man who shook the CUD, for the sake of Ethiopia, has now challenged the TPLF, all for the country once again. Then Meles was right in saying that this guy is the true face of the Ethiopian military in doing to the best interest of the country, when it is his call. It was this incident that weakened TPLF not the war nor the party take over by the new clique at the palace. This was more of the display to the public, of a secured win, over three years earlier.

This was complemented by the role played by a man, a regular family guy, whom you would never assume to be running such heavy-weight missions. As I could see the only thing, he has is a place to live and a government SUV that he drives. his wife, who is also super smart and devoted, works at the ministerial level as an advisor. They live a humble life for the level of responsibility on their shoulders. A friend and

I sat with him at the newly built Skyline Hotel, owned by the Ethiopian Airlines, located right at Bole International Airport.

He oversaw high level intelligence work, which he lastly briefed directly to the former PM Hailemariam, exposing the corruption that took place at the Sugar Corporation, an institution that promised to build ten sugar factories and that saw the Old Guards embezzled the funds in billions, seventy billion Birr to be precise, which was close to two billion USD at the time this happened. It is important to note that the currency value of Birr depreciated already at the time of reporting, while the embezzlement took place much earlier. We are talking about time span of about ten years gap in between the corruption, the investigation and press release.

It is important to note that it was the para-military conglomerate that was contracted to build the factories. His report was composed and televised from the parliament session signalling the TPLF grip over the power of the parliament is also sliming away. I asked him why he chose to risk his life in the city where people would grab billions and keep quiet about it.

He smiled at me and implied in his response somewhat sounding like, 'sile hagere new yarekut' simply interpreted he meant 'I did this for the country.' At the time, not so many among the old guards knew of his mission and what he was up to. But he was not speared from suspicious following and later being threatened for lie by Getachew's right hand man. After having our fresh coffee, he drove myself and a third man who was also with us, who also played central role in the high-end security of the country.

From exposing the Sugar Corporation scandals and leaving the Metek naked due to its mismanagement of the contracts for the Millennium Dam and many others, it was thanks to a network of few brave men and women who risked their lives to enable Ethiopians see government change than the vuvuzelas, and patriots of the dawn, who appeared on local TV or published articles championing 'victory' having no clue about which, and the role of its main actors.

When Darios was arrested, it sounded like a revenge because of his political frictions with Meles. It was only later that people realised this exposed the shadow play behind inflated pricing and financial games the

Metek was doing, which would implicate it back to the Old Guards and the gradual downfall of generals and people of ranks. In this story, the friend of mine who was Darios' girlfriend and his maker into a business rule setter and later crushing his financial bones and tossing him to jail, a question of who is dominating who, is a matter of listening to the stories of the right people.

Ethiopian women are not as far from the central power play as how the western mindset would believe. Simply, in Ethiopia high value incidents happen differently. That is also why there is no special hero or heroine in the story of the 2018 government change. Whether men are the only makers or breakers or if it is not powerful women whose shadows are seen all over it is about having the eye for it.

How you can unscrew the once giant government wheels that were on the hands of a few women than the arrogant man, Gebremichael, who got a shot on his legs at their duty at Sheraton. Helina and Liya, the two women stand to be more powerful than many men in the suits to whom thousands would bow down their heads. Now, looking at her with this in mind, she is not that everyday woman at all. She is a hybrid of tigress and lioness with the brain of several people.

The women in power are hiding in plain sight while several men with lower roles make too much noise to cover their inadequacies. Ethiopia is strangely secretive. If the women who are at the core of power play are not visible in the story, simply put, you did not reach the depth of it.

A few times, I would poke Helina, but now she is poking me as a reverse of it. I have always loved sitting with her and touch on areas of our society, its struggles and a few people who are responsible for it or if lucky, possible solutions. This time, she wanted to hint that she has muscles too, not just the untamed masculinity of men in the city. I am here having it difficult to sort it out whether I am learning about the might of Ethiopian ladies or the setbacks of the underestimating men like Darios Gizaw, who would challenge the like of Meles and get into their nerves is now being toyed back like an old teddy bear by a woman.

Helina asked, "Are you not observing one thing?"

I asked her, "What is it?"

"That women are now overpowering men," she replied.

"What makes you say that?"

At this point, I realised that the state operatives compartmentalised a few powerful people to the point that they saw their own story from what was known to them and what they did. The aggregate of the stories that makes up the bigger picture was not clear to them and they did not know the magnitude of the impact each of them was exerting except they were playing their part of the script. She knew she overpowered Darios Gizaw, and he also had ties with the Old Guards, but seeing the chain of events and making the full picture was not why she did what she did. He was in jail and she was telling the story. That is all, or so it appeared.)

Helina's helper was pouring the second round of coffee, as the cups are much smaller, also lifted the kolo so that we grad some. We were staring at the TV at this point. Helina said, "We are in politics, in economy and social sectors. We are dominating."

I asked, "Are you sure?"

Helina replied, "Yes, I am very sure."

"How much of the Ethiopian economy do you pretty ladies of the country own?"

Helina replied, "That comes through time."

"Without this, you think you have overturned history and time?" I commented.

Helina said, "Don't be mean."

"I am realistic," I said.

Helina asked, "What do you mean by that?"

"Show it to me that you are equal, let alone overpowering men."

Helina said, "You will see."

"Isn't this what needs to be achieved first?" I asked her.

"We are better off now anyway," she replied.

"Congratulations then."

A few weeks later, she travelled to Norway as she often did; I thought she would go to the US when she said she had a travel plan. Normally, a few of such people travel overseas get some sort of indoctrination to rock the fundamentals of the society at its core, most of the time towards a good end. I was aware that some of her trips were not like most of our middle-aged ladies who snap some photos, do a thing or two and comeback with western cut styles and perfumes.

As curious as I was to learn what she brought back with her, we sat again after her return. This time around, I don't know if it was the Norwegian effect of seeing the world differently or if she contemplated on it on her own, I was not sure about it. But I was expecting she was to throw a word or two that would be half-feminist and half-religious for that week everyone was talking about some incidents that involved religious institutions, and somehow this popped up.

"By the way, Andualem," she started.

"Yes?"

"We need to accept that we are not equal and that men are higher, and possibly there would not be a war and misery in the world," she said.

"But then isn't this what we all are up against?" I said.

Helina replied, "Sure, it seems it is not working."

"So, we are correcting a mistake by another mistake, in that case."

"what do you believe?" she asked.

"About equality; you know my stand and that I am not bluffing."

Helina replied, "But we are not equal."

"Not equal yet is one thing, but you sound definitive," I said.

Sleeping During the Day

In our multi city trip in 2012 where we travelled to Rio de Janeiro, Sao Paulo and Minas Gerais, Helen Berhane, Eritrean human rights activist, and I were invited to a house of Brazilian Award nominee Fernanda Brum, who dedicated a lot for the Eritrean human rights cause, where I met her husband and music producer Emerson Pinheiro, tried vocals with his drummist and himself on tuning Ethiopian beats with a Brazilian touch in his studio.

Fernanda's emotional attachment to Eritrean people is unthinkably amazing, making it obvious with the way she treated Helen and me with the utmost love and care one can ever imagine. In this department, Brazilians are a special breed of exceptional people I would say. I wished Ethiopians would be tender to others, and more so to each other. Without having any need to have ethnic, political, economic or social links or expected reciprocity. Clearly, there was no way we could honour enough of how greatly Fernanda was towards us. It made me yearn for this level for treatment for all Ethiopians alike.

During this travel, I met a man who designed the modern-day electricity network for the entire Sao Paulo with his team.

We are talking about a city of twelve million, which is an addition of two million on top of the population of Sweden. Such is the size of a city that just puts heavy expectations to meet the needs of diverse people's groups and visitors alike.

Addis Ababa on the other hand, is not even officially five million dwellers if we can be confident to use the official statistics at all. If such big cities can have power grids, water pipes, Internet, telephone, policing and service delivery, I do not see a reason why this cannot be done in Addis Ababa unless adapting to poverty is to be taken as strength and the rosy resilience NGOs talk about.

I must say here that I believe Addis Ababa inhabitants can have better schools to send their kids to, quality health care to rely on, much more smooth access to transport, cheaper and advanced connectivity via internet and phones, enabling and empowering financial services, fit-for-the-day service outlets, mushrooming accessible and affordable malls, un-cutting electric streaming, unstopping and super clean water, not-so-smelly sewage and disposal systems, oiled and not-so-quirky bureaucracy and above all, safe and secure places to find themselves around.

This said, in the eye of seeing a city that is awake during much of the night, Addis Ababa is a place dozing during the day for reasons unclear; whether it is because of the hangover or if people are oversleeping every day. As a lot is just slipping through to the level that people pray away their problems and complain off their challenges. one would just want to know who feels owning the city in a real sense.

Comparing Addis Ababa with much richer cities such as London, Stockholm and Sao Paulo, that also have different history, topography, demographic and geopolitical facts, may not seem fair, but learning is not fair too. Though some Ethiopians do not believe in their blackness, we are as black as all, and as beautiful or handsome as Ethiopians can get. Blackness is an undisputable identity of Ethiopians. Addis Ababa shares with Nairobi, among other factors.

It is important to mention that the main source of the Ethiopian blackness concept is from Wolaita. The Wolaita call themselves Amado's blakcs, more than they would confess being Wolaita. Blackness is sense of pride and strength among the Wolaita which made its way to the central policies of black lion ideologies. This is about integrating blackness daily in reflection of their self. Yes, I know, in the era of cosmopolitan identity, talking about ethnic representation can sound lame, but guess who is more into this! I rest my case here.

As we know, Kenyans eat ugali, the maize porridge, the Wolaita call it shendera. Shendera is eaten also by the Gamo, the Gofa, the Dawuro, the Basketo, the Konto and many adjacent people of Southern Ethiopia, call it fufu in Ghana or Nigeria we all eat it. One other maize-based food we eat is called sul'a which is a hand fist pressed maize dough (with meat, lentils, spinach or so on), boiled in water and is eaten with many types of sauce. What we call Halakuwa, the moringa, is the food eaten in areas starting from Wolaita made its way to most parts of northern Kenya, bordering Lake Turkana as regular long before the world knew of it. I can mention cultural mobilities, migration and so on. Turkana used to be where war horses were getting their water, in the era where the Wolaita ruled beyond Turkana all way to the shores of the Indian Ocean, which the people of the time used to call s Afriqa Gita Aba, the name the colonizers changed.

But hoping this suffices to get the conversation going, Nairobi is a place we can use as a mirror to Addis Ababa so that both cities can check spots in their looks for reference and shared betterments. From frequent daily flights to land transport, trade and socio-political ties of the two countries are much more intertwined than how it is presented by the media.

As I mentioned earlier, I had the chance to travel to Nairobi a few times. I was privileged to travel around the coast; the gracious Mombasa, Malindi, Watamu and Kilifi are my favourites, but Nairobi is a place that brings you back to reality before you head on to your destination and welcomes you back to the world in some way.

My interest in Kenya, particularly Nairobi, was triggered by a man I met in Sweden, while I have several Kenyan friends in Kenya and overseas. This particular man teased the African Union as a toothless lion that it was good for nothing. By then, though, I listened to his arguments as an unsuspecting listener, only to learn that there is this untold rift between Addis Ababa and Nairobi.

While Addis Ababa is the political capital of Africa, Nairobi is the capital of the continent for social affairs, or it appears so in a few bold talks. This is because of the simple reality that the African Union presides in Addis Ababa where several diplomatic clutches roam around; and most international civil society organisations, at least at the time, were stationed in Nairobi by following the queen Elizabeth's footsteps than the political arrangements of the continent.

From this, Addis Ababa is the voice of Africa while Nairobi is pretty much the voice of the queen, but not to hurt some feelings, it is the voice of the rest of the world that wants to gravitate even business HQs of Africa to Nairobi. This is kind of interesting on its own. Leaving these themes of differences, as much as the Halako and Ugali are eaten in both countries, the two cities can cooperate and learn from each other while they can keep competing for the interests that want it to be so, for competition would presumably mean mutual improvement.

Instead of the socio-political talks, I would prefer the composition and dynamic intricacies in the two cities and how the interaction of the dwellers created two different vibes.

Now here is how I compare Addis Ababa with Nairobi, though I do not hold all the litmus test papers for every curiosity I have, more so for the diverse perspectives of readers, we have something at least. Addis Ababa dwellers can be described as unreceptive to new cultures, ways of life or even styles except for the second-hand / high copy products of Nike, Adidas, Armani or Gucci you may find, thanks to products made in middle income countries and are available at cheaper prices in Dubai.

People are tricked into something that is halfway through for almost everything. Let me put this observation as simple and tolerable to the taste of the reader. Much of the time spent by the women, and some men alike, during the evening and weekend hours in Addis Ababa is spent on Kana TV than a total of hours spent on movies, football and all other sport events whether live or in the media. Much of the content is not Ethiopian or western, rather Turkish and the like.

At some point, a colleague of mine and I was sitting close to the now Amora Building, back in time called Imperial Hotel, which used to have live music every now and then. It was at this Hotel the then 'popular party in the cities' had its plots to topple the Meles regime and were then wiped out, and that the military intelligence that got to the heart of the story spent excess amount of money to acquire the hotel and convert it to an office for the para-military business conglomerate that is now under the control of the PM's side.

My friend and myself sat at a restaurant in front of the Amora building at the late breakfast time. One thing peculiar is that the cheaper the breakfast gets, the loudest the TVs are and the chaotic the service gets. As the loud voice called for my attention, I turned to the TV, and it was Kana TV again.

I said to my friend, "Isn't this more like the Turkish and Mexican movie drama series?"

He said yes.

I then asked him why do people of Addis need to have cultural transit in Istanbul of Mexico since we all know the destination is not Bollywood, it is Hollywood?

He said, "What are you saying?"

"Why not buy a one-way ticket to Hollywood than freezing people first in 'Ethiopian culture', then lure them into Turkish culture and indicate to them that Hollywood is next. It is not just boring, it is fooling the masses as if there is no one left who can think and ask.

"Please be quiet, there are people listening to mean informants of the paramilitary business conglomerate."

"I think this is worse than the situation itself," I commented.

"What is the worst situation then?" he asked.

"It is that what people watch on Kana TV is designed as a collective anaesthesia for the people not to focus on important issues."

Breakfast was served, and we started our bites to forget the fact that the TV was still loud and that the scenes where the women and the men appeal to the viewers that they are in a love they would not reach to. The movie as the mirror to the very intention of selecting them in the way of showing that the civility and modernity of the west is what we are not getting to, while whether we want it or not is still unclear. This is, of course, discounting the idea that most families would want to send their kids for graduate studies to the western schools. It is a self-conflicting phenomenon in Ethiopia, or at least in Addis Ababa.

While enjoying my breakfast in the midst of Kana TV noise, to my own abrupt laughter, I just said, "They don't learn, they don't teach or keep quiet and mind their own businesses."

My colleague and myself looked at each other, and he laughed to the roof. I felt he had also observed a few things. Addis Ababa needs a lot of cooking oil, but also oiling of the social wheels that just are very noisy in every turn and all the moves. The wheels and cultural expressions are not only too old for the present-day world, they are rusty and collections of rumbles and shackles that just need to graduate and kept at museums.

Speaking of culture washing, looking back at the arrival of the aggressively self-propagating Judeo-Christian culture and the mix of the Islamic presence much later on, not just Addis Ababa, even the entire Ethiopia can be taken as a cultural bank without interest.

You see, if you give certain style of expression to the people in Ethiopia, in a form of cultural heritage to be protected, instead of housing them in museums, once they are old enough making their way to everyone's life, we keep humans as the dwelling place for the cultural expressions. Therefore, cultural midwives of premature 'Ethiopian-ness' reserve them without adapting, developing or sharing with the rest of the world.

Perhaps this is why people who believe in Shoa conspiracy are good at preserving religions and the ways of dealing with matters in a collective manner. What I remember as a quick example is actually a situation that happened right after the war with Italy was completed and that the American missionaries returned to Otona, Wolaita Sodo, Sudan Interior Mission SIM compound.

To welcome the guests, the then converters of protestant Christianity sent their leaders to Addis Ababa. The Americans saluted them, all who missed each other greeted, hugged and kissed as to the custom of the Wolaita, you would contact two cheeks together and hold them there, and then roll your head slightly to the left and right.

All is done and talks of what happened by to the Italian generals in Wolaita and across the country, how it was to the newly growing church. In the middle of the conversation, I assume, the Wolaita elders saw that the Americans came with a dog and all of them left the guest room and rushed outside.

Confused by the actions of their soon-to-be hosts, the missionaries were afraid something terrible had happened which they did not know much of yet. When asked why they ran outside, they said, "You have taught us, and it is in the Bible to stay away from dogs."

Everyone burst into laughter after clarifications were made of what the passage meant. That the message in the verse was not literal meaning, so on and so forth. This way, even the much-evolving, reform-adaptive and progress-thirsty South was once confused about what is to be preserved and what is to be updated through time. To give a picture of this situation though, regardless of the Italian occupation and attempts of Catholicising, these poor farmers who were only twenty when the Americans left, converted tens of thousands of people and just became forces of cultural change, whether the new practice would be pronounced good or bad.

This clearly shows that it did not take even a decade for the Wolaita to share their learnings to their neighbouring ethnic groups than keeping it to themselves, as compared to the northern Ethiopians who fought to keep Judeo-Orthodox and Islam to themselves, while the west had to come to Africa to convert to Catholic and protestant while the Arabs came to preach Islam to the rest of Africa. Abyssinians of the time were exposed to all three major religion categories as early as the Israelis themselves, but they thought it was not to be shared, rather to be kept like in a zoo.

Yes, the arrival of the Americans to Wolaita made real difference in the way people lived, thought and did things. The culture was not only redressed, at some point, the people seemed to have liked the practices promoted by the missionaries to the level of taking it too far. History tells us that the earlier kingdom of Wolaita was established by a queen and that it used to be a woman-led society only until the spoils of war and bringing more women from other ethnicities incorporated in the then-Wolaita structures changed the status of women and their roles.

It also meant some harmful cultures were also adopted from the newly included tribes, among which was the way women are perceived. But now this has changed to its old state of seeing women as a blessing. I must say that women are treated far better than in most northern areas of the country, even better than the situation in Addis that is dominated by the same group. While this is true to a significant level, the newly adopted culture of Wolaita would mean, if a girl were born, she would be buried if the family wished to have a boy.

The logic of this was that the once architects of the entire society, the women, began to be perceived as burdens than any helpful creatures on the face of unending serial wars, conflicts and instabilities that demanded that every family would give a young man for a war, since war is a collective responsibility and that even the king has to assign a child like everyone else, and no one is spared from doing this unless they don't have a child, in which case the father would take a bigger responsibility to make it up.

From such practice of seeing women as weak members of the society, to the newly adopted, or rather re-adopted view of how women are looked at, mostly due to the protestant Christianity, the people already were questioning if this were something that respects the values of the Wolaita.

What I would want to highlight here is that it shows that cultural change is not necessarily a guaranteed good thing; cultural infusion into society and progress would mean to adopt bad practices as in killing girls, and when the right ones are prescribed, it signifies the re-advancement of lifting their status back to its place and seeing women as vital members of society.

I have learnt that the appetite for change and sincere progress still exists in Wolaita in the same way as when the Americans arrived in the area. I noticed this from the conversation I had with one of the executive committee members of the then Tigray's governing party some twelve months before the war broke out.

Well, the person confessed that all of them regretted that they did not help Hailemariam and that their practice towards the Wolaita was not just out of proportion in treating badly, it was what an adversary does than an ally. After a few sorry-s and we will make it up-s, which I would never trust nor give it a serious consideration of course, and that he was sure I went there for answers more than anything, we talked in a great detail about what went wrong. I was pressing more on the role of their dominant few just to hear him admit that Ethiopia became a mess due to his party, and after a lengthy conversation, he finally said it.

In today's Ethiopia, according to this man, to my astonishment, the Wolaita were presented as a force of change in the country. I then asked him a few questions.

"Do you see that many southerners and the elites are stuck in time?" I asked.

"Stuck as in?"

"That they are not seeing that the people are moving on," I explained.

He replied, "Yes. We see that."

"What do you think played a role in this?" I asked him.

"The fact that they are receptive of what they are taught," he answered.

I said, "You must have been proud then."

"Why?"

"Because you have succeeded."

"To be honest, Andualem, we never expected to be this effective on the Wolaita. The elites are just so good."

"What would other Ethiopians say?" I wondered.

"In the matter of Wolaita, forget about other Ethiopians. Let's talk more about the Wolaita."

I must admit that Ethiopian engineers, architects, topographers and interior designers frustrate me the most when I think of the urban situation in Ethiopia the incompetent and poorly educated politicians, whose flaws are super clear as compared, while most among the former groups are the 'best' and the 'brightest' to make it worse. If these are the best, and their product is a mess, I don't want to even think about what the average can make. Probably most city life is a nightmare in Ethiopia, due to this. And if you don't mind making your cities into dysfunctional camps, you fulfil the criteria for the 'top team competing to make a country poor.'

Addis Ababa, though it is a city of a yet-to-develop country, is not left without contacts that can transform it to something much better than it looks like this time around. The presence of the African Union, the European Union, the United Nations, None Governmental Organisations, faith-based organisations and general civil society organisations on one hand and international companies, embassies and representations of different offices shows that greatest proportion of those that come to the city for more than a month are knowledge-enriched, highly skilled, heavily invested on, and ready to engage type of family members that follow with them.

I am not implying organisations don't have their own policies, and the country would not have justifiable argument over some of the questions. Yes, there are a thousand other ways of doing this, but you start, perhaps, with available and affordable methods before getting it take the highway if I am right. This said, what Nairobi has learnt, and Addis Ababa has not yet begun, is using the wealthy resource that roams in its streets, visits its cafes and restaurant idler than being an engaged change maker.

Nairobi is one of coolest places in Africa, if not among the rest I have been to a few times, without any question. A place is the best sometimes because of a criterion its openness to allow me to visit without hurdles as for the visa issues to begin with. And to enter Nairobi, I do not need a visa. This said though, it is not free from few issues, but then, which city is without these? Starting with the very fact that you are greeted by curious and open-minded working class would just hint you that the village people have a lot of wisdom to share than to take in a real sense. The city of Nairobi may not be as safe as Addis, but Shegar is losing its grip of safety in recent years.

As for me, Nairobians are the learning type that would not be shy to share their skills; of course, if you pay upfront that is, but then I would pay extra than being kept in the dark from getting to know what is happening, relevant, must-to-know and must-to-do matters. The comparably much fluent and clear thinking of many Nairobians would just want you to bring a few Shagarians here for a good length of time to loosen up their mind, open up towards the world and have more space for learning.

The sense of international ambience you get at the bars and restaurants and other service areas would just wake your sense that this is exactly what you are missing in Addis Ababa. The connectivity, whether Internet or telephone and digital services are much better as compared, remembering the use of SMS to transfer money was invented here before the whole world followed suit. I am not sure how much Swedes paid the Kenyans to acquire similar technology we use here.

On the shady side of Nairobi though, the city presents itself with some sort of unspoken class and some way of subtle segregation where the Europeans are treated higher, the Indians seem to have secured a second place and the Kenyans as third-level ranking customers if you look around in some service areas. In Addis, you may get disappointed if you expected such secluded treatment that one enjoys in Uganda, Kenya or in similar places. Nairobi is also not yet owned by Kenyans for as much it is owned by foreigners as how it appears. Addis Ababa might be on its way of following Nairobi than keeping the leading on, but time shall be the arbiter. Yet Ethiopians do own significant portion of the country's economy, of course except for questions of proportionality and even distribution. I would not go all way in beyond this line.

On the part of orienting you about the country, assume that you lived in the country for over ten years, any time you meet a new person, they possibly tell you about one thing repeatedly, 'you know Ethiopia is not colonised by Italy'. Anytime people raise this topic, I am not sure if it is only me who feels this is the only thing we did in the span of almost a hundred years.

To me, this makes me notice that we either sound ignorant to assume the person as unaware, or that we assume someone before us has not mentioned about it at all. We all are here to lecture you about it until your last day you would leave the country, or even in your country.

Void of The Truth

"He who eats alone, dies alone"

After I came to Sweden, a little longer than a decade ago, I was sharing an apartment with this man from Sri Lanka who is a former member of

Tamil Tiger Guerrilla fighters. Two months down the line, he said, go back to your country."

I said I was not done with my studies and he had to chill.

He said, "You know what to do, you are capable, and you should just go back and do it. I would argue, and he would not listen even if I attempted a thousand times. He would still say go back.

In my heart, though, I wondered, *To where? We are freaking people in the country that do not know how to manage competent and creative people or be led by them. Do I have a place to go back to really?*

So where did it go wrong with the game of Meles? My father said it from the start! Yes, from the start. I re-quote former President of the United States, the eloquent Barak Obama where he said, "a politics that's based on ethnicity is doomed to tear a country apart. It is a failure — a failure of imagination."

As I said earlier, I agree with him to a greater length, especially in the American, European or other contexts. In Ethiopia, though, I saw a different reality in the same algorithm he argued about. In what he said, he sounded like my father when I was a little child. My father used to tell us that we need to get good education and that intellectual people would not think in ethnic lines.

I agree with my father too, but again to a greater length while the reality I have observed tells me that there is something more to it, intellectualism suppresses ethno-centric minds, and yes, ethnic politics is a lack of imagination, at the same time ethnic grouping is also a sign of loss of protection, and that when social contract or a constitution of a country as we know it fails while you are upholding it, you resort to organise in ethnic lines as your final line of defence. This is true at least in the present-day Ethiopia. It is not up to you to decide what goes around; it is up to those who managed to secure a complete state capture.

As a son of a farmer himself, it was an opening of his inner eyes to see the world, to be part of the then socialist-lenient political movement assuming that had now joined the global force acting for good.

The political life my father went through has taught me that his sacrifice of being demanded to drop from his college, recruitment to the army and returning with bullets in his bones, prison during question of structural justice, economic sabotage to keep him poor and social harassments happened for reasons.

These all signalled that when you are hit to your core, it is often because of your ethnicity — college; when they recruit you to the army — too smart to play around; imprisonment — uncompromising on common interest; and economic sabotage — he refused to accept clan arrangement of Meles' politics.

I may sound voicing conflicting ideas, but if we look closely, these are perspectives that demand us to understand the contexts, the beliefs, sacrifices and lifetime commitments of a man and his son believing in exactly the same thing but doing quite the opposite. I championed the idea of country-level politics and ended up establishing ethnic-based party; he fought country-level politics till this day except when he had to join local grievances due to structural justice for zonal demands.

Well, it is with this family reality I put about my father's assertion of 'the Weyane are Gabrovos of Africa' argument and my observation of what I thought were serious problems of Meles' algorithm of political economy for Ethiopia, the Horn of Africa and the rest of the world.

A former ambassador, and intimate comrade of Meles once implied in our discussion about post-Meles scenarios and said that he was assassinated and that his illness was human interference over his health. His own party was allegedly the cause for his death, according to her suspicion.

My father calls the Old Guards as Gabrovos of Africa and refers to the well-known Ethiopian proverb 'he who eats alone, dies alone'. He always said, their greed has no end and their lie does not have a human face. Their motives are wicked, and their souls are deeply corrupted. They don't have any humanity in them. The good of them is the worst of a wild beast and the most kind among them is like the sharp teeth of a midday snake.

I left back to the field work as an expatriate to Iraq, though I had an invitation or two, I refused to take part in a caged system whereby you are just HR tally in the payroll than doing anything meaningful except your face being needed to fill in gaps. Above all, you must show allegiance by hating the Amhara and many others. It did not stop there. You must hate a few people among those you grew up with. I have never allowed myself to be alternated or taken for granted either. I rather chose to stay out of the country at least during the refurbishments of the Old Guard power ranks.

I got a phone call; it was a usual voice and sounded urgent.

He said, "Hello, how are you today?"

I replied, "Am doing very well."

"I have something urgent," he then said.

I was like, "What is the matter?"

The woman refused to leave the palace.

I asked, "Is it Azeb?"

Azeb is the wife of the Late Meles.

"Yes" he said.

"What would you like me to do?" I asked.

He implied that I appear on the media.

Is that advisable? I asked. As I understood he was not safe. Meaning, the Prime Minister is not as safe either. In this case, my safety would be compromised severely.

He said, "Or leak it."

Two of my friends who studied here in Sweden went back with the euphoria of doing good and paying back to society. One of them joined the Clinton Initiative for Health Care after they made his life hell on earth while he was as the Ministry of Health, by then controlled in absolute monopoly of the Tegaru. The trick here is my friend is an outspoken person and is more of technical buddy than the wild political beast that could survive the jungle of lethal counterparts. In less than two years, they spiked and put him into a mental breakdown, and he eventually ended up in a psychiatric condition.

This was my second time realizing that sometimes neuropsychiatric conditions are not what are believed as true disorders more often than people can imagine. There are clandestine forces that use several triggers to force a person or a group into the hands of doctors whose training tells them that the person in their office is to be diagnosed more than a human that may have a story to tell, and that sometimes diagnosing everyone who comes to the clinics is wrong on its own. It is also due to such incidents that I took hours of learning how the security and psychiatric and psychology industry collaborate and at times cross professional lines for political reasons.

In a few advanced countries, the military is also involved in research and developing practices to ensure total control of a given population. It is serving as a population control tool to the least I can mention. I am not casting doubts on the professions, but I would do injustice if I would not mention the level of abuse by the very professions that were supposed to improve people's lives.

When this happened, Kamuzu Kassa, the famous Ethiopian music star, came and told me this in person so that I do something about it. This friend of ours messed up with me in an attempt of taking political advantage, though it was me who linked him with the files and ranks of the TPLF's power play, in a failed attempt of painting dark of my image and walking over my shoulders, and lately cornered himself. If I went to see him in this situation, it would not do him a favour, mentally speaking. I could not walk away either. I had to do something about it. I had to arrange and sit with the second friend of ours who studied with us in Sweden to take charge. This guy is a 'God sent' cool guy who would take it in and still be kind again.

Our friend was not polite to him either, but he had a better threshold of tolerance, obviously better suited than me. He took charge, parents were called, and relatives were summoned from Wolaita Sodo to assist him in his needs. Well, the guy became paranoid so that whenever he saw a car, he would jostle and say, "It is their car" or when he heard a car horn, he would cry out loud, "They are coming". He went totally dysfunctional for quite a long time. That was when I learnt that mental state is not necessarily a disease, at times it is a staged condition people are forced to walk into.

That was when I said to myself, "Serving or not serving this country, we suffer." I am not denying that personal characters do make it worse, yet, using the security apparatus to dislodge his intellectual competencies, made him lose himself and pushed him into the thorny patch of mental state, is obviously the fault of the system. Simply because, they are not angels themselves who had the audacity to be moral police, on top of ethnically targeting him. Worse, most of them had war trauma, intolerable military behaviour against civilian populations, exacerbated by their failure of getting rehabilitated and prior to integrating, they had the need for a process of getting 'converted back to a civil way of life' after the war was over.

To have a clarity on this matter, I sat with an intern who did her practice at St. Amanuel Psychiatric Hospital in Addis Ababa and I learnt the types of patients who are enlisted in the hospital. A number of them were diasporas whose dreams where shattered, ideas stolen money confiscated and are left with suffering. While others are political figures artists and people of prominences, there are regular people among whom the illness is not caused by harmful human interventions for most parts of it.

After few months, I travelled to Addis Ababa and met the Lady Ambassador there. She invited me to her home in Bole where we sat to discuss a few political matters. As I recall it was during a sunny day in August 2013, when the Ashenda festival was smelling up in the air of Addis Ababa, though it is highly celebrated in Tigray where this woman came from, and several areas of Amhara calling it Ashenda, Ashendiye, and Solel. She dropped a joke or two when she was at ease.

She said, "Andualem, make sure you don't date a Tegaru lady during Ashenda."

I gestured for an explanation and asked why.

She replied, "All ladies look pretty by then."

I asked, "Is that a problem?"

She said yes.

"What is the problem?" I asked.

She replied, "All the makeups and excessive focus for beauty means beautiful ones start to show up much more later for one. Even if the prettier ones are with them, the not-so-pretty ones will eventually show who they are, and you will regret it."

"So you are saying if I were to date Tegaru girl, I have to wait until the rainy season is over then?"

"You got the point."

Sure, the rainy season was getting very intense, strangely except the day I visited her place. But I was feeling the woman was not just telling me about the literal rain, apart from hinting that to access power and resources, I was to date a Tegaru girl, she also meant something deeper than that. She was forecasting that there would be a huge crisis to come and that I must be guarding whom I chose to spend my time with, as far as political matchmaking was concerned. I took a serious note out of this speech. She actually opened my eyes to see with better clarity.

The Ethiopian Truth

The Old Guards could not figure out the secret that was hiding in plain sight. I believe that two things clouded their judgements. The first one was heavy reliance on the data they had than getting more curious with the idea that there may be something more to learn. The second one, also tied to the first, was that because they were not paying attention to their surroundings, they fell to the level of not feeling almost anything in the end. The Ethiopian concept of mutually assured destruction in that you may not team up and cooperate, but you would eat together. Even enemies may somehow be forced to sit and eat together in some instances.

As many of the evil forces use food poisoning, spiking drinks and arranging for toxics to get into the body, the best way to manage in the local concept is that if I die, we die together. If you live, I too must live. But the funny thing is that no one says it out loud, but in practice this is what it is. Collective form of safety from the unknown threat, while it is covered by the 'eating together' is to show 'love and togetherness' as it can be said. We do not say it, we just do it. Most of us even do not know its truest purpose.

At times, in a society that has wax and gold, you may have to scratch deeper to actually get to the real meaning of why people are doing what they do. This is also one of the methods of hiding the gold in a plain sight and call it '*sem ena werq*' or wax and gold. If you know the wax, the gold is in it, not elsewhere.

Just look around, or closer or deeper. And imagine being overly consumed to the point that when you are given the gold covered with wax, you fall for the wax and forget that there is gold. The Old Guards did not only fall for the wax, they fell on it too. And getting up and walking again was so slippery they had no idea they were getting washed away.

Because, just as a computer is slow and weak to process data once it is hit by data overload, the mind of the Old Guards and their players was so crowded to the point that they could not see during daylight and feel anything when millions of stimulations were taking place. Overwhelming with excess information and poking makes anyone weak and slow to process, to a point of dysfunctionality. No one is more powerful than a determined few that can line up millions behind them for a true cause.

While they were eating with their enemies, they did not even notice that much was going underneath the smiles and overly respectful gestures they get every day.

The aspiration for dominating the public life, controlling the resources and seeking a deciding role over the fate of individuals and groups in Ethiopia, serves as a generational source of contention between the Tegaru and Amhara. On an average, war has taken place every quarter of a century for the contest of alternating state capture. These two groups have an assumption that the rest of the people would not be enlightened enough to figure it out for themselves, and that they would fall for their religious, historical and contemporary prescriptions of life geared towards serving their interests. If one wants to understand why Ethiopians are poor, the lens has to focus its sharpest pixels here.

Simply put, there used to be two routes to international legitimacy. First it begins in Jerusalem, passes through Cairo-Alexandria- comes to Axum and stations in Addis Ababa. This is the historical and religious pipe.

Second, the plot begins in Gondar, comes to Addis Ababa, goes to Jerusalem (and at times reaches out to Moscow, Greece or even Syria) and comes back to Addis Ababa. The first trail is political Ethiopian vein. This second one is ethnic (that includes Ethiopian Jews) and interchanges depending on the need, meaning, it becomes religious, historical and political both national and international.

The Gondar Amhara also have the links directly to Jerusalem. This is plausibly the truest explanation of elites form both the Tegaru and the Amhara claiming their Jewish link as their gateway for legitimacy in the state control and religious dominance and tracing it back to Jerusalem.

Needless to say, the Ethiopian state building has been left for the northern groups as history is my witness.

Furthermore, one can study how King Yohannes bought a plot in Jerusalem, which is serving as an Ethiopian monastery in Israel, why the Egyptians had to break a fight on one of the monasteries frequented by Ethiopians, and what it means to these two groups (not necessarily every Ethiopian) in terms of international relations and ecumenical ties to the western world.

Perhaps this is where my friend said that God is Amhara and where Dhugasa said that Christianity is not for Oromo nor is it for Wolaita. Again, if there is any secrecy at the state level, which is accessed only by the northern brothers and sisters, and their contest for its dominance spills over to the rest of the country, costing lives and wealth, and that every few decades all has to be undone; then people have to make up their minds as to whether they want to see the very definition of what it is to be Ethiopian, whether its fundamentals shall remain intact or if this generation has to design its own idea of Ethiopian identity and co-existence in its own terms instead of allowing it to be shaped by unending wars that they must pay for.

Clearly the Ethiopian identity that was founded in secret, having its basements in monasteries in Jerusalem, is unfortunately related to wars, poverty, injustice, and social unrest. Perhaps the new Ethiopia must be founded with all its transparency tools such as laws and agreed social contracts, all laid down in Addis Ababa alone.

Obviously, this is what makes the mainstream celebrated version of the Ethiopian Truth a circle with no way out. Meaning, perhaps truth means an illusion in Ethiopia and fact means what you want to tell people than anything measurable with any little sense of objectivity. This would then mean truth does not exist. What exists in its place is then that the ethnic preference, and the will of those in the ethnic groups, meaning you have to accept what you are told as a truth, and worse never question it. This becomes the Ethiopian Truth, it is now crowned by Cairo and blessed by Jerusalem and legitimised by the West.

I personally don't think that God has anything to do with this. I do not think that what people with state capture aspirations believe as 'Ethiopiawinet' as in Ethiopian-ness is what Ethiopians believe as their collective identity. Perhaps that is also why there has never been a consensus in Ethiopia in strategic matters of such significance. The question is whether citizens should still believe in the Ethiopia that has to attach itself with Cairo, Jerusalem and the entire west to feel whole. This goes against the very Ethiopia people who speak about a none-colonized, independent nation and so on.

Gondarians are now on the frontline to what the state players have devised as a powerhouse central to the pro-Russian players dressed up with the pro-west mask. This cost the Amhara during the time of the Old Guards, and now with the algorithm to set them up as the blame to the future crisis, that is inevitable regardless how many would want to believe. In this sense then, in its overall appearance, exploring the Ethiopian truth means then circling around and around then circling around again. Where it brushes itself with Gondar, the heart of it is in Shoa and the brain stays in Jerusalem.

With all this going on, China is the silent guru that knows the way around, is the best in test and keeps lowkey unless excessively provoked. What the Chinese accumulated as the skills bank of operational precision to adapt the circling around, means that the USA-West pair shall get enlightened more than its attempt to do so to those who created the 'circle-around' context as engineers of the state reality. China has its issues too, but then it seems that buying the Chinees risk is paying off than its counter parts. It is up to the USA-West pair to outcompete, or even better, enter game of equals, with the Chinese or even Russia.

In my personal debate with my leadership professor, when we met in Uganda, he was complaining saying that Europe had at least 50 years of modern time partnership with Africa, and Chinese interference hurt it. I told him, the Chinese pay us better, the west can pay even more and see what happens after that. Smarties, it is the economy!

Aggrieved Famers

Hurting Oromo farmers means a fire that once you set just captures the rest of the country very easily; over eighty-five per cent of Oromos are farmers and any grievances around Addis Ababa means social unrest in other cities. All you need to do is call for strike and do a great job in mobilisation and the rest plays out on its own. As a mobiliser, Jawar Mohammed did just that.

Previous practice of the land acquisition for building houses, apartment or malls and service centres is in a very informal price arrangement and traditional dealership where the buyer and the farmers would have a negotiation possibility through brokers. In this, the problem with brokers is that most are not educated and that the way the land is sold does not fit any practice of financial, legal, city plan and smart handling except that it is oiled and enhanced for a much smoother process.

The farmers were better off and that the buyers also did not have the financial intelligence blockage as some were blacklisted later. It was helpful to avoid setbacks by the previous system's intelligence that tends to sniff around and stop unwanted buyers very easily. The new land policy looked elegant from the outset, at least if there was a proper legal system, regulation and human capital to handle it in a way that favours the city, the farmers and the buyers.

It also looked like theft and illegal trade as well as hastened land grabbing would be monitored and stopped. That is, all the papers presented, and politicians tried to defend. For one, can you trust papers (policies and operational manuals) and politicians, and then can you trust institutions and the human capital at the civil service that are handling cases? A hard question, with obvious answer.

What the reality presented was that instead of the city being the facilitator of the processes of land acquisition, it was all Old Guard's newly blessed brokers either from among Tegaru or their proxies from Oromia that took the place of the brokers in the market.

It also happened that the middle players are either officers in the city administration or their family members, making it appear like the government is the broker and law enforcer while the farmers and buyers started to face undue challenges. It did not stop there; some brokers would assemble their family members and take empty land lots for nearly a piece of penny and became millionaires overnight evicting farmers in the name of development and following the new city masterplan.

In this arrangement, the traditional brokers were out of job, making it hard for farmers to get any chance of trying out alternative buyers. This meant, the government has just collected its lethal enemies in one track and gave them a free ride. To my shock, its key informants that amassed all its big benefits were not even listening to its cancer growing into inevitably terminal malignancy.

When the farmers go for complaints, it is the family members of the 'new brokers' that handle the cases, and when they turn to higher government offices, they face their proxies on the tables, that the farmers and politicians who plotted this through prime minister's office have become invisible forces that are gradually bonding around common and crucial social, economic and political grievance.

In short, the land policy served as a double sword cutting through barriers of bringing the farmers and all Oromia opposition and civil servants and political actors together and that it was high time to then start plotting a season to take down the government. Added to the Amhara outcries, the overall dissatisfaction at the country level, disgruntled USA over Ethiopia's affairs with China and losing its grip in the entire Africa, fuelled by the EU migraine of losing its century-old dominance over Africa and Prime Minister Hailemariam's mood of getting fed up with their obsession to control the security apparatus, the fight between The previous system and the then Army Security Chief General Samora Yenus, and excessive thirst of power and Old Guards also having unquenching appetite for money embezzlement using Metek — wanting it all for themselves at the Sugar Corporation — exacerbated by Egypt's anger due to GERD (Great Ethiopian Renaissance Dam or later called as Millennium Dam) negotiations, Ethiopia was already cracked into pieces, that majority woke up much later once the masterplan issue fuelled uprisings in cities after cities and finally the Irreecha massacre that claimed the lives of young women and men, and shocked the entire country to wake up to a reality that the government was about to go.

One day I checked out of Bole International Airport, on my transit and was sitting with a friend of mine, a young man with Eritrean origin who grew up in Tigray. Hagos, a family member of mine, and I sat at a fast-food restaurant in Addis Ababa, Bole area.

In this regular day in 2016, I returned from another field work and was on my way back to Sweden, and just during the transit, I wanted to go out of the Bole International Airport and visit Addis Ababa city to meet with friends, have a lunch and board the plane again sometime later. It does not hurt to eat some injera or even a good slice of pizza, enjoy some fresh macchiato with a friend, and dark black coffee with family before checking in again, I used to do this as my pills to sooth whenever I missed Ethiopia.

We were talking about light issues, a bit of certain religious books, then obviously politics. In our discussion, we mentioned about the ongoing uprisings in almost thirty-seven townships and cities all at once that the government security personnel were totally drained, and that Addis Ababa was almost empty. He was happy that it is getting better and that the reports of the last two days show that things are getting much calmer from the way they were.

I asked them a question, rather I aimed it at Hagos. I said, "Have you ever thought why the Axum empire collapsed?" and both the gentlemen looked at each other.

Then we all went silent, as this became the moment of truth and a time of deep soul searching. It was unexpected, but a very unusual question that needed real reflection before uttering a word. It was also clear to realise what I was trying to say, but more importantly why I was saying without saying. One thing you like about young leaders like Hagos, at least many of whom I sat with, they have a common trait, they listen well, speak well and ask questions when a question is heavy and has no short answer.

I told them that I wished that I would read not just the history books, but the events and the underlying causes of state collapse that happened in the world, particularly in Ethiopia and especially something that explains what made the Axum empire crumble into pieces and be a forgotten kingdom apart from having obelisk, Axum city, churches, history and some fables left behind.

"Why is that?" said Hagos.

My answer was that I have two reasons; one is understanding if my anticipation of the recent processes as indicative of the soon realisation of the demise of the Old Guards but also to see if there is clear empirical resemblance between the two empires. He said, "But is Tigray an empire?" and my answer was both yes and no.

If we looked at the structure and its status before the international equivalents, the answer may seem to be a 'no'. But if we look at the landmass size that it is influencing today, the political leverage it has and the security and economic muscle it can flex, literally it is an empire in East Africa whose influence extends all the way to Yemen but adds Kenya, South Sudan, Sudan, Eritrea, Djibouti, Somalia and partially Egypt. I am not a political scientist per se, but if a sub-state has this level of significance and direct strategic partnerships with the likes of the USA, EU, Russia, China, Japan, the UK, India and the rest of Africa, what would you call other than an empire. It is shy to call itself, either to become so once it may secure independence or disappear trying to do so.

He then asked me, "Do you think it will disappear?" and I asked him back, "How do you understand what I say?"

He responded, "You are saying this government will fall."

I said yes.

"Oh my God!" he exclaimed.

I elaborated my argument, tried to make my case and proposed that someone shall write a book and I want to have a good read with a macchiato on my table. I want to know the backdoor games and identify key players of it. He was sweaty on his face, was super uncomfortable and his view was that I needed to pray so that the government would continue to function and that the peace and life would return back to normal. I said no. I think it is foolishness to pray about something that you know is going to be broken into pieces, I would rather pray and work hard so that the impact of this would not hurt the masses, or is minimised, and that it would be a bearable and peaceful process.

One thing that makes me uncomfortable to talk to faith leaders about, for as much as I booked such moments in my own initiative, is not just that I can talk about hard topics, it is just that it is very difficult to show them that something destined to failure is not worth a prayer and that our efforts shall be on managing and limiting the damages this may incur and that civilians would not be affected very significantly, though zero effect on people is not realistic. Most would insist for prayers and meditation, this gives me a headache. Now look, you sit with a leader you pictured would cause a collapse of the government, and he tells you to pray so that the police have better skills to stabilise and that God gives the political leaders the wisdom to handle the situation and restore peace, what do you make of this? It is terribly annoying.

What I wished was that he would call all the faith leaders within his circle and guide people so that they don't hurt each other and that if it is time for the government to go, they would make sure that the crisis would not come close to regular citizens apart from being managed at the government circles, if worse in their close networks than going down to the law-abiding mass. It really is very hard to even open up knowing this. Then not getting the message across, even if all the link was within a reach, frustrates the hell out of me to know it is unresponsive in due time.

Our conversation with the gentlemen went well, except its intensity and my frustration that the discussion was not meant for a table and that it was a timely message for all that were concerned. The thought of this just suffocates my chest. I am not blaming this young leader, but just that my country was going to go through hell, young people were to perish from Moyale to Mekele, from Harar to Gambela; even at my hometown, my Wolaita people were to go through a designed and deliberately executed collective trauma, that a person was to be burned alive, the skin was to be peeled off, eyes were to be scratched out, limbs chopped, and homes burnt, farms set on fire, factories destroyed, women raped, pregnant were forced to give birth on zebra crosses and hundreds of bullets rained on a single man, and while this was told to people in time who ignored and did not act on time, this would just mean we failed as a collective. Solving the political issues on the political tables and accomplishing this without bloodshed were why one had to know it in advance. It just sickens me to the core of my stomach and makes my heartbeat go slower every time I think of it.

In an honest reflection, I see grievances when I see atrocities, not just of the victims but also the perpetrators. During such instances, the reasons become people instead of wrongful policies, actions and sustained injustice. I am not defending and justifying atrocities, not do I imply its continuation, not at all. But just the fact that a sane human being is not capable of hurting another fellow human unless the core of their humanity is broken by prior lengthy and inhumane treatments and perfervid repression to the point that they would not bear life without taking away the reason for it. At this point, anyone who commits this is as wild as animals, void of human reasoning and full of beastly appearance without any droplet of humanity left.

I know the feeling myself, after all the good work we tried to calm the situation, reconciling the Wolaita and Oromo and worked on people-to-people relations and so much individual and group attempts wobbled and that the government became more hostile for every good we tried to do. I would not forgive myself for even expressing on talks, and never carried through as peace is more powerful tool than violence in the world where peace is valued. The question of hurting the mass is not inscribed in the playbook of my people. We do it differently, but time and again Ethiopia as a state not just tested our limits, but also tried to overpower having the international players on its side. Therefore, it really breaks the core of humanity as we know it as this means shoved off on diplomatic tables, dashed out by journalists' note, unread emails by international lobbyists and taken as a piece of joke for perpetrators before all forget we exist in about a second. It is denial of our existence and utter cruelty to every person whose limbs were chopped or whose child had to be born on the street.

Standing at this point, what is human rights, or women's rights, minority voice or the NGO terminology jargon in a true sense? After all, what is humanity and what is to be civilised? And to fellow Ethiopians, without mentioning the internationals, did anyone deserve that we hid all other ethnicities from getting killed even by potential unnoticed infiltrators? This would mean my people would be like everyone else, playing by their books than our own that hid over two hundred priests of the Orthodox Church that came for sanctuary, escaping death from many cities during Haile Selassie's fleeing to England until the Ethio-Italian war was over and that his majesty would be reinstated to power again.

It was also true that the state cruelty became even harsher, even if other areas that killed, looted and burned were left alone, the Wolaita had the burdens increased up on them. Ethiopia has been so cruel to my people regardless of the mercy we display or the empathy we show.

Peace is becoming traded on and played with by world global powers, power brokers, journalists and policy thinktanks. Why this pains most is that among the perceived minority, people like the Wolaita become collateral in the process where no audits are done, and all global powers get away with it, without even a scratch. Because the Wolaita are not listed among the people group they would want to care about. The world fails to recognise the Wolaita exist, what if it is returned in kind? Who is to blame? Who is the sinner and who is righteous in this world where the sinners are the winner?

Sure, all hundred and ten million people went through hell. The world must wake up and realise that it is just a little better far away from the primitive way of treating each other, except that I have the privilege to write on a laptop and people can access this on their fingertips.

It is clear that the global community created inflated self-perception to justify such incidents with one way or another and shifting the blame instead of exploring the way of ending such collective madness that needs a cure. The collective madness to just change government, a known future back then, hurt the foundation of our communities, and the farmers were hit the hardest.

When incidents affect so deeply that their impact will be prolonged, most likely this means that the act is committed with a planned and thoroughly analysed mission statement. Such mission is normally calculated having the deep-rooted feeling of hate and revenge intending to break the backbone of a community. The hurt is still aching as the wounds are fresh and they are preparing for even more.

All previously mentioned horror happening to people of Wolaita means a crushed spirit, destroyed morale and losing the strength of getting things together as the political hit was collective at the scale of a war about two years before the formal war was declared. At this point, it became very clear that this needed a systematic response.

Fast forward, the party was established, people who were expected to stay around and develop the organisation were elected, and I sought through the whole process. A major event took place that made the whole country go shaking. We staged a rally with 1.5 million people, women and men, mostly youth-led, very peaceful to the point people gathered at 06:00 in the morning and at 10:00, everyone was back to business.

What made the rally powerful was that we have over forty thousand soldiers fired from the army recently. This was without accounting for about thirty-one thousand more who were fired distantly and were working as farmers, security guards and so on who were rather stable.

Again, this was also by skipping the more seniors that participated in the wars during the Dergue regime and were supposed to abstain from conflicts.

These are said to be about forty thousand able combatants, while there are reserves of over 31,000 Dergue era and earlier soldiers during the former regime. We then have over 30,000 militias and police force retirees. All of these make a hundred and one thousand soldiers trained, tested and prevailed. The active and recent combatants were selected and forty thousand were in lines of different ranks; from special forces, commandos and republican guards, brigadier generals, colonels of sorts to regular soldiers with their green uniform made the country go mad.

Three top leaders of the country started immediate meetings at a sofa of one of them, as they contemplated that if they have forty-thousand soldiers ready on one spot, then what is to be next? Some people said that it was for retaliation while others feared a potential state capture. The people on the other hand, wanted their rights respected and intended to send an open message that any plan of ethnically targeted attack on the Wolaita people would have organized response.

It was a true moment of solidarity, showing off collective strength. We went quiet not because we did not know how to retaliate at a mass scale, we just respected the constitution, the laws of the land and above all else, our people live upholding the core of humanity. Well, to me, this is what the United Nations Charter declared on its humanitarian imperative. But hey, we don't exist until we exist, so for now it is us.

After a while, I came to Addis, and the ruling group did not take time to have a plan to dismember this united front we created together with my friends and concerned ones. This would mean every inch of my moves were measured, and for once I was to be kept away from any financial source, my personal work was to be shut down and any chance they had they would send hustlers who would drain my money, even at government offices. Some hotels started to charge me more, not all but a few restaurants started having attitudes. I started to sense that I am an enemy to some people that I do not consider as my enemy.

But then, high-level politicians, influencers, journalists and lobbyists were all supportive and that I felt they took me more seriously than I wanted to. I am a passer-by until my people say your job is done, and we have someone who can replace you or until I say so. As participation in social movements came almost five years ahead of my plan means, my life is altered and that this would bring serious strain in my personal freedom.

New Players

On a beautiful day in Albufeira, a resort city of Portugal, I sat with Clinton's advisor for what turned out to be a very lengthy chat. After listening to my stories, he asked me one question with a straight shot. It was about how good my communication with the Ethiopian top officials was. He said, for the brain capacity you have, that is the kind of support you need to realize your dreams. Since there is change in the political climate, I would find out about my odds of being able to work in Ethiopia sooner than I anticipated.

On my return to Addis Ababa, I sat with Hailemariam once again, this time talking about the worrying situations regarding the stability of the country, the mistakes of the leadership and possible ways things could get better. It was on a good weekend, we had a lengthy time to socialise and had those moments to ask real questions and have real conversations. It also gave me the chance to know who my true enemy had been and why no one including myself had done anything about it apart from seeking the answers. I hinted this to him.

Hailemariam said, "I am sure you would want to know the answers to your personal challenges."

I replied, "I would be glad."

"It is only now that I have realised you were personally persecuted, even recently."

"I have survived."

"Sure. I know it has been too much on you."

"What can I do other than taking it as part of my story?" I said.

"You have outlived your challengers," he said.

"Who are we talking about?" I asked.

"You know what I am talking about."

"Who is behind forcefully shutting my humanitarian organization and sending me to exile?"

I was thinking that he may say as if he did it, but it is clear now that it was Meles who wanted to squeeze the civil society organizations."

"How about you?"

"By then, we all agreed to it."

I asked, "What was your role?"

He answered, "I was overseeing the policy we generated for the action."

He was noticing me that I was wrestling with questions raining over my head.

"Do you regret?" I asked.

Without even saying it, he saw it on my face as I took a good stare at him. He replied, "We learnt later that it was not good for everyone."

"Many people, organisations and the progress of the country was impacted negatively," I stated.

He nodded. "Yes."

"It is both a time lost, and an opportunity missed."

"It is unfortunate," he said.

"What was Getachew's role in this?"

"Getachew Reda?"

"No, the other guy."

"He oversaw all our operations."

"To what end?" I asked.

"To the level where the country came to its knees" he replied.

I was wrestling with what I could make of this conversation, and whether my thought was right as I was listing names of higher officials that should have been behind bars and to follow their cases in the military court, not just in the civil arena. I for once thought that several individuals had outlived their purpose on earth and having them on this planet is an injustice to human existence. I was not even feeling that I was judging, I had this level of clarity with how things should have been managed. People cannot, rather should not, just toy with the lives of millions and then want to walk away from it just like that. And some wanting to come back to do more of it.

By the time Hailemariam was telling me this, what distressed me was that the national treasury had tens of billions of USD trade deficit, which is worse by now, and worse, the Ethiopian Airlines was about to be taken over by the Chinese in exactly the same way as they had seized the Zambian airport and similar state infrastructures for debt defaults. African leaders must be transparent to their people about what collaterals they give out to China in their sweetened debts secured. The valuations and price setting of payment structures must also be studied and determined by experts against the secretive method of doing business with China.

At that point, the Ethiopia did not only default on its debts, political functions, and security control but also shown deterioration in its capability of overseeing the daily lives of its citizens. Such depth in the crisis was caused by the greed and thirst for power throughout the two decades before Hailemariam came to the scene of premiership. Anyone could see that he was to take the blame for the misdoings of others if he did not play it safe for himself and for the country. It was so obvious that the country needed a change.

I started thinking, who is even there to be held accountable for all my sufferings and those of millions? Sure, I understand that it was the repressive and unforgiving system that is to blame not individual actors in this regard. Yet, all the money I lost, I was tortured and went through hell and I have no one to point a finger at. Such a place where helplessly people are conditioned and have just been effective in hurting each other and the lives of millions.

Members of the previous leadership made several fatal mistakes and were auditing it themselves to realise that they had been ruining lives for no gain. In the end, what is the meaning of all this senseless cruelty and the bad will towards aspirants and people who just wanted to be change makers and regulars that would live their lives like everyone else? How many more must suffer for this to stop? Should people react in aggression and retaliate or shall they just 'forgive them' and continue to suffer if the perpetrators are not quitting their madness? My mind was pouring questions after questions, it is just that I would not allow it to limit my time with the prime minister. Because at this very moment, what worried me more was the future than what had happened in the past.

About the past; people were hurt in Holozo, and this was something that couldn't be changed, for a peaceful co-existence it had to be mended. It should never give the impression that people can get away with their misdoings, especially when they blame the incumbent system which is a road that takes nowhere, that creates a vacuum, in contrast to their hurtful approach, those who have suffered are real people that need real answers.

I concluded that if a system is hostile to me, I will deny its existence as it does mine. As this affects millions every day, there must be a way around this to avoid what had happened in the past because of a glitch in the system.

I believe that people who are harmed systematically must either override or create a parallel system of their own where they can live their lives just like everyone else, or even thrive if they have the appetite for it. No system should escape accountability and from being held responsible for what people do against others. At least there must be a way to put the perpetrators on check.

I have also realized that systems have hurt notably intelligent individuals who I have encountered in Ethiopia, Sweden, the USA and a few other countries.

In this sense what everyone blames the system is actually a collective body of a bunch of people, sets of documents, prescribed practices, skillsets and competencies. In all this people are the most important part of the spinning body, not some lifeless machine. People stand as manipulators rather than the other way around, at least for the most part of it. Knowing that it is people who harm each other and conceal it by using the system as their excuse, or rather accountability-proof, is a heinous crime.

No system is neat, I get it, but why be cruel and kill someone for only wanting to do good? This is difficult for my mind to comprehend or make any sense out of it. Not because it is too sophisticated for my understanding, it is just that people use the system as a vehicle to decide the fate of others, and in this the system is a helpless machine which is not able to think on its own, yet, as it depends on people, who have bias, jealousy, hate, flaws, prejudices and issues with competencies. Some of these people made it through political, social, ethnic, religious or other enhancers or just by being in the cue ahead of the rest.

I also realized that almost any individual who has noticed gaps in their systems either hate it, or even worse, curse it occasionally. But they carry on with their lives just like they do every day. For those who attempt to break the cycle of a subdued life, the most effective way is to withstand and overcome a repressive system by disregarding its vocabulary and its language all together.

You don't take their perception of good and bad. Their sought-after best character must be savagery in your language. The worst people they think must be the best type you are looking for. Do not fall for their values either, and never apply their perception metrics or any scale of personality measurements that are in use. Their standards are outdated, and their sense of quality is a mess.

You will start to see people as a mass of voluntarily enslaved souls who are feeding the beast or are oiling the machinery wilfully. You will meet engineers, doctors, teachers, nurses, chefs, technicians and carpenters all in the same boat perceiving the same treatment but with different mindset. They all went to universities, colleges or had personal skills training through family culture but have missed this point all along.

Remove yourself from their rhythm prescribed for your daily activities. For instance, in almost every city, people wake up, do exercise take a shower, eat breakfast and head for work between 5:30 and 8:00, and eat lunch at 11:30—13:00, work until 16:30—17:30, drive home between 16:30 and 19:00, and repeat this the next day. Simply put, they wake up, wash, eat, travel, train, sleep, make love and wake up at the same time. Humans become rhythmically synchronized animals. The only difference is that they live in big cities, speak several languages and are paid in currencies. This is horrible.

In every major city, most streets are clear between 5:00 to 6:30, 09:00 to 11:30 and 13:00 to16:00, and after 20:00 in the evening. It appears that even people who move around during these hours decrease the traffic congestion, obviously useful to the climate, are somehow attached to planning their activities within the time range with the rest of the masses.

You must break away from this collective beat, and create your own music, compose a new song. Get a new job, or a source of income totally different from the normal working hours. If you must, do a business, get into coaching, newly emerging jobs, content creation or anything that can enhance this. Once you put this on autopilot for a year, look how much your life has changed and the level of freedom you start to experience.

When you feel that you oversee your freedom, you will realize that you are truly at your best self, potent to overcome any challenge, and thrive like a soaring eagle.

At this point, you have reached a level of total detachment from the regular masses, or rather a mob. Talk to your soul if you want to return to normal, where you are a tally, a code, a case, or a subject; the choice is yours.

I said, "The government has passed on its power and transferred it to the new actors who seem to be doing their job so far, not without gaps though. I am worried about what will happen with the Old Guard issues."

He said, "What Old Guards?"

I said, "You know what I mean."

He replied in Wolaitic, "*Salawu hola shin etawu attumateta oyiqidi mirqichogeta!*" Meaning, 'we already have got their balls'

I was frozen.

He was silent.

We both looked at each other, he added a Wolaitan expression tone '*a-a*' and we both burst into laughter.

This sounded like what Mr Tekleweld reflected about the war the previous dictators engaged against the rest of the country, and he said, *"Hega malaba, kutiya para qakawusu ges Wolaiti,"* — meaning, in such circumstances, the Wolaita would say 'a chicken kicks a horse'.

About a year earlier than this, also after the massacre that took place in Hawassa, and devastating experiences during the transition, the Wolaita came up with a thought that we need to have our own region to ensure dignity and respect. The regional statehood quest was enflamed so that the whole country heard of us. The rally we arranged with 1.5 million people also had this as its major theme of questions.

The government may have a stand, but it was not impossible to get to the statehood achievement. It was by this time that Getachew sent someone to me. The person said to be on a visit in Addis and would want to have lunch with me. We sat and raised many issues among which the situation of the minorities was, how the new administration was handling and what must be done to fix the issues. Then came unexpected suggestion as half a question and half a statement.

The person said, "I was wondering if you would like me to book you a time with the man."

I asked, "Which man are we talking about? Not the PM's guy, I presume."

The person replied, "No."

"Who is it?" I asked.

"It is only one person left whom you have not reached out to."

"Is it a good idea?"

"It is up to you," the person said.

I was rushing for clues of the intent to meet this man, at this phase of the leadership collapse. Why me, why now and to what end?

The person asked, "What are your thoughts?"

"Well it does not feel like the right thing to do."

"Why is that?"

"Things have changed. And it is both late and a bit silly to assume that I would want to sit with him. Don't you think so?"

The person said, "It is up to you."

"Getachew had decades to reach me out. His good days are over as you know. Thanks for your attempt, but there is nothing in it for me," I told him.

"How about the people?" he asked.

"People know what it means to partner with him," I replied.

"What if they ask you to?" the person then asked.

"If Hailemariam's making it to the rank of prime ministerial post was not beneficial, given the circumstances, what else can he propose beyond this in Ethiopia?"

The person said, "It is up to your imagination."

"I run out of imagination, sorry."

"I know you don't."

"Has it occurred to you that I was targeted all my life and was subjected to immense pain?" I asked.

The person answered, "There can be a way to make it up to you."

"It cannot bring what is lost, I am sure you would agree."

"You know what this means."

"What would that be?"

"They will retaliate for your rejection."

I replied, "I will take my chances."

"You may get locked out of this system too." "You mean the new players would also reject me taking my refusal to Getachew's proposal as their justification."

The person responded, "Sure."

"The question would be who rejects who," I said to the person.

The person asked, "You mean that?"

"Yes."

"Isn't this why they want to get back to you."

"Why?"

"They seem equally determined as you are," said the person.

"In what way?" I asked.

"By not taking no for an answer."

"Do they assume a will is thrown out just like that?"

The person replied, "They own pretty much everyone's will."

I am aware of this, I said.

The person said, "Isn't this what you will be cornered into, and be left out to dry from both sides?"

"My decision about not partnering with Getachew is not based on the treatment of the new players, it is based on the merits of him independently."

"You seem to have made up your mind long ago," the person noted.

"What did you expect?" I asked.

"I assumed you may give it a chance."

"Too little too late for this, don't you think?" I said.

"Most Wolaita people are persecuted and there is a need for help."

I replied, "We may have to explore other options to handle this."

The person took his fork, inserted it on the chicken leg, sliced it and sat quietly thinking.

Old Rules

When the army entered Wolaita en mass in 2020, and started killing a total of reported number of 36 people, with a pregnant woman and a child, also seeing their friends, families and loved ones were not even touched while the Wolaita were being killed, all other ethnicities questioned the judgement of the prime minister, his cabinet and the army in the decisions they made in this case. They were roasted and repeatedly grilled. I was getting calls from the US, Europe, South Africa, China, even as far as Japan and Australia, people were on our side.

This is because I was campaigning to encourage our youth to continue peaceful protest, and refrain from attacking or disrespecting the army. The youth obeyed and we managed to disarm the army.

Once the violence subsided, and all activists and politicians were thrown in jail, I was almost the only one who was among them in the fields and is now voicing out for the cause. Of course, there were a few people, but for some reasons they were not quiet.

We took lessons from the experiences of our seniors. These are that people who betrayed the Wolaita people's cause. They worked for the previous system and its network, and choosing to work being their own matter, they wanted me and a few well-meaning people to take their fall. I took this not just as an act of cowardice and betrayal, but also utter failure and absence of humanity. If they are trained in London, Moscow, Tel Aviv, and several other cities I am astonished by the idea of people not asking themselves if they are not supposed to outperform their compatriots, for their countries are self-sustain to the point that they could share to our country from their excess. And Ethiopia needs a lot of work to compensate and narrow the gaps.

Here I am discounting calling the boss, do I need to mention though? These guys were astounded by the buildings, the beautiful ladies and the functionalities of their societies and brought with themselves toys of electronics they apply to ruin lives than enhancing the experiences of their citizens.

There must be a gap in the logic these countries are founded on and the one Ethiopia is established at. And these were supposed to narrow the gap, not choke individuals with the trained hands and in the end shoot on their own feet. Among well-intentioned, great multitudes of their kind, such lame ducks are a waste of resources, it is also lack of competence on the side of decision making.

For such people, we have a term in Wolaita called 'Basha' meaning several of the maize happen to grow empty when they are supposed to carry their buds. These are cut and thrown for the cattle or chopped and put back in the field as fertilizers. My frustration came from the fact that all the seniors and the youth, most of whom had cheap suits from boutiques in Addis Ababa, were sitting like stiff statues and spoke with this intellectualism, but the prime minister sitting on the stage had climbed this ladder through serial riots, killings, wounding, burning factories and manoeuvring some of the darkest state capture projects ever seen in recent years that the protocol and measured speech were obviously boring to him which people were not either changing or making him change his view, or at least draw him an inch closer. No, they would not.

I on this side was burning and wished that this meeting would never have happened and that the key decision makers and selected few individuals would have sat and had an honest discussion as for why he would not accept on his side, why they were rigidly making clear that they would not back off. I would call this a negotiation. But all that happened to me was both sides played it difficult to create this possibility and are now on official deadlock trying to prove to each other. I was aware that some seniors wanted the deadlock for their personal gain by appearing as a saviour in the last minute. I realised that many of our new politicians were being played at, to engage in conflict with the prime minister and make it hard to penetrate the South and were clearly being set up for a disaster. It had become clear now that a war between the army and the youth in Wolaita was inevitable. What I was not sure about was whether it would be select individuals or if it was collective destruction they wanted. And knowing about this would mean selecting the effective strategy to minimise the impact. For as much this may sound more like simple political trickery, the upcoming conflict was both internal and global as many foreign actors had a stake in it.

In their turns, the players that are acting as the faces of the interface between the present and former southern intelligence have also had their own inspiration as to how the change of the government should play out on individual's lives, some using others and abusing to their end. If you are sensing enough, you would see the shadows of competing actors moving around yourself or others.

The southern interface group also working with the Oromo side, pushed off a skinny postured, come-get-me type of lady who goes by the name Lelise to my car in what was supposed to mean a holiday trip to one of the cities close to Addis Ababa. I just wanted to do away quickly with deciphering the first layer of the thing and get her in the wheel or show her that our days won't last if she would not come out clean.

I just stared at her with the look.

Lelise knew what I was thinking and asked, "Why are you staring at me like that?"

I replied, "Did I write something on my forehead?"

She said, "Feels like that."

I asked her, "What do you see?"

She stated, "You are curious."

"Sure, I am," I said.

She went silent.

I cleared my throat and stared again.

She said, "Yes, you can say I have been part of them but not any more, you know."

I smiled.

She was like, what?

I said, "No, nothing."

If you are attached to a former Oromia's president, and his family circle, and a southerner throws you in my basketball ring, sure you are not in it any longer. For once though, the Oromo are both sharp in what they do and coming out clean once the sense of shared learning is what you wanted out of it than chasing or being chased.

A key point was how to solve when there was a serious dispute with the Oromo elites among the likes of the PM, Lemma, Jawar and Addisu Arega.

Lelise looked around and said, "Well, you know they will grill me for this and possibly punish me, but I have got to tell you."

I commented, "We all are being punished."

She said, "You guys have got very deep into the situation as I see it."

I nodded. "Yes."

She said, "Gather the Aba Gedas and get them to accept your side of the argument and it will all go fine."

"Not even a table talk?" I asked.

She replied, "That is the desert."

"So the Aba Gedas cater the main menu in your side of the planet," I said.

"Sure."

A few days later, Lelise came to me and said, "Nothing will change."

Do you mean we still have old rules?

She said "yes."

"That is why I fight" I said.

She asked, "Are you not making it difficult for yourself?"

"How?"

She said, "By wanting change that involves your people."

"Instead of…"

She replied, "Focusing on yourself."

I told her, "I am not wired like that."

"Shouldn't you fix your issues first?" she asked.

"My issues are not personal any more; it is a collective suffering,' I replied.

"Perhaps you may want to start with yourself."

"Or else…" I waited for her answer.

"You will not have an economy and will either give up or leave the country," she replied.

Somewhere down the line, we ended up ripping off our perpetrator's stories and bruising their egos with a little satisfaction as a revenge. But all on a table and without making a move. And she went on to say, *"Chir sil atwedim"* — meaning, 'You don't like when they leave you alone'.

"We are paired in a tango," I said.

Lelise asked, "Who will break the heart?"

I answered, "Me as always."

She said, "You don't mean that."

"You will see."

"You know they are cold and heartless."

I said, "I Have grown not to care."

She then asked, "Don't you want people to treat you normally?"

"The normal is long gone," I stated.

"What is there then?" she asked.

"The reality the day brings," I told her.

She said, "They must have hurt you so many times."

I asked her, "Are you expecting that I cry now?"

She said, "I am not your mommy."

"You are not my sister either."

She asked, *"Min abah eyalk new?"* — meaning, 'What are you saying?'

I said, "Nothing."

A few weeks later, we sat at a resort hotel and I saw the friend who hooked us up was in a hoody and sat watching us from a corner. We both realised, saw each other and said, "Just pretend we have not seen him."

"You don't have a woman around."

"Marriage is gone, and I'm tired of plastic-looking ladies in Addis."

"Why is that?" she asked.

"I hate impostors," I told her.

"Looks like the thing of romance has disappeared."

"Good luck with that," I said.

"Not loving, not loved, is it not boring?"

"Your company is un-boring me."

"Is that all?" she asked.

"Was I to invite you during the valentine's day?"

She said, *"Mozaza!"* — meaning, 'You are a jerk!'

"I know that."

"Atishenefim eko," — meaning, 'You don't let us win, do you?'

I said, "We may win together."

"That is the problem."

"Why is that?"

"Because we are not good-hearted as I said."

"I am not you."

"It does not matter."

"Fine."

"Are you sure?"

I asked, "Of what?"

"That you are not one of us?"

"I do not have a boss, for the most part."

She said, "You just did not make me feel more dissed than ever."

"Why?"

"It used to be my world."

"You can walk away," I said.

"You think it is an open stadium, don't you?"

"So, we are agreeing that you are still in love."

"I had to survive long since I left, but my life is an inch away from their pinching at any given time."

"A priest, a soldier and a nurse never retire."

She said, "Well, a soldier must."

"Tell them that. Thankfully I am not any of it. I even said this to my father."

She asked, "Isn't he a former soldier?"

"Yes."

"What did he say?" she asked.

"My father believes that I am a combatant."

"You need support, you cannot do it on your own."

"Perhaps I can retire. If I start it on my own, I can end it on my own."

She said, "You are your own boss."

I nodded. "Since a long time."

Having an MA in management, and training as a soldier, she knew her way around. She was a lecturer at the security academy on the boring side of her job, as she put it. One day, Lelise was on an excursion and went to a hotel resort swimming on the hot spring and spending a lazy day in the spa when she saw a young man. Rather short and looked like someone with a big story. I was listening with the filtering mind to picture if she was sent to snatch a well-off diaspora guy at the spa or if it were a coincidence, but the guy being the guy it could not be like every other people stumbling on each other.

While she was at the swimming pool, she saw that he was coming towards her after several incidents of locking their eyes and blushing at each other. He introduced himself as a diaspora who was just on his vacation. They dated, he was brought home and presented to her father who happened to love him for her more than herself, while she started to love him less for every day after a few months of dating. He would make frequent visits to her working place, to the point that it felt he was her colleague. And the guy happened to be a poor soul, grandson of Emperor Haile Selassie who was living in the US.

"Let me tell you the story," she said. "Every time we meet, he laments to me about his back pain. I thought for a long time he had some sickness on his spine, but he meant that his family was deposed and that he felt his entitlements were taken away from him. What started as a love story ended up as a therapy session. I just walked away. I had enough headache in my life, I would not sit and listen to complaints of former monarchy." She said no to his proposal and walked away.

What was so strange was that by the evening she was telling me this, I sat with a sister of his ex-wife over a lunch; Helina, who also was a girlfriend of Darios Gizaw herself. These people are surely the affluent circle of Addis Ababa. The girl he married, Edna, was from a well-off family in Addis Ababa, who knew millions and billions before many in Ethiopia did not count money more than six digits.

She was highly smart, well-mannered, elegantly tall and super pretty. Her family was in banking, logistics, shipment, construction and real estate sectors; they were among those who had been running Shagar since the time of Haile Selassie. Super tall for his short height, but very much smarter too, she left him later and ran away from his house in the US. He would lock her in her room and would not allow her to see or be seen by anyone else. She could not trade her freedom for some royal status what felt to her like from another planet. It was almost around this time that he visited Addis Ababa and met with my other friend, Lelise.

For me, seeing different cities of the world and some civility in what people think and do, I find most of what happens in Addis Ababa as a waste of time, resources and lives of generations. Here is the thing, the 'All this for what?' question leads me to learn how much all this jibe create in the economy, how much registered dollars we make as a country and how many of us are getting lifted from poverty and whether the country is advancing or at least getting better by the day.

Do we even have a logic of making things work instead of dragging people down, at least for once? Who is to blame for our poverty, ignorance, poor life quality, lack of having entertainment and sense of lively culture? What has been my role in this and what have I done to mess things up myself? You would ask all this hurting each other, rushing to destroy ambitions and crushing each other's spirits, guarding literally empty banks at times lacking money, at times the financial intelligence, are we even a wholly grown-up, full-fledged state, and if there is a state, where is it?

While I was pondering among my conversations with someone who meets on daily basis with The previous system, whether he was the one who sent Soliana, in what appeared as slipping of the tongue, he just mentioned that they had concerns fearing that I was a short-termist and that maybe there was something I needed to clarify about my intentions.

Let alone me, I did not want any competent and future-looking young intellectual from the South to be linked with the former tyrants at any strategic level. This was also one of my reservations when it came to some of Oromo activists. As an idea, what they championed existed as a threat to me during its best days and being chick-y to contain my mind would just tell me that something existential is perceived to go down hard and no romance would be a remedy for that.

This said, I was not without being honest about our situations, the needs we had and where our people were. In case people regret, they may deserve a second chance as the whole country was contemplating on this.

This was clearly communicated that it was what they had done to the people of Wolaita and they were either to fix it or face further detachment of what was left. They took us for granted and would throw personal pennies and act as if the rest of the people did not exist meant that most of intellectuals and politicians had already lost the game and were trapped in the glucose drops of financial benefits that only keep them alive. Speaking of the cost, what it took the Jawar team to paralyse the entire security system of Ethiopia, jam all the digital control posts and claim the upper hand at the police military and special forces would shame all the old guards. I wondered what the previous one would do if he knew how much was spent to buy out his security dominance not only in Ethiopia, but also the entire horn of Africa and extended arm all the way up to Yemen and UAE.

Team Jawar spent only 4.2 million USD to take down a once super grand government and its tight security system. Yes, you are reading it right, it was only 4.2 million dollars that sufficed to kick out the previous system and corner its security chief and the ruling class long before the national army waged the recent war.

One may argue, referring to the recent war (2020-2022), but from the look of it, having that vast control and leverage in East Africa to just be sized down to bunkers means way more than 4.2 million dollars in the real sense. This is the expense in the USA and Europe including London, Paris, Berlin and other major cities.

Much of the expenses within Ethiopia in local currency Birr was collected and spread among actors within Ethiopia. But again, this is just financial cost we are talking about, not loss of lives, body parts, psychological trauma, crack of social fabrics or frozen services, divorces and separations — it was all madness. The material damages are unimaginably so big that you would not want to know how many factories, shops, hotels, restaurants, large scale farms, bridges and institutions burned into ashes. We all were going through some collective madness and we really needed a healing. We really did!

We have not yet touched the young lives lost across the cities of Oromia, Amhara, the South, mass graves in Somali region, displacements of the Afar, burnings in Gumuz and Gambela.

Literally, people paid in bones and blood regardless of which group they come from or which identity they present. Houses, factories, shops, restaurants and cafés, hotels and service centres were set ablaze, farms were destroyed, mining fields were ploughed up on, cars and trucks either turned upside down or burned to light up the nights or for smoke effect during the day.

The Tegaru were, as a people group, among the hardest hit with the hellfire going more intense on them than many others. And the cost was many more times felt on the shoulders of Tegaru than anyone as the rest of the country had started to gradually gather against them, literally hundreds of thousands of people added to the hostile side than even those who decided to remain neutral.

Religion lost its role, faith collapsed, social bonds were broken, humanity faded, laws tarnished, constitution mocked at, justice joked about and moral and ethics squeezed and trashed on site meant the cost of losing a government is not redeemable for only 4.2 million USD, not in million years I would say.

While 4.2 million USD is the sum that brought down the government, it also means every fraction of money people earned in exchange for information mean the government was sold just like a slice of pie in the soil of a sovereign state. Just think of it as a ministry of the government worth few hundred thousand dollars maximum. If you want to call this a country, you better build it so that a trillion dollars would not be enough to buy the cheapest of its office in any ministry, let alone selling out the entire country for this money which is less than a bonus for a well-performing CEO. What I am bluntly saying is that we have citizens that can sell the country for as little as 5 million USD.

A country is built by institutions as we all know, and institutions are constructed by people as its pillars. Anyone who aspires to build Ethiopia must start the work in building the country in the minds of the people first than erecting high rising tower offices, mega projects and large companies, which we need of course. I believe this was what was missing in the Tegaru led Ethiopia.

Above all, the Tegaru lost their dignity, except that they don't show this side of them as humans and remain fixed as the concern about this being remembered in history. This tarnishing the previous sense of historical prestige meant pain is endured in silence, and aching sounds are to be swallowed at any cost.

Such suffering, added by the war waged by almost the entire world going against them, or paying silence to the least, presents a new sense of how we set a price value to decide the cost of defending a government back then, and now losing power and standing in the middle of an arena where everyone else throws stones at a group of people. Seeing what happened to a common Tegaru that has got nothing to do with what the tyrant group has done to people and standing in their shoes would mean the Tegaru are too generous for not wanting to cut out Tigray and put it on another planet to make sure no other cultures would be in touch ever again. This is super intense.

The level of the intensity became deep as the world was undergoing the COVID-19 monster that claimed millions of lives, infecting more millions and putting the world to a standstill before a way of making things move forward became possible. The world was enduring this with all it had and there came the war in Tigray. It was less than three months following the military campaign conducted at my hometown. Tigray was punished by the whole world, and COVID-19 meant that real hell on earth was just unleashed, putting everyone in the mental and emotional test of holding before all went to the wild side of the breaking point.

Ethiopia being one of low-income countries, and Tigray a region that endured severe famine just fifty years ago, COVID-19 and an all-out war would not be easily bearable for a common person in the villages. This is for sure one of history's darkest season for the people of Tigray, much worse than Ecuadorian city and many others like it that had a challenge to bury its citizens. What happened in my hometown Sodo was just ignored as if some mosquitoes had died.

We have a deep-hate-based relationship in which anyone with the likes of my mother's links were to be kept down. If you are born to royalties of Ethiopian kings and queens, you face an imposed poverty for the assumed sins of the past. And the kinds of my father who figured it out long before they won the war and took overpower, were to be humiliated and kept languishing in economic chains. And being their child, my siblings and myself were supposed to have a lifelong suffering, not just see a short-term wrath of an angry and hate filled powerful group. How can you call this a short-termist play? It sure was not short-term crisis when my NGO was closed three times, business doors shut and threatening my existence, and forced me into exile.

While Jawar spent 4.2 million USD, what did I have to lose to see this with my own eyes though? How about millions of people? Money, sure I lost so much, more importantly my childhood and early youth age, my aspirations and all the pain I had to endure, meaning nothing compared to seeing the collapse of this monster government closely. And no one will ever narrate this better than the master mind who orchestrated the scripted role plays of shattering the government into pieces. This is one of my reasons for spending time with Jawar although we went beyond chitchatting about the past and helped shape Ethiopian politics towards peaceful political contestations than aggressive and violent approaches.

Select few from my hometown that are loyalists of Getachew Asefa wanted me to sip the final cup with him. They arranged so that I meet and agreed to push me off the cliff. This was a very deep betrayal by the people who organized social movements with me. The group that plotted to throw me under the speeding train did not know what I had in mind, and that long before they left Addis Ababa, and long before the news of their collapse would be told to the country, I had all the road maps in my hands.

As they are religious people, many of whom also went to the same church I went to, a biblical code was used to perform this, and I was notified of it finally. I am not to preach to anyone here, but let's just see through what this actually means in the story of the cost of what goes around from different perspectives to see what is happening all around us.

What is the cost of putting down a government? Well, it is refusal to be sacrifice lamb when evil people try to play smart.

Rolling the curiosity wheel means that I need to keep searching and asking. As mentioned earlier, most in the community believe in me to do something, depending on the issue in discussion. That is why I was approached to establish an organisation as such a request was forwarded or at times I took the initiative, I did something at some given time.

Looking back, we pacified Amhara elite hostility much efficiently than what my father's and generations before them did. And some coming and asking us to insult the Amhara to show our strength was not just an underestimating of our capability, it was a misconception about self and the position one creates mentally. It was very disgusting, I would say. Now owning a media outlet is mean, you put words in people's mouth. By this we afforded the capacity to protect the Amhara living among our farmers and the urbane. In effect we smashed two bananas with a stick.

One very difficult thing in today's Ethiopian sky is to identify people as a community and treating them the way we want to be treated. And separating, at the mental level, the intents and actions of the political leaders. To me, looking at all the cannibalism and act of cruelty, I decided to focus on what the regular people would do and base my approach using this as a mirror.

With all this craze going on, there are still kind- and tender-hearted people, without whom groups would have been tearing each other apart. These are the people that make up Ethiopia as a country, regardless of all its falws. This is also why we are people of unimaginable level of resilience.

Club of the Conditioned

Something a few of my friends feel about me is that I am highly odd to the point that few of them think I have some sort of anomaly. Probably, by not being like them, I create the contrast that presents me as odd. Anyone can agree though, I am not a usual guy. None of my life experiences, all the fun and challenges put together would be taken as a life of every other Ethiopian. I wish! Or at least I have never had the usual life of every other guy. For good or worse of it, my life constantly puts me in this awkward feeling of being out of the place. Well, many people would say, same here, I can imagine there are so many who may even have more complicated situations than mine.

My issues get exacerbated by the fact that I am not that reserved from living out my life and putting the oddness of the commonly accepted manners off guard. Knowingly or unknowingly. Sometimes, I would challenge the very accepted norms and realise the depth of personal rejection people felt long after it all settles. When I check, I would always say that their feelings are not be legitimate. Imposing their standards on me and not accepting as a free person to imagine of my own, and for myself, just give me a break.

If you are odd yourself, you would feel me, especially on the face of looking thinking and doing the same, and thinking you are the bad guy for not being just that.

This is when you conclude that their sense of oddness and getting hurt just because you don't feel like it. What they want you to be is one of odd ones, that by chance they chose to be the 'common odd' which is probably boring, if not the intolerable average. There is no sense of oddness, demanding conformity to the 'prescribed average oddness,' but then no one is there to do 'oddness policing' as people live their lives and are busy on themselves than monitoring each other.

Speaking of oddness, I would arguably say that Ethiopian urbanists whose mindset is designed to fit the way of life engineered using Amharic interface are not just odd to this planet, but also are possibly the people group that are against everything human; body, mind, soul and spirit. In this sense, as for me, such mentality has an atmosphere that is not just at odds to the natural reality, but also contradicts all the contradictions of the world in any dimension imaginable. In this sense the premature 'Ethiopian-ness' demands you the 'prescribed oddness' people of the Horn of Africa are expected to conform to.

I love my country and my people not any less than a soldier who dies for it or a doctor who would dedicate their good sleeping nights to care for others, or a humanitarian who does that one crazier adventurous trip to a war zone just to save lives, or a teacher who dedicates much of their adult life educating others. This is rather a very honest reflection of my 'countrymen' in an anticipation that people would understand it better and eventually things would start to fall in their rightful place.

I am just saying that I am not that odd, I just see what most of my fellow Ethiopians fail to either see or are not courageous enough to say it out. The oddness of the mindset Ethiopians have is that the normal becomes odd and the odd condemns them. In this sense, I am not odd — perhaps those who think that I am are.

There are those moments when you speak the truth without reservation and realise that it was just a wrong audience, time, place or even to say it at the first place regardless of appropriateness. Recently, I was reading through a group discussion on social media where it was said, "Geez, born Amharic and democracy cannot co-exist in their present form.

Either democracy must be renamed, or Amharic must be a language of this century. No other way, sad to say," before I realised it would be too late to delete it. I did not mean to devalue Amharic or anything of it. It is just that from the observations I had, I found it very hard to arrive at a consensus with the Amharic-shaped mindset that basic pillars of democracy such as tolerance, diversity, justice, equality and so on are vitals of society that trading these off would mean tyranny.

Listening carefully to what most Ethiopian urbanists say, one realises that most people are decent in their thinking and well-meaning for most part of it. It is not the people or their intentions that poses a serious threat to the very minimum I want to see in them in light of humanity. It is the upbringing and the linguistic and cultural effect obstructing the connection between their intents and what they actually are doing in reality.

I tried to put considerable amount of time to study Amharic; one, for making sure my college entrance would not be jeopardised, and more over the idea of understanding the psyche of Amharic-speaking people around me who took a prestige out of their eloquence in lingua franca.

Amharic is perhaps the only African language that has its alphabet and numbers or has its history and so on. Well, this was the motivational factor for me to put so much effort to read books and try to understand literature, cultural dimensions and getting along. But how about the fact that speaking about the uniqueness of the language is not enough on its own? What if we have to look at the very characteristics of the language to begin with, to spare people at least?

For a fair presentation of facts, Amharic is unique in its characters and has alphabets and numbers as I put earlier. It is true that no language I speak matches a few of its expressions. Having this said for fairness, uniqueness does not necessarily mean advancement or the capacity to enhance life quality. It has odd sounds you make and is awkwardly flexible for ghetto talks and slangs that spice it up to ridiculously make it feel special.

There are some sounds and expressions for which there is no verbal representation of a written word. It is also a language of a thousand romances, a sound of a million loves, and that, uhm — thing for your unspoken expressions.

Born from Geez for military purposes and confusing the enemy, it became a language of the camp before it made it to the daily life. This then means that you have that other guy or gal who is virtually against you and you need to withstand their bewitching through some spells. It is also a kind of game play of some sort.

A friend of mine from Wollo area of Amhara region used to say that "Amharic is surely not among 'normal' languages. It is a language of war, of lasting conflicts and unending generational disputes. As a language, Amharic attaches itself with poverty, inequality and inequity even if the rest of the world would have no influence on it at all." As a language family, it is related to Arabic, Hebrew, Aramaic, Chaldean and Syriac for the most part of it. For instance, *arba* in Amharic is forty and *arba* in Arabic is four — while these are somehow played around — *salam, malak, bet, qudus* all have the same meaning of peace, angel, house and holy in most of these languages including Amharic.

In this, it shares many words. What is so spectacularly distinct in Amharic is that while all others are written from right to the left, Amharic is written from left to write. In its written form, it matches the Roman language families, while in sharing words it has more common words with Semitic languages than any in the world. By being so it just self-contradicts in many ways that such oddness is seen in the way most Ethiopian urbanists think and do.

If Amharic language were a mental state, it would locate itself somewhere around Yemen and pretend it is in California. Imagine we have people who are in Addis Ababa physically, pretend they are in Yemen, Sana'a city, mentally and emotionally insist they are in California. I would like to recall that I put a few lines talking about the Turkish drama series getting popularity in Ethiopia as a cultural transit hub before making the way to Hollywood. A question would be why not by a one way ticket to Hollywood instead, or even better, build Ethiopian version if you have what it takes?

The idea of using the advantage of the Turkish experimentation of adapting to the west can sound economical and wise, while the present culture is being lived and that time would have already been lost if and by any chance the Istanbul cultural lab becomes a failure. Even if it would work there there is a considerable probability that it would not fit the Ethiopian contexts and societal preferences now or in the anticipated future.

What people are doing in real life and how Amharic has manifested itself may not be that different apart from each other. I am quite sure that this is as deeply social architectural issue, as it is just that the intent and the act seem to mirror each other while the language is the programming and coding instrument that has more influence over people. Obviously, it is more than mere prescription of entertainment alternatives.

As a principle, Ethiopians who speak and write in Amharic, write antagonistically to that of Arabic, Hebrew, Aramaic and other Semitic-speaking communities of the world. The writing is not the only feature that sets the Amharic-writing people aside from the rest of Semitic-language-writing communities.

It is also that most Amharic writing people do believe in this fable that Ethiopia is the only business of God, with Israel being the only contending country. Well, if heavens chose Jerusalem, Makkah and Madinah, and if any spot of Ethiopia would be any important to the angels, it will always be at the second place. I am not sure if I would throw a party to hear a news that I would be a second guess of heavens.

Presumably, my Ugandan, Congolese and the rest of friends will never invite me to their fest if they hear that they may be third-guessed by heavens, if this hierarchical levels of worth in the eye of heavens were real. I mean, why go through a hassle of prioritisation rollercoaster when you can just have a single place, planet earth and avoid the question of spiritual equity to several countries!

Modern Amharic presented itself with a notion that making it a lingua franca should mean that by choice or force people would have to be able to speak it. Sadly, Amharic was expanded through coercion to the point that the spiritual institutions are caught off-guard, somehow looking complicit to the once state-level imposition of learning the language.

In my hometown, the mass was done in Amharic at times without translation while most attendants speak local language Wolaitatuwa and significant members of the church have difficulty to really understand the spiritual terms with linguistic depth used during sermons. In other spiritual centres, even Geez, a mother language of Amharic is used that would make one wonder — why teach people in a language they don't understand, if what you teach is worthy of a message from heavens and people are to live by it? — no offense here. Shouldn't it be translated to Amharic, Wolayitatuwa, Afan Oromo, Afu Sidama and the rest?

It sounded like while Amharic is not easy to internalise, you add its older mother language and make it harder and more complicated. Would it be unfair then, I would understand them, if someone wonders whether the oddness of Ethiopia's societal problems and their solutions hiding in plain sight is inscribed on the linguistic stone walls, partially at least.

Listening to the mind programming contents streaming from Monday through Sunday, its perfect depiction is that an individual's mindset is codded to read the normal as odd, and the odd as normal. This is the climax of the mass mind-control project.

A controlled odd mindset is the common place, and anyone who is not a duplicate of everyone else is condemned to be cast into the pits of rejection, hurt, economic loss and political repression. In principle then, who is repressing an individual may not just be government or its leader as solely responsible, as the role is divided among the stakeholders that enforce this together.

A naïve mind may think this has to do with practice than the language or intent for imposition on others. Imposition is done in many ways today that a once rifle-guarded language has already set itself as a lifeline to winning daily bread, getting acceptance or fitting in a new place. In being so Amharic has claimed unspoken role in determining the experiences of an individual swaying the tides of appealing pleasant moments.

By the time non-speakers of Amharic learn the tips and tricks of it and get to the comfortable level of easy communication, most people realise that any sense of global advancement they thought would be unlocked via Amharic remains that one more thing they must do. They realise they have to study the global trendy lifestyles altogether for which Amharic has more shortcomings than their native languages, such as Wolaitatuwa for the people of Wolaita. Wolaitatuwa is easier and closer in its linguistic capacity of being enabler to learn the things of the wider world outside Ethiopia than Amharic.

It is an easy jump directly into global rhythm than going Amharic, being stationed in Turkish cultural hub and head for the bigger world. The same applies in other language speakers of the Kambata, Hadiya, Afan Oromo, Agnuwak and so on. This puts Amharic at odds with most communities in different areas of Ethiopia.

Amharic is at odds not only with the rest of the languages in Ethiopia, or the Semitic languages, or Roman languages, it does not match its mother language Geez either. Its alphabet order, sentence formation or the type of lifestyle or cultural environment it fosters all contradict Geez if not are in direct conflict with each other. Some would actually argue if Amharic would ever evolve to become a language of harmony, stillness and equanimity.

Amharic is not a language of peace, co-existence and cooperation. It is a language of chaos, disorderliness, disobedience, unorganised state at the best and that of hate, deep suspicion and enabler of jealousy. The users of the language are not so liberated to thinking the impact of the language has in damaging the social fabric all are trying to repair and that keeps being torn apart time and again, regardless of how hard all are trying to fix. Whether it is the language, the mind programmers or the day-to-day users that have a role to craft it into a useful tool for good remains to be understood more.

As a language created for the purpose of military intelligence to disorient the enemy, its daily users also create a mental picture of some invader or categorical enemy they have to disorient, derail and defeat in their daily lives. In this sense, all Amharic-speaking individuals live as if they are in a real war zone where aerial bombardment, ambushes, bombing, exploding mines, never-missing snipers and pounding artillery are commonplace. They have undisclosed country that waged a war that begun thousands of years back and that the war has no sign of ending today. Their ancestors were born to it the same as their fathers and mothers.

They are born to a war and celebrate every birthday under the live fire raining over their heads. They date, love, get married, have children and raise them in this context. It is either the wider west, Italy, Egypt or UAE or its neighbours in the mentions as hostile states if one carefully pays attention to a few controversial conversations that poke the defence for culture, faith or geopolitical issues.

A friend of mine who used to be my colleague once took up intense talks about Ethiopia, its societal challenges and what it is that needs to be done for improvement and making the country a place to live. He is a licensed psychologist and a very gifted listener, but also one of the most talented individuals who can come up with rich ideas and concepts of collective healing.

To my scary ground shaking, I remember him saying that about eighty-five per cent of Ethiopians need some sort of psychological support to a varying degree. He would say repeatedly that Ethiopians are people of unprocessed, untreated and unhealed sort of generationally dissecting and deep collective trauma. He was so serious that I started to mumble with his unbending confidence of having a firm stand.

Of course, we debated about the accuracy of the 85% needing counselling in a given population. The argument is that over a third (about 33%) need therapeutic counselling that is related to diagnostic disorders while 52% need a preventive counselling as a prevention of disorders. This is plausibly the most accurate presentation of the need for preventive and therapeutic psychological and psychiatric need of a given population under pressures such as war conflict, unrest and poverty.

This makes sense to me as traditionally elders, and wise people of a community usually sit down and offer advice and counselling for younger ones on matters that are delicate and hard to bear for an individual. No one seems to create the time needed for such encounters as time has become unavailable in such a huge contrast with the customary abundance people used to access to enjoy each other's company.

He said this about thirteen years back when there was no formal conventional war. This time around, we have a country that has gone through a series of riots, uprisings, lootings, highly localised war, displacement, mass grave and horrendous brutality for five solid years. Very high societal polarisation, political divisions, fledgling economy, unreliable spiritual figures and a relatively new government all have put almost everyone to go through serious psychosocial challenges as of now.

This is without mentioning the COVID-19 outbreak that has been rocking the lives of billions across the entire world. Ethiopians are going through triple layers of very intense and constant collective suffering without even a break. Can anyone imagine living a regular life, in a peaceful city where there is law and order, with presence of the police, a functioning army and all social institutions to your favour that you have to live in fear and trembling emotionally as if you are in a war zone? Can any imagine that you use undeciphered twisted codes and third party-created communication tools to the point that even those with good orientation of your algorithm are left puzzled to figure out what you said in the middle of every conversation?

Amharic users experience this except that it happens vividly at an unconscious level, to the point that it is manifested in collective behaviours. It is noticeable at individual encounters for the most part too.

Amharic language has not left the war front and forcefully keeps all its speakers as prisoners of war. You are at war if your daily language that you speak and hear from morning to evening is filled with words of war zone where the intent for killing, distortion, subjugation, burning, looting, rape and brutality are embedded in the very words you use while you are not even aware of this totally.

Heavens would agree to the idea that a person is a soldier after subscribing to use a language of war and live by its rules and principles full-heartedly. Of course, no one of Amharic speakers subscribes for conscription in a formal manner. No, that is not what I mean.

But once you are born to it and are caught up in this perceived war for which you have to be a member of an intelligence community comprised of citizens of the whole country, you surely are a warring person walking on the planet that may possibly refuse to call yourself a soldier, even in a very respectful title.

Countless Ethiopians who speak Amharic are soldiers by birth and are conditioned to it. Nothing can be more damaging than finding yourself as an unpaid soldier who was not provided proper induction of a conventional war. It would be more depressing to learn that it would never take place and that the societal expectation to treat everyone you meet as a potential threat to humanity, and fatal risk to survival is all wrong.

Sadly, Amharic is a language that is designed by a ruling circle for a purpose of secret operations of corruption, inequity, injustice, inequality and barbarism, using heavens or spiritual promise as an excuse. Or hang on, isn't it the few murky people who do this though? It is a language that justifies horrible and sadistic treatment of the other making the act mentally easy, emotionally affordable and a collectively supported act. You will not find a direct encouraging notion if you search for it at the surface of the daily use of the language. No, no!

If one wants to have a sense of it, they need to look around and observe what is happening underneath the hospitality and gesture of kindness or appearances of generosity. The language may mean one in a word but completely another in just saying the same thing to two people with the same tone and body language. It needs a high level of sensitivity to really get that something completely different is being communicated with precisely one word and tone. For much part of it, not most are supposed to get you when you say it.

Some dubiously mean people may communicate two or three types of people saying a single word. Such selectivity and audience stratification mean some sort of ranking and prioritising is close to the regular use of the language. Such situations make the impression that some feel more intimately treated than others oddly in a single sentence that is said for all of them listening together. Amharic is odd. Amharic speakers, who endorse this as normal are the odd ones; not me, who sees a highly serious problem in this.

I believe languages and the words we use every day have direct and powerful impact over how we think, do and live our daily lives. Taking the Ethiopian context into an account, war is lived in daily lives. There is a war at the fronts, and another in daily lives. And anyone who feels like waging unending daily war to be normal is at absolute odds with humanity.

Once again, this is also why I believe that people in general are good in their hearts and that it is all about the information installed in their brains from childhood that skews the way they live. It is this installed data that has the power over their fate deciding whether they can experience a life full of love, care, tolerance, abundant wealth and sense of fulfilment.

If a language is the most important part of data creation or even programming, the society is in charge of commanding individuals and groups and owns the prosperity, abundant wealth, informed life and pleasant experiences they produce. This is, of course, if the commanding language is intended for positive outcomes.

As a society is the sum of individuals that were once children in whom we install what we wanted them to produce, then no other country matches Ethiopians in installing a language of a culture that cultivates poverty, violence, disharmony, incoherence, lawlessness and inequity. The most obviously visible fact is that the programmers and mind controllers of Ethiopia have best delivered the collective elite we can call as Club of the Conditioned.

Arguably, no other country does better than Ethiopians in self-conditioning each other into a hundred and ten million poor souls, majority of whom would want to leave the country the first hour if they were given the chance.

Well, wanting to use Amharic as a tool of progress would mean getting back to the very basics of knowing its limitations, the level of societal advancement it stands for and putting efforts for architectural work to fit in not only today's society but also make it compatible with the language capacity of evolving towards the future intended context.

You see, Amharic is not a language of a fast-paced lifestyle, high-frequency productivity, large volume mobility of goods and consumption of wealthy population. By being so, Amharic is not an industrious language. As a non-industrious language, it lacks the idea of social capital, collective wealth, common protection, sense of group and individual security and observing the necessity of wellbeing of the whole.

I am deeply sad to put it this way that the language suffers from traction forces of theocratic secrecy and autocratic show-offs. In this sense, it is meant to cater for rulers, spiritual figures, socially prominent people and some businesspeople. Its selectivity of enhancing life, is its hinderance from being a language of the common people.

This is one of its setbacks that hold it back as it fails to play the role of the linguistic hinting of what is lacking in society. The language is trapped in its state where it kept the people in its bondage. At times, it is the war prisoners taking the language as their captive. It is somehow like role changing in adult play. Where the language attempts to influence the positive thinking, the culture drags it down. And for now, I am not really in the mood to touch issues of our culture at this point. Perhaps, sometime in the future.

The society needs self-liberation from its own practice of conditioning individuals in order to trust, commission and allow them to progress. Because it is individuals that make a society.

The essence of true freedom and free will of the individuals and the groups shall be fostered and cultivated to see any glimpse of hope for change, and the wording we often use to the level of self-deception must be economical. Our wordings must be economically deflated to their normal levels where terminologies are meant when we use them than playing with the minds and hearts of the people in focus.

Ethiopians need to unchain each other and to proclaim liberty of citizens across the country from the cultural, linguistic, customary and traditional conditioning that kept the people poor and in precarious situations for the last millennium. Otherwise, except for the great weather and the few good people, the country may soon turn out to be unbearable to live in except for monks. Or should we not make it bearable, afforded with bare minimum of survival, or even possible to thrive?